D1189871

THE *WAY* OF THE
DICTATORS

THE WAY OF THE DICTATORS

By

LEWIS BROAD

and

LEONARD RUSSELL

With an Introductory Letter by

THE RT. HON.

D. LLOYD GEORGE,

O.M., M.P.

WITH 8 ILLUSTRATIONS

KENNIKAT PRESS
Port Washington, N. Y./London

THE WAY OF THE DICTATORS

First published in 1935
Reissued in 1970 by Kennikat Press
Library of Congress Catalog Card No: 71-112796
ISBN 0-8046-1063-0

Manufactured by Taylor Publishing Company   Dallas, Texas

TIME eateth away at many an old delusion,
yet with civilization delusions make head ;
the thicket of the people will take furtiv fire
from irresponsible catchwords of live ideas,
sudden as a gorse-bush from the smouldering end
of any loiterer's match-splint, which, unless trodden out
afore it spredd, or quell'd with wieldy threshing-rods
will burn ten years of planting with all last year's ricks
and blacken a countryside. 'Tis like enough that men
ignorant of fire and poison should be precondemn'd
to sudden deaths and burnings, but 'tis mightily
to the reproach of Reason that she cannot save
nor guide the herd ; that minds who else wer fit to rule
must win to power by flattery and pretence, and so
by spiritual dishonesty in their flurried reign
confirm the disrepute of all authority.

The Testament of Beauty, by ROBERT BRIDGES.

CONTENTS

of hate against the oppressor. The nightmares of the adult Pilsudski centred upon the Russian superintendent of his gymnasium at Vilna, whose aim was to crush the independence and personal dignity of the Polish scholars. The gymnasium, with the ever-present possibility of corporal punishment, became a place of dread for him. "Looking back on fifty years of his school experiences he said ... "I am still under the impression that system made on me," and "I know ... judge by this fact," although I have since passed through ... and Siberia, and have had to do with a number of Russian officials, it is still the Vilna schoolmaster who ... no small part in every bad dream."

Dictators are made in childhood, the psychologists agree, and some of them believe that Europe would have been a happier place to-day if the pastors and masters of Vilna ... the world had possessed the knowledge that ... does so much wrong from to youth as to ... the ... Certain experts have forgot the tyrants of his ... schoolmaster neither did Mustapha Kemal, whose hatred ... of the hands of a pedant may well have been ... his first ... war on religion.

At the age of eighteen Pilsudski began to consider how he could best spread his gospel of ... rebellion against the Russians must be taken up ... action must be directed by one man ... literature ... The literature of the French Revolution, ... occupied by him in his solitary days, and the one maxim he had gained from it: "If a revolution was to have any chance of success, more than blood and barricades, it must be directed by one stage," already forced himself as the leader.

At the University of Cracow, where he became a medical student, he was brought into contact with ... of his own generation, and he found that those ... politically-minded accepted Marxism almost to a man. Pilsudski, too, became a Marxist, although he did not ... the creed or understand it, but any stick was good enough to beat Russia with, and as a Socialist (though hardly an Internationalist), he began eagerly to form a revolutionary society. In 1887, however, his activities were brought to a sudden halt. He was said to have been involved in an attempt to assassinate the Czar Alexander III. Pilsudski, though not a direct ... in the conspiracy—his name was found in

LIST OF ILLUSTRATIONS

AN INTRODUCTORY LETTER

BY

THE RT. HON. D. LLOYD GEORGE, O.M., M.P.

I HAVE read *The Way of the Dictators* with great interest. It is a most timely study of a problem which is of particular concern to all countries at the present juncture, and especially to those which still preserve the ideals and traditions of democracy and political liberty.

THE account you give of the way of the dictators traces the course of post-war history for a very considerable part of the civilised world. We in this country can learn much from the developments in other lands which you describe. Britain has taught the world the art and science of self-government ; but the breakdown of that system elsewhere sets in a clear light the dangers to which it is subject, and the errors against which it must be on its guard. The course of political development abroad is plentifully sprinkled with warning signs for those who wish to travel safely the road of democracy and parliamentary government.

In Britain we have our own domestic problems—notably that of persistent post-war unemployment. None the less, we can congratulate ourselves on the fact that there is no country where more persistent efforts have been made to better the lot of the mass of the people. During my own public life, the condition of the workers has been vastly improved, their standard of life has been raised, and a new security in the event of sickness, old age or unemployment provided for them to a degree undreamed of a generation ago.

You have been good enough to refer in your book to the part I have taken in dealing with these problems. No work with which I have been associated has given me more abiding satisfaction than the share I have had in securing for the workers these measures of social justice. And there can be little question that these provisions have played a decisive part here in averting, during the economic blizzard from which the world has latterly suffered, those extremities of destitution, disorder and embittered revolt which lead through chaos to the setting up of dictatorships.

Democracy here has succeeded in maintaining a national standard of wealth and well-being which is the envy of nations struggling through political and economic experiments towards some system of government that may give them ordered prosperity.

We have equal cause to congratulate ourselves here upon our success in combining individual liberty with order and stability of government. You have been right to dwell in your book upon the loss of rights and the restraint of liberty which are suffered by the people in the lands of the dictators. Political freedom has ceased to exist under the dictatorial systems of Italy, Germany and Russia.

Each generation has to learn anew the lessons of politics. Much as it may profit by the wisdom and experience of its ancestors, it must ultimately make its own decision as to the course it shall follow. The lessons and the warnings in your book serve as valuable guides to a wise choice.

Ever sincerely,

THIS BOOK

W HEN Thomas Cromwell, Earl of Essex, was all-powerful, says Erasmus, men walked slowly and carefully, as if they feared a scorpion might be sleeping behind every stone. Other times, other bogeys. In this day and age many of the politically timid drive rapidly, as if they fear a dictator may be peeping from behind every beacon.

Theories and criticisms about dictatorship are everywhere. The facts are less easy to obtain. This book's purpose is to give the facts, with commentary where it appears necessary, and to provide a basis for an answer to the question : Could events such as those seen abroad during the last few years occur in England ?

This book is written from the standpoint of observers who would place their faith in old democracy rather than in new dictatorship, in the English Parliamentary system rather than the Fascism of Italy or the Communism of Russia.

Conscious of this standpoint, the observers set out to discover whether the new " isms " of government and the dictatorships in other countries have arisen as a result of abstract political inclinations, or whether they have been the result of hard political and economic circumstances ; and if the latter, whether those circumstances might arise in England.

Properly to consider these questions it is necessary to understand the means by which the governments of the new " isms " have been brought about. It is the aim of this book, as we have said, to provide the facts, personal and political, about the dictators. Something of the achievements and benefits of the dictatorial régimes are included in the survey and something of the failures and disadvantages.

L. B.
L. R.

I

THE CONSTITUTIONAL DICTATORS :
HITLER AND MUSSOLINI

Mussolini and Hitler have devised a new frame for despotism. They have flung out democracy bag and baggage. They have shown their contempt for the ballot-box and universal suffrage as the basis for their system of government. They loom, supported though they be by overwhelming majorities of their people, autocrats as arrogant as a Shah of Persia in older days, or the Grand Mogul.

Considering the matter in advance it might have been supposed that despotism such as this would have inspired a revolt, but, almost to the disappointment of the more vigorously-minded democrats, the new despotisms have been established almost unchallenged. Mussolini and Hitler, it is plain, know how to make dictatorship acceptable.

They represent Germany and Italy in a sense in which no Englishman or Frenchman stands for his country. The Duce and the Führer have as bulwarks for their own safety thrown ring after ring of restrictions around supporters and opponents. But if they were to take off the whips and permit their people unrestricted entry to the national division lobbies they would unquestionably secure re-election by handsome majorities.

Though Hitler and Mussolini have thrown off democracy they took the constitutional democratic path to power. They conquered democracy by observance of her rules. The Fascist and National Socialist Movements were built up principally by means of the instrument of free speech and propaganda. There were bludgeonings as well, and the formation of militant organisations, but in neither case was power usurped by force.

Both dictators were invited by the heads of their States

to become constitutional Chancellors.   Both then proceeded to carry out intentions long avowed of bringing
about democracy's overthrow.   In the career of Hitler
and Mussolini is to be seen the demagogue triumphing over
democracy.   The democrat might almost have preferred
that the citadel had fallen to armed forces.   The danger
from the demagogue appears more sinister than that from
the man at arms.

ADOLF HITLER

1

Hitler reached power by the constitutional means of democracy and then democracy was overthrown. He exploited Germany's spirit of humiliation and a nation gave allegiance to the ex-Corporal who promised to grapple with external and internal enemies.

ADOLF HITLER is the supreme example of the demagogue's power. In the full light of day he has deprived the German people of their former democratic rights and liberties. He warned them in advance of his intentions, and they gave him the authority to carry those intentions out.

Hitler proclaimed that he stood for the substitution of personal rule for programme, policy and principle. He asked for a blank cheque and it became the death warrant of German democracy.

They speak, sometimes, of Hitler's " march on Berlin " as if he had led a *putsch*, but the Nazis took the constitutional path to power, though there was a certain amount of blood-spilling in the by-ways. Hitler made one *putsch* and its failure brought a sincere and lasting conversion to constitutional methods. He promised that heads should roll in the dust when he arrived, but pledged himself not to attempt a second coup. So firmly did he stand by his constitutional undertaking that less constitutionally-minded followers of the militant Storm Troops came to speak of their leader, almost reproachfully, as " Adolphe Légalité."

Great, we know, are the uses of publicity. Powerful is the appeal to the masses of flag-waving and the paraphernalia of brown-shirt uniforms and swastika emblems. Nevertheless it appears fantastic that a publicity campaign could have put across such a monumental achievement in political salesmanship.

Look at the gulf that publicity bridged in less than fifteen

19

years. In 1919 an obscure Corporal, who was not even a
German by nationality, joined a hole-in-a-corner political
party at Munich. In 1934 the ex-Corporal was elected with
something approaching national unanimity to the Presidential chair of Germany ; the obscure party had become
nation-wide, all-absorbing, all-destructive, all-triumphant.

The phenomenon of Hitler is only to be understood by
an understanding of Germany's national aspirations. Publicity made Hitler, created the great man legend, but it was
through exploitation of the hopes and longings of the
German people that Hitler secured national acceptance.

Distress and discontent form the background of the stage
on which the drama of Hitler's rise was enacted. The
economic distress in Germany in the decade following the
War was more severe than anything known in England in
modern times. It fell short, certainly, of the famine in
Russia, but the German people endured privations un-
paralleled among civilised races in our day. As a result
of the Allied blockade, which continued for some months
after the War ended, there was a scarcity of all kinds of
food. The nation lost much of its power of resistance to
illness and infection ; ill-nourishment produced a mental
inertia in adults ; children were to be seen suffering from
hunger madness. These were the conditions that saw the
birth of Hitlerism. The blockade was lifted ; the standard
of living gradually improved, but it remained, and remains
yet, below the level in England and France. The working
classes had a grim struggle for existence. There was the
nightmare for the nation of the catastrophic plunges of the
Mark, when as paper money was churned out by printing
presses the peoples' wealth and savings vanished. There
was a respite and then Germany felt the onset of the world
economic blizzard. The chaos of national bankruptcy
again appeared imminent. Trade and industry collapsed,
men went out of work thousand after thousand, until at
one time it was estimated that the unemployed touched a
figure of ten millions.

This is the background, these are the conditions which
explain the rise of Hitlerism. The older democratic parties
appeared to be failing in the maintenance of the old order.
The people turned to Hitler as to a strong man who could
save the country from Bolshevism. The older parties were

" Hitler poured forth a torrent of words. . . . He proved by experience
that he was a born orator."

conscious of the limitations of their ability and power. Hitler was conscious of the national aspirations, and proclaimed his ability to bring about their fulfilment.

Side by side with industrial and economic distress was a weariness of national spirit, a national " inferiority complex." Germany suffered the humiliation of defeat in the War. The men of the new Republic which succeeded to the old Militarist Empire, disowned the War. The adult manhood had taken part in the struggle, but in the bitterness of defeat they were not allowed the consolation of looking back with pride upon their sacrifices and achievements. Under the Republic the men who returned from the War were invited to become penitents. The Treaty of Peace further humiliated Germany by depriving her of wide possessions. To Germany, too, was attributed the moral iniquity of war guilt. It was in the days of national humiliation that Hitlerism was born. Germany had to shoulder the burden of reparations, and during the years these payments proceeded reparations was one of the most compelling appeals of Hitlerism.

The greater the sense of national humiliation of spirit, the greater was the force of the appeal of Hitler's new nationalism. The people who mourned their lost greatness responded to the cry of the man who promised to re-create the vanished strength, to lead Germany back to her old place amongst the Powers. How could the spirit of Stresemann and Locarno hope to compete with the appeal of the man who, with sincerity and conviction, gave promise of the fulfilment of dearest national hopes.

Here indeed lies the success of Hitlerism. The human mind throughout the world responds with facility to the vision of the fulfilment of its own expectations. Religious leaders have founded creeds on the extravagance of their assurances for the fulfilment of human desire. The political demagogue in an uncritical and unsceptical society can promise his way to power. Hitler's path was paved by promises and hope, and led him to the greatest triumph of a prophet since the days of Mahomet.

The Crescent and the Swastika are emblems of creeds whose exponents have been ready to obtain converts by trading upon men's fears as well as upon their hopes, by coercing where they could not convince. But there must be no exaggeration of the conquests that the Nazis made through the means of physical violence.   There was terrorism enough : opponents were bludgeoned off the platform and off the streets, for the Nazis though sinned against as well as sinners during the days when the streets were a battle-ground for lusty rivals of politics, were plainly the better men in the political struggle in all its phases. But you cannot bludgeon an entire nation into your support. There were bludgeonings on all sides in German politics, for they are more robust in their methods in Germany. But Hitler conquered by propaganda in season and out of season—propaganda that was less subtle than that of his opponents, that succeeded by its very blatancy and the incessant reiteration of its slogans.

In the Hitler conception, propaganda must be carried on at a level not higher than that of the most limited intelligence.   The level must be lower and lower in pro- portion as the mass of persons to whom it is addressed becomes greater and wider.   The understanding of the masses is limited ; propaganda must, therefore, be limited to a few points and catchwords, which the most simple can understand.   Effectiveness must be the test of the propa- ganda—not its truth, and in earlier editions of his auto- biography Hitler made the admission that " the German has not the slightest notion how a people must be misled if the adherence of the masses is sought."   It is a cynical expression of the arts of demagogy.

2

The Austrian of humble birth serves in the German Army.   The youthful Hitler learns to hate Socialists, Trades Unions and Jews, and elevates personal antagonisms into a principle.   He also gains lessons from British war propaganda.

Looking back on his humble origin you can only wonder that Hitler should have risen to his present eminence. His methods may be reviled, but there can be no with- holding the admiration due to the man who has been the architect of such a fortune.   After the War, as a man of thirty, he faced the world without money, without occupation, without apparent prospects. In little more than ten years he brought himself to the front rank in German politics, attained the Chancellorship, was elected as Hindenburg's successor, and was accepted by the German people as a despot holding powers never previously approached by any of their rulers. Such at forty-five was the record of achievement of the man whose life had begun in the obscure home of a minor Customs official in a minor town in Austria.

The life of Hitler before the War can be disposed of shortly. The chief interest in these years is to discover the origins of the opinions which have become the distinguishing mark of the political philosophy of Hitlerism. The brief autobiographical facts are these.

Hitler was born on April 20, 1889, at Braunau-on-the-Inn. Some of his ancestors had been small farmers. His father, Alois Hitler, began life as a cobbler, and after a struggle attained his heart's desire by entering the Government Service as a Customs official. He was fifty-two at the time his son was born, child of a third marriage. The mother was forty-two. Young Hitler had one point in common with a number of other great men—he was a failure at school, and he failed in his early attempts to earn his living. At an early age he went to Vienna and tried to become an artist and an architect. He was reduced to keeping himself by working as a bricklayer's labourer and he learned what hunger meant. Two years before the War he moved from Vienna to Munich, where he was living at the time War was declared. Although an Austrian he volunteered for service in a Bavarian Regiment, and was extremely gratified that his petition to serve was granted. In the year 1916 he was wounded, and at some time or other—his biographers have failed to discover the occasion—he won the Iron Cross. Shortly before the Armistice he was the victim of a British gas attack near Ypres, and was sent back from the front. He was in hospital when the War ended.

There were three determining factors in Hitler's life before the year 1919—that he was born in Austria ; that a Trades Union restriction once prevented him from earning his living ; and that the sight of a Jew on some occasion in Vienna had a startlingly vivid effect upon his imagination. His birth in Austria is the first fact that he places on record in that curious incursion into autobio-graphical literature which he wrote during his period of imprisonment in 1924, and published under the title of *Mein Kampf*—My Struggle.[1] "It stands me in good stead to-day," wrote Hitler, "that Fate decided that Braunau on the Inn should be my birthplace. That little town lies on the frontier between the two German States (Germany and Austria), the reunion of which we younger ones regard as a work worthy of accomplishment by all the means in our power." He goes on to declare that it is essential for German Austria to return to the German motherland, that common blood should belong to a common state. So, as a child, if he remembers aright, Hitler was converted to the idea of pan-Germanism.

As a young workman Hitler came up against the domin-ance of Trade Unionism. He was making a living as a bricklayer's mate, but was not a member of the Union. His fellow-workers insisted that he must join, but the young man who had ideas of becoming an artist or an architect, and was only carrying the hod as a temporary expedient for the solution of the problem of existence, had no intention of throwing in his lot with the proletariat. He refused to join the Union, and was compelled, as a consequence, to give up his work. There is no doubt that to this incident is to be traced the origin of the intense antagonism to official Socialism and Trade Unionism which has dis-tinguished Hitlerism. The crushing of the Labour organisa-tions in Germany in the year 1933 is thus to be traced back to an incident in pre-War Vienna. There is an illuminating passage in the autobiography, in which Hitler speaks of the " free " Trades Unions which " lowered over the political horizon, and over each man's life like a threatening storm cloud. It was one of the most terrible instruments of intimidation against security and national independence, the solidity of the State and individual

[1] This book has been published in England (Hurst & Blackett) in an abridged form. It has been many times revised by the author since its original publication, and many passages struck out or modified. An unauthorised version of the whole was published in France, but Hitler took legal action to have it suppressed. Three million copies are supposed to have been sold in Germany.

freedom. It was, above all, that which turned the idea of democracy into a repellent and derisory phrase, brought shame to liberty and mocked at brotherhood in the words : ' If you won't join us we will crack your skull for you '."

Last of these early formative influences was Hitler's meeting with a Jew one day in Vienna. " I was walking through the inner City when I suddenly came across a being in a long *caftan* (under-coat) with black side-locks. My first thought was : Is that a Jew ? I watched the man stealthily and cautiously, but the longer I stared at that strange countenance and studied it feature by feature, the more the question in a different form turned in my brain : Is that a German ? " Hitler then sets out the process of his intellectual development towards anti-Semitism. We follow the steps to the conclusion that Jews were not Germans of another religion, but members of a different race. Feelings of repugnance followed as Hitler came to associate Jews with the production of unclean products of artistic life in art, literature, the theatre and the cinema, and the terms of denunciation became bitter. " It was pestilence, spiritual pestilence, worse than the Black Death, with which the nation was being inoculated." Jews, Trade Unionists and Socialists came all to be classed together in the Hitler antagonisms. The Social Democrats, among whom were many Jews, were authors of the post-War German Democratic Republic established under the Weimar Constitution.[1] By way of his early antagonism to Jew and Social Democrat, Hitler reached his antagonism to the German democratic system and he elevated his antagonisms into a principle.

Finally the complete anti-Semite was revealed. " Thus did I now believe that I must act in the sense of the Almighty creator ; by fighting against the Jews I am doing the Lord's work." From his anti-Semitism followed the Nazi doctrine of racial purity, the restoration of the German race to the " primeval Nordic purity of its Aryan origin." The blood substance of the German race was to Hitler so " pre-eminent and unique an asset of the world " that the safe-guarding of racial purity appeared to be Germany's duty

[1] The National Assembly which drew up the Constitution was summoned to meet at Weimar because of its associations with the great Goethe.

to humanity. A step more and the Hitler vision is completed with the conception of a pan-Germany dominating the world.

From the War Hitler learned one great lesson—the use of propaganda. The conclusions he arrived at guided the propaganda that created Hitlerism, from which it is to be deduced that the conclusions were sound. Hitler's verdict is that German war propaganda was not only inadequate, but wrong-headed to such an extent that it was actually harmful. It was fundamentally wrong, he submits, for the Austrian and German papers to have made the enemy a figure of ridicule. When the German soldier came to meet the enemy he discovered that there was nothing ridiculous about him ; it was damaging to the *morale* of the German soldiers to discover that the men they had to fight were not the weaklings that had been ridiculed. In contrast with this, the British and American war propaganda was psychologically correct in the display to their people of the German as a barbarian and a Hun. The British soldier never felt that this propaganda was untrue when he came to meet the enemy, against whom his rage and hatred had been excited.

Hitler was moved to admiration by British propaganda and what he terms the " brilliant understanding of the primitiveness of sentiment in the mass of the people." It taught him, he asserts, that " the receptive ability of the masses is very limited ; their understanding small." They have, on the other hand, a great power of forgetting. This being so, all effective propaganda must be confined to very few points, which must be brought out in the form of slogans " until the very last man is enabled to comprehend what is meant by any slogan." Whether or not British propaganda was the inspiration, here was the principle which guided the master-in-chief of Nazi propaganda, which built up the National Socialist Movement and installed Hitler in the seat of Hindenburg. Hitler went marching down through propaganda all the way to power.

3

*Hitler joins the German Workers' Party and becomes chief of propa-
ganda. He wins his spurs as mob orator and obtains control
of the Party. The founding of the Storm Troops and the
troubles they caused.*

It was midsummer of the year 1919. The War had
been over for nine months. Soldiers had come back to
Bavaria to civil life, bitter and disillusioned. To their
minds their Fatherland had been betrayed, first by the
rulers of the Imperial House, who had deserted their posts,
and then by the Marxists who reigned in their stead—
Marxists who disowned their predecessors and all their
works, disowned in particular the War and the men who
had taken part in it. There were murmurings of discontent. On all hands the malcontents were forming
themselves into new parties and organisations, each with
its own programme for remedying national wrongs.

One July day, at a beer house in Munich, members of the
German Workers' Party were holding a meeting. There
were a couple of dozen people present listening to an
address from Gottfried Feder.[1] There was nothing to
indicate that this gathering was a decisive moment in the
history of Germany.

There marched into the room a man of military bearing,
who was made welcome by the chairman. Corporal
Hitler took his place in the audience and listened with
politeness, but no particular interest, to the address. A
" Professor " followed, and chanced in his speech to refer
to the Austrian-Germans. An Austrian-German himself,
Hitler's attention was aroused, and so was his indignation,
at the views the speaker was expressing. When the Professor
sat down Hitler rose and asked leave to reply, and he
launched out in a speech of fiery denunciation. It was his

[1] Feder played a considerable part in the formation of Hitler's
political opinions. It was from him that Hitler heard the first
discussion in his life on international banking. Feder was part
author of the Nazi programme of 25 Points. When Hitler came
to power a minor Government post (under-secretary to the
Ministry of National Economy) rewarded the services of Feder.

first address to the German Workers' (later National Socialist) Party, and such was the effect of his scathing eloquence, that the Professor fled from the room " like a drenched poodle," as Hitler said afterwards.

A few days later Hitler received by post an intimation that he had been elected to the Party, and a summons to attend an executive meeting for his formal admission. Now it was Hitler's intention to launch out into politics, but his ambition was to form a party of his own. There seemed no particular reason why he should depart from his plans to join this hole-in-a-corner organisation, but for some reason the German Workers had caught his imagination. He answered the summons and found that there were six members of the Executive. He put them through a cross-examination regarding their intentions, and left to consider further the matter of his membership. He tells in his autobiography that he sensed this to be a critical moment in his life, and in his mind turned over at length the question : to join or not to join. Ultimately he decided to become the seventh member of the Executive, the decisive influence being that the Party was so nebulous in its programme, so lacking in organisation, that there was little appreciable difference between joining this and forming a new organisation. Here, in effect, was a new party, only waiting for a leader to give it life, character and purpose. Thus it was Adolf Hitler was enrolled as the seventh member of the inner circle of the German Workers' Party.

The German Workers had originated some months before as an organisation founded by Anton Drexler, a locksmith, under the title of the Committee of Independent Workers. Its original aim was the promotion of the conclusion of peace with honour. After the War ended Drexler reconstituted his movement as an organisation for the working classes, and secured as president a journalist named Karl Harrer. At the time of Hitler's visit there were forty members, with an inner circle of six.

It was not entirely by chance that Adolf Hitler attended the meeting. He had been with his regiment in Munich when Eisner's Bavarian Soviet was overthrown by *freikorps* soldiers of the counter-revolution under Ritter von Epp. Hitler was one of those sent out to investigate the activities of local political organisations. He had brought himself to the notice of his superiors by his talent for ready speaking, and had been appointed Education Officer for the troops, a post which gave him his first opportunity to develop his gifts of rhetoric. As member of the German Workers' Party he found new scope for training as mob orator, found scope, too, for his talents for organisation and propaganda. The German Workers were without a programme, without a leaflet, without even a rubber-stamp. He devoted himself to filling in the blanks, contriving to secure his appointment to the control of propaganda. He soon showed that he had a flair for publicity. More than anything the Party required to become known, and the best means thereto in Hitler's view was to arouse the opposition of antagonists. Flags and posters made their appearance in Munich in flaming red colours, the red of Socialism and Communism, but his red slogans proclaimed anti-Communist sentiments, denounced Communism in biting and aggressive terms. The device was successful in attracting new members and engaging the opposition of the Left Wing organisations. Attendance at Party meetings mounted.

When he first joined, eighty invitations, partly typed, and partly written out laboriously by hand, were issued. The seven members of the inner circle would assemble, and after an hour's delay, in the vain hope of new adherents, the meeting would proceed. Within a space, Hitler had increased the attendance to a hundred. For the first time, he himself took the platform. He had faith that the power of words had been conferred on him, but he had not put it to the test at a public gathering. When the night came he had no stage-fright, but, confident in his ability, he poured forth a torrent of words for thirty minutes. What he knew within himself to be the case he proved by experience—that he was a born orator. His eloquence resulted in the collection of the sum of £15 necessary to defray the costs of the meeting.

In addition to publicity and organisation, Hitler provided the German Workers with a programme of twenty-five points. First and foremost was the declaration that all Germans should unite in a pan-Germany, a fundamental matter for the man who was born over the frontier in Austria, and who still lacked German nationality. The next three points concerned the position of Germany in the eyes of the world, embodying declarations of her equality of rights, the necessity for wiping out the treaties of peace, and for the grant to her of colonies for her surplus population. Point six proclaimed the anti-Semitism of the Party ; Jews could not be members of the German nation, were indeed only foreigners living in Germany, who should not have the right to vote, nor to hold office in municipality or State. Point seven embodied the pet principle of Gottfried Feder, that the " tyranny of interest " must be broken, and unearned income abolished. Point eight required the nationalisation of financial and industrial trusts and combines. There were other points calling for land reforms and the creation of a strong central government. Any tendencies exercising " disrupting influence " on the national life, whether in art or literature, should be stamped out, and non-members of the German nation should not be allowed to control newspapers.

The year passed, and propaganda and publicity under the inspiration of Executive Member No. 7 saw the Party firmly established. Hitler submitted that the time for a mass meeting had arrived—to this Herr Harrer demurred. It was a personal crisis in the career of Member No. 7. Had he given way then, his growing prestige would have received a set-back. He carried the day. Herr Harrer retired from the chairmanship, to which Anton Drexler succeeded.

The Munich mass meeting marked a new stage in the programme of the young Party. Hitler himself made all the arrangements. Flaming red posters announced the gathering for February 24. A crowd of nearly two thousand was attracted to the hall. A third were supporters, a third were merely curious, and a third were opponents from the ranks of Socialism and Communism. Hitler was the second speaker. He opened his remarks to the sound of uproar. Interruptions rained on him ; as he spoke on, disturbances broke out throughout the hall. Soon, half a dozen free fights were in progress as the stewards dealt in summary fashion with hecklers. At the end of half an hour the interruptions were drowned by the applause ; at the end of the speech the audience rose to cheer ; for the first time the cry " Heil Hitler " was heard in a Munich public hall.

In the month of April, 1920, Hitler left his regiment to
devote his whole time to his new party. He now took a
step which had a decisive influence on the growth and
tactics of the movement—of organising what he termed
" defensive troops " for the movement, now renamed the
National Socialist German Workers' Party.[1] Attack, they
say, is the best means of defence. The troops, which were
to defend free speech at Nazi meetings, were soon carrying
the attack into the other camp. Hitler proclaimed the
principle that the movement must ruthlessly prevent, if
necessary by force, meetings or lectures calculated to poison
the minds of fellow-citizens with Marxism. Munich
learned of " cold friction " as the new political argument.
The halls of opponents were invaded and there were frequent
skirmishes in which blood flowed. Hitler on one occasion
was sentenced to three months' imprisonment for his
violence, of which sentence two-thirds was remitted. Political meetings in Munich became more notable for feats
of physique than for their intellectual appeal.

A landmark in the inaugural stage of National Socialism
was the acquisition of a newspaper—the *Völkischer Beobachter*.
This weekly paper had been heavily in debt, and Hitler
obtained the funds necessary to purchase it through the
good agencies of Captain Ernst Röhm, No. 60 on the list
of members of the German Workers' Party. Röhm was one
of those soldier politicians who occupied himself after the
War in the organisation of military forces, then forbidden
to Germany. The soldiers who led the counter-revolutionaries of Bavaria needed political support against the
Left Wingers they had ejected, and it was in furtherance
of this policy that Röhm had joined the Workers' Party,
to which Hitler had been sent as investigator. When the
opportunity of purchasing the *Völkischer Beobachter* occurred,
Röhm secured the interest and support of General von Epp,
and thus was provided the 60,000 Marks necessary to
acquire the newspaper.

The propagandist-in-chief of the National Socialists was
now provided with a complete battery for publicity, and the
Party flourished accordingly. It developed outside Munich,
local branches being established as far distant as Frankfurt-
on-Main. Membership mounted from the original 60 to

[1] Deutsche Nationalsozialistische Arbeiter-Partei.

3000 by the close of 1920. In 1921 Hitler was able to fill
Munich's largest hall, the Zirkus Krone, with an audience
of 8000. As his fame spread he looked towards Prussia
and Berlin, and thereby brought about a crisis in the Party.

Up to the summer of 1921 Hitler was no more in the Party
than propagandist-in-chief, under the nominal authority of
President and Committee, but the propagandist obviously
counted for more than President and Committee combined.
This position caused no feeling of personal jealousy until,
with the spread of activities beyond Munich, others began
to cast eyes of envy upon the position and fame Hitler had
built up. Hitler's rivals began to work upon the feeling
of Anton Drexler, the locksmith President, representing
that Executive Member No. 7 was arrogating to himself
prerogatives of leadership. Drexler allowed himself to be
persuaded ; a curb must be placed upon No. 7's activities.

Hitler's ascendancy was such that the conspirators did
not dare to face him openly. They sought, instead, to
undermine his position by underground methods. They
attacked him through an anonymous pamphlet, which
accused him of lust for power and personal ambition, and
charged him with bringing disunion and schism into the
Party ranks. It declared that it was his purpose to use
the Party as a spring-board for his own personal aggrandise-
ment. It sought to represent that he was furthering the
interests of the Jews, and the conspirators attempted to
exploit his reticence regarding the sources of the money
which he was successful in obtaining for the Party chest.
National Socialists were warned that Hitler was a
demagogue, a man who relied solely on his talents as a
speaker, who was capable of leading good Germans astray.
Members of the Party were urged to attack him and to
support the founders of the movement.

Hitler had been in Berlin while the conspiracy was
maturing. When news of it reached his ears, he hurried
back to meet his accusers. He faced them squarely,
characteristically. He threatened resignation. He turned
the attack on him into an attack on the attackers ; he
overwhelmed the executive ; he convinced the Party ; he
triumphantly secured the defeat of his rivals. Drexler
found himself seconded to the rank of honorary president ;
Hitler was promoted to the presidency ; to crown his

ADOLF HITLER 33

personal victory, the Party constitution itself was amended
to give him unlimited powers.

By this means did the propagandist-in-chief become
recognised leader of the National Socialist Party. His
first concern was to evolve a new section within the Party.
This revealed his sense of political realities. He had already
known intrigue. He now determined to place himself
beyond the scope of intriguers. This could be done only
in one way. He must have a group of supporters whose
loyalty was unquestioned—followers upon whom he could
rely to overcome any possible future rival who might covet
his throne. To this end he reorganised the defence troops,
and out of them formed a new offensive force to which was
given the title of Sturmabteilung, or S.A.—the famous
brown-shirted Storm Troops. This corps was given a
uniform entirely brown—shirt, tie, breeches, tunic with Sam
Browne belt and peaked cap. On the left arm was worn a
red band bearing a black swastika on white ground. Then
he had to explain why these troops were formed. He
declared that they were a sub-section to be devoted to
gymnastics and sport. Never was a bodyguard so skilfully
explained away. These are Hitler's words : " Men and
comrades of the S.A. By the Treaty of Versailles the enemies
of our nation, both internal and external, have forbidden
us the right to organise our defence. According to their
wishes our technical disarmament should have been followed
by a spiritual one. . . . It is the aim of the National Socialist
Party to set up a new Germany in place of the old ; this
can only be possible if a spirit of national honour is intim-
ately allied to an unlimited desire for freedom. The aim
of the S.A. is to prepare for the nation a body of young
Germans who are morally and physically ready to defend
her . . . out of hundreds of thousands, the S.A. will weld
one single, powerful disciplined organisation. . . ."

With this force at his command, Hitler reckoned that he
would be able to face any personal adversaries, but the
new force became the means of involving him in a dispute
with Captain Röhm, and in the danger of losing the Party
leadership. The troubles in the Ruhr were at their height.
Captain Röhm, who was a soldier first and a Nazi second,
urged that the S.A. should form part of a secret army, the
peace treaties forbidding the overt formation of military

forces. Hitler objected. He wanted his troops for the political ends he had in view for his Party, to assist in guarding his meetings and wrecking the meetings of his opponents. Röhm, however, had his way. Reichswehr officers took over the training of the Storm Troops, and placed them under military orders. The S.A. might have passed entirely beyond Hitler's control, and he might have been robbed of this essential backbone of his organisation, but for the Munich *putsch* which, though it failed and temporarily damaged his prestige, led to his complete freedom from the Reichswehr.

One notable recruit (later destined to play a mighty part in the revolution) Hitler gained just before the *putsch*. This was Hermann Göring, formerly flight captain, one of the most courageous of the German airmen during the War —an " ace " respected by armies, whether German or Allied. Even amongst the daring members of the Richthofen Circus, the most destructive air squadron in the German service, his courage stood out and he gained the highest German decoration for valour i n the field—the Order Pour le Mérite. His detractors say that he nerved himself on drugs,[1] but drugs cannot make a coward into a brave man ; nor can drugs induce efficiency. Since the close of the War, Göring had worked for a Swedish air company, and had married a baroness. Returning to Germany he listened one day to Hitler addressing one of his Munich meetings, and sought to become a member of the Party. He found ready admission, for his wealth made him a desirable recruit in the days when the Party finances were not flourishing, and he was appointed Leader of the S.A. Göring was a man of brilliant personality, but liable to outbreaks of sudden passion, relics of the days when his nerves were taxed by the strain of aerial combat.

[1] It seems an unnecessary slur on the reputation of a man who served his country in the War to have dragged against him the slander that only morphia nerved him to his exploits in the air. His morphia addiction was not attested before the Courts until 1926, during a lawsuit over the custody of his wife's child by a former marriage.

4

*A march on Berlin stops short at Munich. Hitler marches with Luden-
dorff and is sent to prison to write his life story. Party
successes follow a set-back.*

It was the eve of the fifth anniversary of the Armistice.
Five years of tribulation for Germany had passed and the
new Republic had survived, despite bitter denunciations
from the extremists on either side, Communist and
Nationalist alike.

There had been five years of privation and further inflation
of the currency had come to rob the people of such of their
life savings as remained. The Government printing presses
were turning out Marks by the million, and the purchasing
power of the single Mark faded away into insignificance.
A life's savings vanished with a meal ; a fortune was
needed to pay the rent. Thousands of German families
were reduced to penury. Children died from malnutrition.
Discontent increased—discontent, the best auxiliary of the
agitator. Communist and Nationalist alike gained more
adherents as they cried " Down with the Government."

The French occupied the Ruhr. The street-corner
orators fanned the flames of German patriotism. If poverty
and distress were sapping vitality, they were spurring the
spirit to get something done. Hitler and the Nazis from
their strongholds in Bavaria quickly summed up the
situation. They threatened a march on Berlin to turn out
the Government of betrayers. There must be a " Night
of Knives " they declared, against the Jews, who flourished
on all sides, despite the afflictions of the people. Heads
must roll in the dust, the heads of the enemies of Germany.

It was the eve of the fifth anniversary of the Armistice.
Hitler, the man of destiny, faced a great assembly in his
hall at Munich. A sea of upturned faces, expectant,
enthusiastic, fanatical, greeted his eyes as he surveyed the
scene from the platform. Beside him stood von Kahr,
Dictator of Bavaria, General von Lossow and Colonel
Seisser, Chief of the Bavarian Police.

Suddenly Hitler drew his revolver. There was a report
and a bullet embedded itself in the ceiling. The upturned
faces became more expectant—more fanatical.

It was the moment of crisis. The revolt was now due to begin : the march on Berlin to be announced, the overthrow of the betrayers and the establishment of a new government of the German people proclaimed.

Dictator von Kahr and his two companions were invited by Hitler to withdraw to an ante-room, to be informed by Hitler of the roles allotted to them. He begged their Excellencies' pardon for not having consulted them before appointing them to their new places, but there was need for prompt action. Thereupon there was produced to Dictator von Kahr and his two companions a " Proclamation to all Germans " bearing the signatures of members of the Provisional Government—General Ludendorff, General von Lossow, Colonel Seisser and Adolf Hitler, of whom only the last had had foreknowledge of the proclamation's existence.

To his three companions Hitler announced the impending deposition of President Ebert. Hitler was to be Chancellor, von Kahr, Regent Governor of Bavaria ; and General Ludendorff's office would be that of Regent Governor of Germany. There were also posts for Seisser and von Lossow.

Now was the moment of crisis for the leader of revolt. Would the men upon whom he sought to thrust the role of fellow-conspirators consent to conspire ? He turned and harangued them as though they were a mass meeting. With tears in his eyes he pleaded with them. With his pistol in his hand he threatened them. " Here," he declared, " I have four shots. Three for you if you desert me, and one for myself."

General Ludendorff drove up by car to the hall, and was immediately conducted to the ante-room. He was ready to undertake his appointed role. The others were uncertain.

Hitler went back to the hall to announce the overthrow of the government of betrayers, to seek the sanction of his supporters for his self-made appointment. The upturned faces radiated fanatical support ; hundreds of voices rose in acclamation.

Hitler returned to the ante-room. Now that their appointment had been publicly announced and endorsed, now that they had been committed to the revolt, would von Kahr and his companions consent to play their part ? The three shook hands with him. All now had tears in

their eyes, and he took this as a sign of assent. Back went
Hitler to look once more upon those upturned faces. In
their presence he felt confidence in the hour of crisis.
They nerved him to go forward. " To-morrow," he
declared, " the betrayers will be overthrown. To-morrow,
Germany will have a new government, or you will have
our corpses to bury."

Only Ludendorff of the five men who met in the
ante-room found sleep that night. There was no rest for
Hitler, who had his marching orders to complete. There
was no rest for Dictator von Kahr, who had his orders
still to obtain. By telephone the Dictator of Bavaria
consulted his master, Rupprecht, head of the Bavarian
house of Wittelsbach. Rupprecht would be King of
Bavaria if the revolt succeeded, and he might have fallen
for the bait had not Ludendorff been in the conspiracy,
but Ludendorff had inspired the hatred of the former
Crown Prince. Over the telephone wire came his curt
refusal to be associated in the *putsch*.

Dictator von Kahr was a loyal servant of the house of
Wittelsbach. Before morning the broadcasting station of
Bavaria announced to the German people that Dictator
von Kahr and his two associates would not take part in the
march on Berlin. Their participation in the revolt had been
obtained under threat of Hitler's pistol, and now that they
were free they repudiated the Nazi leader and all his
putsch. The broadcast concluded with the announcement
of an official ban on the National Socialist Party and an
order for its immediate dissolution.

There were no upturned faces radiating fanatical support
in the morning. In the cold light of a November day,
Hitler had to make his choice between withdrawing with
damaged prestige, or to face armed authority in the streets
for a march which he knew must lead to a Munich prison,
if he were to escape with his life. Better, he decided, to risk
liberty and life than suffer ridicule and loss of prestige.
So, with his Storm Troops behind him, with Ludendorff
in frock-coat and top-hat at his side, supported by Göring
and Röhm, he marched through the Munich streets. A
few of the Storm Troops were armed, but most of them
were lacking in everything but enthusiasm, and to keep up
their spirits they sang Nazi songs as they marched.

An aide-de-camp hurried up to announce that an armoured car was being brought into action against them. The man who had won the Iron Cross in the War was not to be intimidated. The march went on. The procession came in sight of armed soldiers. Hitler marched on. The soldiers made ready to fire. Still Hitler marched on.

A volley sounded. In the front ranks of the advancing Nazi column many were seen to fall—Röhm, Göring. Hitler marched on no more, but to escape the fusillade, threw himself on the ground with such force that his shoulder was damaged. Ludendorff marched on ; marched into the crowd ; marched out of sight. Fifteen of the Hitlerites were killed, many were wounded. Those who had arms flung them aside. The column melted away. The revolt was over. Hitler escaped without irreparable loss of prestige and with no more damage than a bruised shoulder. The bullets had missed him, although he marched at the fore. He owed his life, it has been stated, to the fact that Ludendorff was at his side. The soldiers took care that their bullets went nowhere near the Generalissimo.

Hitler fled, and was arrested in the Villa of a Princess before he was able to cross the Austrian frontier. Göring fled too, and made good his escape. He was smuggled by his wife and friends into Austria and when he had recovered from his wound he went on to Italy, land of Fascism.

Hitler had escaped the bullets, but what was to be his fate ? As leader of a revolt, guilty of high treason, he was liable to the penalty of death. It was not a man expecting the death penalty who appeared before the judges when the judicial sequel to the failure of the *putsch* took place in the spring of the following year. With Hitler there were placed on trial Ludendorff, Röhm, Dr. Frick and a few more. The accused were in a cheerful mood as they took their places in the court-room—the mess-room of the former military academy. It was the mildest of mild indictments that the State Prosecutor submitted to the Court. There was testimony to the patriotism of Hitler. The patriotism of Ludendorff stood above testimony.

The speech of the occasion was made by Hitler. His

defence was a justification by way of attack on the Government he had tried to overthrow. The old tactics again—never be on the defence but attack, always attack. After a few moments, while he warmed to his words, Hitler was haranguing the Court. He spoke, not as a man addressing his Judges, but as if he were facing fanatical supporters. It was not he who was on trial ; it was the Government. Even Ludendorff was roused.

The Court's verdict reflected the effect of his address. There could be no prison, it was decided, for the Generalissimo ; Ludendorff's release was ordered on the ground that he had been carried away by the excitement of the moment. For Hitler the sentence was one of five years' detention in a fortress, but it was mitigated to the extent that his release could be ordered after a few months if his conduct merited it. Sentences passed on the minor offenders were minor indeed.

So ended Hitler's *putsch*, the only attempt he made at insurrection, his only deviation from the path to power by way of propaganda. It was a deviation which cost him more than a few months' confinement in his fortress prison, passed in the writing of his autobiography. His failure and his absence from the political arena formed a set-back to the Nazi movement. The improving state of Germany, the lessening of the discontent, combined with his absence to set back the Nazi clock. When he left prison he found the National Socialist Party languishing. It was swaying, too, towards the Socialist Left, and Hitler had to labour with renewed vigour. He had some consolation in finding that the movement was not flourishing in the absence of its leader. What greater tribute could there be to his own indispensability !

The *putsch* brought about one development which Hitler could regard with complete satisfaction—the freeing of his forces from the influence of Reichswehr. Because of the illegal rising the National Socialists were declared illegal, and for a time the movement had to be carried on under the title of the Popular Party. During his imprisonment Hitler gave much thought to the problem of leadership, and on regaining his liberty after eight months in the Fortress of Landsberg, his first act was to reorganise the movement on an autocratic basis. He lost the assistance of Röhm,[1] who left Germany to find a sphere for adventure in the service of Bolivia, but he had gained two important recruits. The first of these was Gregor Strasser, who was to perish in the clean-up of July, 1934, and the other, Dr. Paul Joseph Goebbels, who has been termed the Nazi Mephistopheles.

Everyone now knows of Goebbels, the cripple boy, the Minister for Propaganda of Germany, first person to hold such a ministerial appointment in Europe. Goebbels came into the movement as a result of the influence of Strasser, by whom the Nazi gospel had been carried into Northern Germany. For a time there was a prospect that Strasser and Goebbels would lead a conspiracy of the Socialist wing of the Nazi movement to capture the leadership. Hitler was alarmed, but he contrived to detach Goebbels and sent him to take charge of propaganda in Berlin. Here he rendered fine service to the cause. He had to take charge of a branch of the Party which was split by the rival jealousies of would-be leaders. He carried out a purge, and under his leadership the conversion of Berlin vigorously proceeded. The apostle of Berlin is one of the few eminent members of the Party who did not see service in the War, for which he was rendered unfit by his lameness. He is a man of small stature, which is counterbalanced by his intellectual energy. He had served an apprenticeship in propaganda as a journalist.

Publicity and propaganda, the beating of the Nationalist drum, and the organisation of workers and workless, particularly of workless, soon made up for the leeway lost as a result of the Munich rising. The National Socialist Party transcended the territories of Bavaria and became an organisation on a national scale. It advanced with gathering momentum. Membership rose with increasing velocity. When 1926 began Hitler could count on less than 17,000 members ; he could look upon 40,000 in 1927. By 1929 membership had risen to 120,000.

[1] There was a further dispute regarding the role of the S.A. which Hitler wished only to be a subordinate adjunct to his political organisation, whereas Röhm, the soldier, considered that the Storm Troops should be kept clear of politics. Röhm sent in his resignation, and his letter, despite his services, remained unanswered. He went without a word of thanks.

The growing distress which Germany suffered at the onset of the world depression provided a further stimulus to recruiting. Unemployment mounted by leaps and bounds, and the politically discontented linked up with the political extremists, either of the Right or of the Left. By 1930 the Nazi membership had reached a quarter of a million. At the elections in September, six and a half million votes were cast for Hitler, and the Party gained 107 seats in the Reichstag, forming the second largest party, ranking after the Social Democrats.

After ten years of propaganda Hitler had arrived as a National figure. He was now supreme head of the Party, combining leadership of the Storm Troops with that of the Party. Röhm had been summoned back from Bolivia to become his Chief of Staff. Hitler's position was safe-guarded by the existence of the S.S., his personal defence force, *corps d'élite* of the party.

Hitlerism had now arrived on the political stage on which the final struggle for power was enacted.

5

A tale of intrigue in politics with a moral for politicians who tamper with democracy. Tells of a forgetful plotter, the rise and fall of the arch-intriguer and the men who gambled with Hitler.

Depression descended upon the world. Trade began to cease, production to be curtailed because no one would buy. Currencies were threatened as confidence was destroyed. After a period of comparative tranquillity, all was unrest again in Germany. World depression and international mistrust destroyed the results of years of patient international negotiations.

There were new masters in Germany now. President Ebert had gone ; Stresemann, the pacificator, was dead. Hindenburg occupied the presidential chair ; Dr. Brüning sat precariously in the Chancellor's seat.

An able man this Dr. Brüning, industrious, well-inten-tioned and correct, but not the man to ride the whirlwind of depression. German fears of chaos and confusion were

not to be stilled by the precise voice which declared :
" We are firmly resolved to proceed along our chosen path,
waiting the time which soon must come when international
co-operation will save the world from sinking into misery
and chaos." Not by words like these was the spirit of
Locarno to be perpetuated when Germany was swept by
the economic blizzard. German ears were more responsive
to the fiercer tones of Hitler. " Ladies and Gentlemen "
and the " Spirit of Locarno " could not prevail against the
impassioned barrage that burst in torrents from the Führer.
" Men and Women of Germany " produced more response
from the sea of upturned faces than the formalities of
" Ladies and Gentlemen " and the " Spirit of Locarno."

The Nazi programme had now reached the full flood
tide. The Nazi sail was spread to catch every breath of
discontent. Redress for every grievance, right for every
wrong, a catchword for every class were offered by the
propagandist-in-chief and his lieutenants. Workers were
promised higher wages, but employers would gain higher
profits ; tenants would live in lower-rented houses, but
house-owners would receive higher rents ; peasants would
get more for their produce, but the middle classes would
buy cheaper food. Under their all-embracing title the
Nazis contrived to set their appeal to Nationalists, to
Socialists and to workers, or, what was more important in a
state where eight or nine millions were unemployed, to
workless.

As the effects of the depression became more severe, the
burden of reparation payments under the Young Scheme
became more oppressive. More strident grew the Nazi
denunciations against reparations and the Peace Treaty,
under which the burden was imposed. The " Diktat," as
they called it, placed on Germany the responsibility of war
guilt, and thus justified the exaction of reparations. For ten
years every statesman in Germany had been protesting at
home against this attribution of war guilt. The nation had
been convinced long since that the Treaty of Versailles
embodied an international lie, but statesmen who had
declared German innocence at home, had abroad to conduct
international negotiations on the basis of Germany's war
guilt. Statesmen proclaiming German war innocence at
home found it difficult to justify to the German people the

agreements reached abroad. The fundamental contradiction undermined their position. Hitler had freedom to
fulminate against the Peace Treaty, and the Reparations
Plan, a " scheme for the enslavement of the German people,"
with all the extravagance of his eloquence. It was the most
formidable weapon in his armoury of propaganda.

Germany faced bankruptcy once again. Dr. Brüning
had placed burden after burden upon the taxpayer in an
effort to make the budget balance, and drastic economies
were enforced. In the Civil Service, salaries of employees
were reduced 10 to 13 per cent ; Reich Ministers were
required to yield up to 30 per cent. The German Treasury
was at the end of its resources ; the German taxpayers could
support no more. The President proclaimed to the world
that the limit had been reached of privations that could
be expected of the people. There was throughout the
country a sense of impending catastrophe. A *coup d'état*
from the Right or from the Left was momentarily expected.

Dr. Brüning no longer thought it expedient for the
Reichstag to meet,[1] and an adjournment of six months was
announced with the President's sanction. The Chancellor
ruled by decree under Article 48 of the Constitution.
This provided the means whereby the Cabinet, in a state
of national emergency, might authorise the issue of decrees
without immediate parliamentary authority. It was a
dangerous step for the Chancellor to take, a perilous
weakening of his own position, a dangerous precedent for
any successor. The head of a Government who disavows
democratic control thereby loses democratic support and
places himself at the dependence of the head of the State.
Dr. Brüning escaped from party difficulties in the Reichstag
to be involved in the perils of intrigue. In his fate may be
seen a warning to the democratic statesman who is tempted
to tamper with democracy's institutions.

[1] Brüning took office in March, 1930, on the break-up of the
great coalition in which Stresemann was Foreign Minister under
Müller. The Brüning Ministry was a move to the Right, the
Social Democrats being manœuvred out of office. He had no
majority in the Reichstag, but was always hoping to gain the
support of the Nazis. Hitler was approached on several occasions,
but refused to co-operate with any Ministry of which he was
not himself the head.

While Dr. Brüning was trying to meet the economic blizzard with his decrees, adding to the unpopularity of a ministry perpetually forcing the nation to tighten its belt, Hitler found a previously unexploited opportunity for propaganda. Hindenburg's first Presidential term elapsed and Hitler stood as candidate, German nationality being hurriedly conferred on him by his appointment to the Legation in Berlin of the National Socialist Government of Brunswick. The Field-Marshal was returned by comfortable majorities, but the results were not disappointing for the ex-Corporal. In the first poll Hitler received eleven million votes against Hindenburg's eighteen and a half millions ; in the second the margin was reduced so that he gained thirteen millions to the President's nineteen. " He is eighty-five and I can wait," was Hitler's reflection.[1]

Shortly after the Presidential election Hitler received an unexpected blow from the Chancellor with the issue of an order banning the S.S. and S.A. It was a step for some time contemplated, but not previously dared, or considered politically expedient, for Brüning in his negotiations with foreign Powers found it an advantage to be able to point to the strength of his adversaries. " Look at the wild men who will overthrow me and take my place " was a not ineffective argument for a man seeking concessions. But at length Brüning solemnly announced that these illegal Nazi forces must be disbanded, it being " exclusively a matter for the State to maintain an organised force," to which political truism was added " as soon as such a force is organised by private persons and the State permits it, law and order are endangered." Germany received the order with incredulous cynicism. It seemed late in the day for the Government to come to a realisation of the dangers of long-tolerated illegalities.

Brüning's blow was disconcerting for the Brown Shirt leader, but the last laugh was with Hitler. Brüning was deposed, and the suppression of the Hitler forces was revoked.

Brüning, once regarded by the President as " best since Bismarck," had been falling from Presidential grace. His

[1] Ernest Thälmann, the Communist, polled 4,983,000 ; Lt.-Col. Duesterberg, joint leader of the Stahlhelm and Nationalist Candidate, 2,500,000.

expedients for budget-balancing moved him further and
further to the Left and the Presidential entourage was pre-
eminently of the Right—landowners of East Prussia, and
the comfortable gentlemen-philosophers of the Herrenklub.
There was alarm in the Herrenklub and among the Junkers.
Brüning was threatening the break-up of the bankrupt
East Prussian estates. " Agrarian Bolshevism " declared
the Junkers; " Bolshevism " echoed the Herrenklub.
Hindenburg was particularly sensitive regarding the estates
of East Prussia, for he had recently been presented, as a mark
of respect, with Neudeck, a former ancestral holding in
East Prussia that had passed out of his family. His sympathies moved with those of the Junkers and when they
pronounced the Chancellor to be " Bolshevik " he began
to see the blemishes in the " best since Bismarck."

It was represented to the Chancellor that he should
make way for the formation of a coalition, to lead to a return
of parliamentary government. Brüning was graciously
informed that he might retain the Foreign Office ; National
Socialist participation was contemplated at the price of
the grant of a couple of minor offices ; and the Ministry
thus provided with a parliamentary majority was to be
led by Baron Franz von Papen. Brüning had a final
interview with the President, brief, but extended over two
days, for an octogenarian President could not be expected
to endure the strain of long-continued conversations. The
President had been led by his Herrenklub advisers to believe
that Brüning would consent to take the subsidiary post in
the Coalition ; he was undeceived. Brüning refused
flatly to be associated with any such Ministry, and he
walked out. Hitler was equally uncompromising in his
refusal. So Franz von Papen had to take office without
allies in the face of the united opposition of National
Socialists, Catholic Centre, Social Democrats and
Communists.

Von Papen, who had been brought from the obscurity
of his Westphalian country home to succeed the " best
minister since Bismarck," had stood only once before on
the stage of history, and then, discredited, had disappeared
behind the falling curtain. By 1932 the world had forgotten
the escapade in which the German Military Attaché at
Washington had been involved not long before the United

States entered the War. The Military Attaché had been concerned in a plot to prevent the Allied powers from drawing supplies of war from America, then a neutral, to which end he had organised a band of conspirators to blow up factories and railways, to place bombs on British ships. But his conspiracy stood revealed when he lost his case of papers on the New York underground. The papers contained a complete list of his secret agents and much other information, and the forgetful Attaché was sent back to Germany, to be rewarded with the Order of the Red Eagle (fourth class).

The world had had fifteen years to forget the tale of the careless plotter when President Hindenburg was recommended to look upon Franz von Papen, genial and popular member of the Herrenklub, as the man who might succeed in ruling the Reich by more strictly constitutional methods and with a less Radical policy than Brüning and his decrees. Brüning and Hitler might damn the scheme by refusing to be associated with the new Chancellor, but there was still General von Schleicher to support von Papen, and von Schleicher had the Reichswehr behind him. The President had much faith in Kurt von Schleicher as a soldier with a flair for politics. Von Schleicher, a Prussian aristocrat, had been on the German Army Staff almost throughout the War. Then he installed himself at the German War Office and made himself into the indispensable link between the Army and the politicians. More and more he intruded into the sphere of politics, and whenever intrigue was on foot his influence could be detected.

Von Papen, with von Schleicher as his lieutenant, took office at the head of the "Almanach de Gotha" Cabinet, which is distinguished in German history for having the smallest numerical representation in the Reichstag. The elections on July 31, 1932, gave him no parliamentary basis for his power, but provided Hitler with a new triumph, 230 seats falling to the Nazis, an increase of 123 since 1930. The House was permitted to meet only for the transaction of formalities and was again dissolved. Again the elections failed to give von Papen a majority. He secured the support of only 10 per cent of the electorate, although he had the satisfaction of seeing the Hitlerite poll fall off by about 2,000,000 votes. But, ominous sign from the Left, the Communist vote increased by 700,000 and the Party's seats rose from 89 to 100.

Brüning had set the precedent for ruling unconstitutionally within the Constitution. Von Papen gave new examples of the manner in which the Chancellor could play the dictator. In the Prussian Diet the elections had gone against the Socialists, but Braun and Severing refused to leave the offices Socialists had held for ten years. The head of the Barons' Cabinet of the Reich was not the man to tolerate the Red Cabinet of Prussia, He followed Brüning's precedent of looking up the Constitution and discovered a clause suited to his purpose. This provided that if public order and security required, the ministry of any state might be supplanted by a Reich Commissioner. Von Papen pronounced that public order required the dismissal of Braun and Severing, and when, in defiance of the emergency *congé*, they declined to vacate their offices, the Chancellor had them bundled out unceremoniously. Here was another precedent for Hitler—a quick way with Socialist dissenters and effective, too.

There were new intrigues in Presidential circles. The Cabinet fell and von Papen again withdrew from the stage, this time consoled with a Presidential portrait and the inscription, " I had a comrade." Von Schleicher ruled alone. He was no Party man and had no Party following. He attempted to rule by means of a German Ministry of all available talents, aiming to establish a new state on an enlightened military despotism. But the economic blizzard would not tarry while he evolved the intricacies of a new despotism which should appeal to the masses. There were plots and counter-plots, von Papen organising opposition to the man who had supplanted him, von Schleicher weaving threads and cross-threads in his web of intrigue to maintain himself in power. Behind von Papen was the Herrenklub. Von Schleicher, the arch-intriguer, had no substantial backing, but only the opponents of von Papen, whom he had manœuvred to his own support.

Intrigue and counter-intrigue proceeded at the Presidential Palace, and amidst the shifting play of personality Hitler found he held the key to the situation. Von Papen approached Göring ; von Schleicher made addresses to Gregor Strasser, leader of the Left Wing National Socialists.

Von Papen met Hitler in Cologne.   Old adversaries at last
became allies.

Towards the end of January the Junkers delivered their
ultimatum to Hindenburg—von Schleicher must go.   He
had dared, like Brüning, to meddle with East Prussian estates.
Von Schleicher appealed for the dissolution of the Reichstag.   The President said " No," and issued the order of
dismissal.   Von Papen was ordered to negotiate with Hitler
for the formation of a new coalition.   Von Schleicher spun
his last webs of intrigue.   If he could find supporters, he
would dare the last gamble of a military dictatorship and
march the Potsdam garrison on Berlin.   Another *putsch* was
threatened by the Communists, who made their plans for
a revolution to begin with a general strike ;   railways were
to be cut, barracks and police stations seized.   The situation
in the country was critical.

At length, on the last day of January, 1933, a leap in the
dark was taken—Hitler was made Chancellor of the Reich,
a Chancellor in chains, but Chancellor at last.

It was a political gamble this Hitler ministry—a gamble
for the National Socialist leader and a gamble for the two
other predominant partners, von Papen and the Nationalist
Hugenberg, the Titan of the Ruhr, who were installed at
his side.   Hitler risked the chains for the sake of office, for
he feared the crumbling of the Party he had created.   There
had been growing discontent in the Brown Shirt ranks over
the Leader's obstinate rejection of office except on his own
terms.   The feeling had grown that it would be better to
temper the uncompromising refusal, to accept any ministerial spoils that offered.   A mood of despair is fatal to a
mass movement based on the emotions ;   and lack of success,
doubts and debts are the sure road to despair.   Even the
optimism of Goebbels was affected, and he was heard to
voice a fear that the entire movement might collapse.
Gregor Strasser threatened to split the Party by advocacy
of association with von Schleicher, and it needed the full
resources of the Leader and a full flood of tears to dispose
of the Strasser malcontents.   Strasser was driven out, and
Hitler's tears were the inspiration for renewed pledges of
loyalty to his leadership.   But the events were a warning
that the tide must shortly lead to victory or it would be too
late.

There was a warning, too, for Nationalists and industrialists in the Nazi slogan : " If the National Socialist
Movement collapses there will be another ten million
Communists in Germany." The last election had shown
that as the Nazi tide receded the Red tide flowed, and to
Hugenberg and the industrialists the Nazis were infinitely
preferable to the Reds. Hugenberg had need of Hitler,
and hence the meeting between the Nazi leader and von
Papen at a banker's house at Cologne. Thereafter there
was angling for position as the new associates by necessity
sought to turn the position each to his own advantage. At
last when the pact was made von Papen had some difficulty in
persuading the President to accept the Nazi leader, but
ultimately Hindenburg was persuaded to give his acquiescence to the appointment of Hitler at the head of a Ministry of National Concentration. He gave his consent, too, for
new elections on Hitler's pledge that whatever the result
might be the Ministers forming the Coalition should remain
in office thereafter. And was this pledge not enough ?
Göring might be the Prussian Minister of the Interior,
Dr. Frick[1] the Reich Minister of the Interior, but there was
von Papen as Vice-Chancellor, the Conservative von
Neurath at the Foreign Office and the substantial figure
of Hugenberg doubling the roles of Minister of Trade and
of Agriculture.

So Hitler took office, and eyes were turned forward to
the elections with varying degrees of hope and assurance.
Hindenburg looked to the Government to obtain a majority
which would permit the normal functioning of the Constitution to be resumed, for as a strict constitutionalist his
political conscience was uneasy over the long-continued
rule by decree. Von Papen and Hugenberg, in uneasy
proximity to Frankenstein and his monster, looked for a
result which would place Hitler in continued dependence
for a parliamentary majority upon Nationalist support.
Hitler looked forward with contrary expectations. Göring,
characteristically, looked nowhere, but got to work.

It is small tribute to the political sagacity of the men

[1] Dr. Frick, Chief of the Police Office in Munich, was among
those sentenced for participation in the *putsch*. In January,
1930, he was appointed Minister in Thuringia for Education
and Interior—first National Socialist Minister in Germany.

who sought to keep Hitler in chains that they allowed Nazis to have control through Göring and Frick of the forces for maintaining order in Berlin, Prussia and the Reich. How is national control to be effective against your adversary if he is in control of the guardians of law and order? Göring in the space of a month contrived to place the instruments of law and order at the disposal of the Nazis. There was a purge in the civil service and the police force. Administrators, officials and officers of Left Wing tendencies were dismissed or given leave, and were replaced by Nazis. From the S.A. and S.S. an auxiliary force of special constables was recruited. Göring called for ruthless measures against the enemies of the State and terrorists—meaning Nazi opponents, Communists in particular. " Every man," he proclaimed, " who in pursuance of his duty makes use of his weapons will be protected by me regardless of the consequences of his action. On the other hand, every man who from any false scruples does not use his weapons can anticipate proceedings against himself."

Göring provided for the Nazification of the guardianship of law and order. Hitler made tentative steps towards the control of the Press and the political platform. The precedent of the von Papen decrees pointed the way. A new emergency was declared by Presidential proclamation to provide for the " Defence of the German Nation." Power was thereby conferred upon the guardians of the law and order to prohibit public meetings where there was ground to fear that public security might be endangered and to suppress newspapers guilty of incitement to civil disobedience or the publication of false reports. It was an effective means for gagging opponents.

So approached the day of the poll which was to decide whether Hugenberg and the Nationalists had exploited the Nazis or were the dupes of Hitler. Had the years of Nazi propaganda, the fervour and the frenzy, been spent to provide a prop for the leaders of reaction, or was the poll on March 5 to free Hitler from his chains? The result was still unpredictable when the flames of the Reichstag fire transformed the German political horizon.

6

The mystery of Germany's Guy Fawkes and the profit and loss account of the Reichstag fire. Communists were placed on trial in Germany and Nazis stood accused at the bar of history. How Hitler's chains were burned away.

The burning of the German Parliament House on the night of February 27, 1933, is an event which will take its place on the calendar of history. Like the fall of the Bastille, it marks the passing of an old order, although no one on this occasion was heard to remark how great, how altogether admirable. The flames that destroyed the Reichstag emblazoned the passing of Germany's democracy.

Who was the Guy Fawkes of the plot against the German Parliament House ? We do not surely know, may perhaps never know. The identity of this German " Guy " may remain as impenetrable as that of the man in the Iron Mask or the author of the Letters of Junius. There are rival solutions favoured by controversialists of rival Parties, but controversy has not yet elucidated the truth.

Who did set fire to the Reichstag on the night of February 27, 1933 ? Hitler, who had first word, declared that it was the Communists. Hitler's enemies replied that he and his National Socialists, by this monstrous device, sought to turn the scales in their favour at the elections. Hitler averred that the Communists set the Reichstag on fire as the signal for a national rising. His opponents replied that no such rising took place; that, indeed, no possible advantage could have accrued to the Communists ; that, in fact, the conflagration resulted in their ruin and contributed to Hitler's ultimate triumph.

Rarely has truth proved more elusive. There has been all the paraphernalia of a State trial, the phantasy, too, of an international " inquiry." Publicists and controversialists throughout the world have set forth conclusions, built up on a mass of statement and asseveration, but the truth has not yet been conclusively established. One man was claimed a victim by German justice and paid the penalty of death, but his condemnation and execution did not advance the solution of the mystery.

Poor van der Lubbe. In whose cause did he yield up his life ? Was he a victim of Communist or of Nazi plotting, or was he no more than a victim of the workings of his own distorted brain ? If fame was his desire, then his desire has been granted, for his name will echo for years in the corridors of time. Was it possible that this half-demented Dutchman was responsible alone and unaided for this con- flagration which installed Hitler as dictator ? Was he in his weakness the fateful pawn on the chessboard of world history ? It seems difficult to credit. Almost incredible, too, that after months of effort on the part of rival and interested investigators the partners in this conspiracy should not have been revealed. If, indeed, the Communists were guilty of this crime it is noth'ng short of the incredible that the resources of the Nazis and the Prussian police, whipped to action by the indomitable Göring, should not have produced the evidence of guilt. Difficult, too, to believe that had the Nazis themselves been responsible for a monstrous "frame-up" their many opponents should not have ferreted out their guilty secrets.

Communists and Socialists may not have had facilities for running Nazi conspirators to earth, but there were Nationalist members of the Government whom Hitler later dismissed from office. They were in a position to discover the truth of the matter, and when they were dismissed they had the incentive which impels fallen Ministers to declare to the world facts embarrassing to the man who has dismissed them.

The established and indisputable facts concerning this history-making act of incendiarism can briefly be stated. It was somewhere in the region of fifteen minutes past nine o'clock on the night of February 27 when policemen on duty discovered the Reichstag building to be on fire. Flames were rising right from the centre of the building, and appeared to be already well established. The alarm was given, and some of the policemen made their way inside. In a lobby was found the Dutchman, Marinus van der Lubbe, who was overpowered in a struggle which was described as violent. The first persons on the scene in response to the call of alarm were members of the Storm Troops. They had received the order : " All at the double to the Reichstag ; leave your weapons ; you are wanted

for cordon duty ; the Reichstag is on fire." Twenty of them
had already arrived by the time the first fire brigade
appeared. Göring was not long behind, and Hitler and
Goebbels followed shortly afterwards, with von Papen, to
whom Hitler turned and said : "This is a God-given
signal. If this fire, as I believe, turns out to be the handi-
work of Communists, then there is nothing that shall stop
us now from crushing out this murder pest with an iron
fist." To a Press correspondent Hitler declared : "You
are witnessing the beginning of a great new epoch in
German history. This fire is the beginning."

By then the fire had spread throughout the building.
The brigades laboured heroically, but were unable to check
the onrush of the flames. The central portion of the building was burned out before morning. The Sessions Chamber, with the tribune and corridors, were destroyed. The
damage ran into millions.

That same evening the Berlin and other wireless stations
announced to the nation that the Reichstag had been set
on fire, and shortly there followed the statement that the
incendiary was van der Lubbe, a Dutch Communist, who
had made a full confession after having been caught in the
building. He was described as having been clothed only
in a pair of trousers, but nevertheless to have had in his
possession a Dutch passport and a membership book of the
Dutch Communist Party.

There is no doubting the effect of these announcements
upon the German listeners. To the foreign visitor to
Berlin there was nothing particularly impressive about the
Reichstag building, with its portico resembling the entrance
to one of the heaviest of the classical style of London churches
and with its dome and cupolas—a St. Paul's Cathedral,
lacking the impressiveness of St. Paul's. But to the German
people their Parliament House was the revered symbol of
their liberty, a token of their democracy.

A few days previous to the fire there had been reports of
the raiding of Karl Liebknecht House (the Communist
G.H.Q.) and the discovery of incriminating documents.
The papers had reported a bomb outrage in East Prussia
and a fire in the Berliner Schloss attributed to Communists.
These events had paved the way, psychologically, to secure
the fullest credence for the announcements made in the

staccato tones of the broadcaster, the modern voice of plenary inspiration. Within an hour or so of the discovery of the flames it had been established, almost beyond refutation, in thousands of German minds that it was the Communists who had set the Reichstag in flames. In his paper in the morning the German reader found confirmatory details of a nation-wide Communist plot, a rising against the Government, for which the fire was to have been the signal. Instructions for the carrying through of a Communist terror on a Bolshevist model were reported to have been discovered by the police in the search of Karl Liebknecht House—plans for the looting of Berlin, to have been followed by terrorist acts throughout Germany and the beginning of civil war.

Then after an accumulation of reports of Communist intentions, sufficient to make the stoutest heart quail, there followed assurances that General Göring had taken all necessary steps to meet the terrible danger. The first attack of the criminal force had been beaten back. Measures had been taken to preserve the peace of Germany, and therefore of Europe. As a sequel to the discoveries, the Communist papers, periodicals, leaflets and posters had been put under ban for a month. A similar interdict was to be enforced in the case of journals of the Social Democratic Party, this step being justified on the ground that van der Lubbe, in his confession, had admitted association with the Social Democrats.

Within twelve hours, therefore, of the fire the Government had placed under a ban of silence all sources of information except those which they themselves inspired. By emergency decree, restrictions were imposed on personal freedom and the right of free expression of opinion ; the privacy of correspondence, of telegraph and telephone was suspended. Thereafter there was absolute monopoly for the voice of the Government as heard by broadcast and through the Press, not merely as regards expression of opinion, but for the statement of fact on which opinion must be founded. By broadcast and through the Press the guilt of the Communist Party and the complicity of the Social Democrats were proclaimed and driven home with a multiplicity of detail. Communists who had set fire to the Reichstag as a signal for insurrection and civil war had planned to violate wives and murder children, to poison water in the wells and food in the restaurants. Terrorist acts on the widest front had been systematically prepared ; public buildings were to be set on fire ; wives and children (not presumably otherwise disposed of) were to be seized as hostages. Now was the Government campaign against the Communists to be conducted with the utmost rigour. "It will be my principal task," declared General Göring, " to extirpate Communism from our people. Let me tell the Communists my nerves have never given way up to now, and I feel strong enough to repay their criminal activities in kind."

Göring had lost no time in carrying out a round-up of all the prominent leaders of disaffection. No scruples regarding the apprehension of the innocent were allowed to become an impediment to the effective locking up of all suspects. The fire was discovered at 9.15. By midnight the first arrests had been made. Police officers and Nazi Storm Troopers went out into the highways and by-ways and returned with Communists, Socialists, Pacifists—Nazi opponents of whatever description. By morning, some hundreds of persons had been incarcerated.

As a result of the control of the Press no word reached the German people of the suspicions regarding the origin of the Reichstag Fire which outside Germany were being expressed more and more. In the World Press the reports of Communist plottings were received with growing incredulity. On the first day the announcement that the Communists had fired the Reichstag had been published by newspapers throughout the world, but as the investigations of special correspondents proceeded, there came doubts and then, in some directions, denials. It was roundly asserted that the National Socialists had fired the building as a means of discrediting the Communists and Social Democrats in the eyes of the German electorate in order to provide Hitler with a clear majority at the impending election. Of these allegations the German voters had heard little.

The effect on the poll on March 5 was indisputable. When the ballot-boxes were opened it was found that the Government had gained 52 per cent of the votes cast. The Ministry was thus assured of 52 per cent of the seats in the

Reichstag. The National Socialists themselves did not receive a clear majority, Hitler's poll being 17·2 million votes, or 43·9 of the total. On the result of the election Hugenberg would have been left in a position to determine Hitler's parliamentary fate, but the election result was already nullified by the decree under which Communists could be placed under lock and key. Without the eighty-nine Communists to divide against them, National Socialists could outvote all opponents. Such was the parliamentary significance of the Reichstag Fire. But though the Hitlerites profited so substantially from the circumstances of the conflagration, you cannot from that decide the identity of the plotters.

Van der Lubbe confessed his guilt, but it was obvious that van der Lubbe alone could not have carried into the Reichstag building all the apparatus of incendiarism. He could not alone and unaided have set the place alight, for the widespread flames indicated that the building had been set fire to at many points. Who, then, were van der Lubbe's confederates ? Four persons were placed in the dock with him when the trial at length took place : Ernst Torgler, head of the Communist Party in the Reichstag ; Blagoi Simon Popoff, student of law, and Vassili Tanev, a cobbler, two Bulgarian Communists ; and Georgi Dimitrov, one of the leaders of the Bulgarian Communist Party. For eight months the proceedings of this impeachment dragged out their course, first in Berlin and then in Leipzig. Communism was on trial before the German nation, and before the Bar of world opinion the National Socialists stood impeached on suspicion of complicity in the affair. After eight strenuous months, the proceedings ended in the conviction of the self-convicted van der Lubbe, the discharge of the Communists actually before the Court and the declaration of the guilt of Communism. It was " established," the Court found, " that van der Lubbe's accomplices are to be found in the Communist Party of Germany. Communism is equally guilty of the Reichstag fire ; for the German people stood in the early part of the year 1933 on the brink of chaos into which the Communists sought to lead them, and the German people were saved at the last moment by men of reliability."

Before the Bar of world opinion the guilt of Communism

was not so transcendentally clear, the innocence of the men of reliability not so confidently accepted. Since the findings of the Court, it has repeatedly been declared that Goebbels planned the scheme for firing the Reichstag, and Göring carried it into effect. It was pointed out that Göring beyond all others had the opportunity to cause the fire, for his ministerial palace communicated by underground passage with the Reichstag, and only through some subterranean channel could the paraphernalia of incendiarism have been smuggled in. This argument would have pointed more conclusively to Göring had not there been another subterranean approach to the Reichstag building to which access was gained from the street and not through the ministerial palace.

Van der Lubbe himself—in what capacity did he set fire to the Parliament House? Confederates he must have had. Were they Communist or Nazi? Of whom was he the tool? His voice can never tell, for he was silenced by the axe of the executioner. Was he incited by the Nazis to play the part of a Dutch Guy Fawkes? Was he promised rewards if he would allow himself to be taken red-handed, and to accept full responsibility? If you believe this you must assume that he was a dupe of the trick that Scarpia played on Tosca and her lover. You remember that Caverodossi was to face a firing squad, and his lover Tosca was told by Scarpia that it would be a pretence, and the squad would only fire blank shot, but to the officer in charge of the squad he gave directions that ball should be employed. Did the Nazis delude van der Lubbe with a promise of the formality of conviction, with release and rewards to follow, and then, Scarpia-like, turn pretence into reality? At some such supposition you must arrive if you are to believe van der Lubbe was a confederate of Nazi incendiarists. It is a terrible accusation.

The verdict at the trial was that the case against the named Communists was not proved. The verdict at the Bar of history is that the complicity of the Nazis was not proved. The Court found that the named Communists had acted suspiciously. At the Bar of history there are suspicions against the Nazis.

7

*The Nazi terror descends on Germany, falling without discrimination
on Socialists and Communists. The goading of the Jews.
Political parties are suppressed, the Press is silenced, the Nazis
are made supreme in the totalitarian State.*

The flames which destroyed the German Reichstag on
the night of February 27, 1933, were supposed to have been
the call for a Communist rising. They proved to be the
signal for the Nazi terror. The elections over, the Nazis
fell upon their enemies hip and thigh. Germany was given
over to an orgy of brutality. From above Trade Unionists,
Social Democrats and Communists saw their organisations
decreed out of existence by Government interdicts, their
propaganda silenced, their property confiscated. From
below their members were attacked by the Brown Storm
Troopers. Throughout the years of discontent, Social
Democrat and Communist had eyed each other with the
jealousy of political rivals, and had failed to present a
united front to their common enemies the Nazis. Now the
Nazis imposed common suffering upon them both, making
no distinction between the violent red of Communism and
the paler pink of the Social Democrat as they carried out
their campaign to eradicate Marxism, to bludgeon out
opposition in the creation of the totalitarian State.

For years the followers of Hitler had listened to harangues
about the poison of Marxism. For years they had heard
the promise of ultimate vengeance. Now, at last, was the
time for revenge, for settling old scores. In city and town
throughout the Republic, the Storm Troopers took toll.
Their opponents were fetched from their homes, carried
from their beds, to be hurried before the mockery of a
Brown Court.

The stories of atrocities, exaggerated as undoubtedly they
were, gave a terrible picture of a country surrendered for a
space to barbarism. Dog whips, horse whips, rubber
batons, steel rods were the instruments with which the
Brown Shirts were accused of having worked their will on
Marxists. Many of their opponents were beaten into
insensibility, some were permanently injured. It is a
pitiful chapter in Nazi history, and not to be explained

away. There was no sanctuary to be found by the victims ; no helper from whom they could obtain assistance. The police stood aside, officials of State made a mockery of complaints.

For the action against the Marxists it is possible for the National Socialists to put forward the excuse that these were their political opponents, who, had the tables been reversed, would have been equally ruthless in suppression of the Nazi organisation. But there is no such excuse available, no such pretext to be offered to explain away the treatment of the Jews. The hardships and misery that the Marxists had to suffer for their politics, the Jews had to endure because they were members of their race. Suffering has been the badge of Jewry throughout its history down the ages. In Germany the Jews had to suffer because of their eminence. Jews in all countries have been prominent in the politics of Marx. The first President of the German Republic, Ebert, was a Jew ; Kurt Eisner, a Jew, was a temporary dictator in Bavaria. Jews have always been astute financiers and there were some who prospered in Germany despite the economic whirlwind. Jews rose to eminence in the German professions, particularly that of the law. Jews of culture were notable figures in art, music and literature. Their names provided targets for the Nazi propagandists. The Jew and Marxist had shared pride of place in Nazi tirades of denunciation. The day of vengeance against the Marxists was to be a day of reckoning with the Jew, a modern St. Bartholomew's Day, a night of knives. The promise was fulfilled by Hitler's followers. Merchants were taken from their business, poor people from their homes ; even the synagogue was invaded and the Rabbi borne off. The energy with which the Storm Troopers carried out their leader's anti-Semite exhortations became a source of embarrassment to Hitler the Dictator. Jews who were citizens of other states were made to share in Brown Shirt persecutions. There were official diplomatic protests from Poland and the United States. A German-wide boycott of Jewish shops and stores, Jewish lawyers and doctors, was organised by the Nazis. Jews of the world began to organise a world-wide boycott against Germany on behalf of their brethren.

Hundreds of Jews left Germany, a country which forbad them the means of earning their livelihood, for officials of

State, lawyers, doctors, teachers and university professors were deprived of their posts. All Jewish judges were given leave of absence. An appeal was made to the sense of national duty to prevent the use of Jewish chemists, dispensers, opticians and dentists. In the universities Jewish lecturers were dismissed. Jews were removed from their posts as journalists. They were debarred from acting as assessors and jurors. They were made outcasts in the world of sport. Bruno Walter, a musical conductor known throughout the world, might no longer take his place at a German concert ; Arthur Schnabel was turned out of the German Academy of Music ; Max Reinhardt might no longer exercise his theatrical genius in Germany ; Elisabeth Bergner might no longer display her talents on the German stage ; Lion Feuchtwanger, creator of Jew Süss, and Emil Ludwig, the historian, were proscribed in Germany ; Einstein, greatest scientist since Newton, went into exile with a call to friends of Jewish civilisation to concentrate all their efforts in order to rid the world of a psychological disease which was bringing brutal force and oppression against the Jews in Germany.

Let the curtain descend on this spectacle of the terror. The scene is one at which democracy must look as upon the warning-board of danger. The " psychological disease " which smote Germany may infect other democracies if the people are not vigilant in the defence of their rights and liberties. When Germany emerged from the terror many rights and liberties had vanished. There was no longer a free press. Before the Reichstag burning, prohibitions had descended like hail upon German newspapers. Thereafter newspaper criticism of Hitler was suppressed out of existence. In twelve months German daily papers decreased from 2703 in 1932 to 1128 in 1933, and weekly papers fell from 348 to 217. Over 250 journals from abroad which once used to circulate in Germany were refused admittance.[1]

---

[1] A censorship was attempted on reports sent out of Germany by special correspondents of the foreign Press. In 1933, for instance, Mr. Noel Panter, special reporter of *The Daily Telegraph*, was arrested for having sent out a despatch describing the militarism of the Brown Shirts reviewed by Hitler. Mr. Panter was incarcerated for nine days on charges of treason and espionage before diplomatic pressure effected his release.

For the totalitarian State there must be totalitarian public opinion, and Dr. Goebbels was, in March, 1933, appointed as High Priest of public opinion, the first Minister of Propaganda in Europe. Under his control were placed all the influences which mould the people's thoughts, press, broadcasting, cinema and the theatre. With Paul Joseph Goebbels to supervise and censor, there was no chance of the disruptive influences of truth disturbing the placid lives of German men and women. Within the totalitarian Reich they were as secluded from corruption as girls guarded from the world in a convent school.

Political freedom vanished. The offices of Marxist organisations and Trades Unions were raided. Documents were confiscated and many headquarters set on fire. Political organisations in any way associated with revolutionary propaganda were outlawed. Within twenty-four hours of the first May Day of the Hitler Republic the dissolution was proclaimed of all German Trades Unions and the substitution of a committee for the protection of German labour with Dr. Ley at its head. Under his guidance was conducted a campaign to expose the corruption of the Trades Unions, the first step towards the confiscation of their money. A week later was issued an order for the confiscation of the property of the Social Democratic Party with its newspapers. Similar steps were taken against subsidiary organisations of the Social Democrats.

On May 13 Dr. Ley assumed responsibility for the confiscation of the entire property of the Trades Unions. Communists and Social Democrats passed into political oblivion. Democrats and the Catholic Centre followed them, even the Parties of the Right were dissolved. The National Socialist organisation was declared to be the first and only Party of the State. July 14, 1933, is the crowning date in the history of the National Socialist German Workers' Party when its complete monopoly of politics in the German Republic was by law established. Whosoever thereafter undertook to maintain the organisation of another political party, or to form a new political party, became liable to punishment by penal servitude or by imprisonment from six months up to three years.

There yet remain in the Concentration Camps reminders of the Terror, effective stimuli to totalitarian opinion.

To-day life behind the barbed wire has been robbed of its worst rigours, and the prisoners, the Schutzhäftlinge, are greatly reduced in numbers, so that not more than 2000 are believed to be subject to this form of incarceration. At the height of the Terror 20,000 inhabitants of Germany were, at the lowest computation, living behind the wire in conditions which remain a perpetual reproach to the governors of a supposedly civilised community. The brutalities inflicted, even allowing for the exaggerations of atrocity-mongers, have had no counterpart in England since the days when the rack stretched the limbs of victims in the Tower. The Konzentratsionslager has been humanised since the Terror, but it exists, symbol of an Oriental despotism which, at will, can order a man's detention without even the formality of a trial.

8

The Reichstag commits political suicide and despotism is established by law. Hitler stages a " Yes Day," provides work for the compilers of genealogies and conducts a moral purge.

From the beginning of February until the middle of July, 1933, was the period of the Hitler Revolution and the birth-throes of the Third Reich. In that time the entire basis of the German Republic was transformed. The Liberal democracy was shattered. The new totalitarian State was founded. A unified Germany, its constituents knit together as never before, was called into being, and over all presided Chancellor Hitler, in chains no longer. The gamble was over, and Hitler was proved conqueror. Of the two colleagues who had been placed at his side as guardians, one, von Papen, was suffered to remain. The other, Hugenberg, was cast off, Hitler conveniently forgetting the pledge he had given that whatever the result of the election might be, he would make no change in the Ministry.

The Reichstag was summoned to meet and was induced to vote its own suicide.

The assembling of the Deputies was made the occasion

for the first great State festival under Nazi direction. The ceremonies were staged at the Garrison Church at Potsdam, historic last resting-place of Frederick the Great. President Hindenburg was present to give his benediction to the Government which, appointed, as he said, with his confidence, had gained a clear majority from the people. The Deputies had to find a new place of assembly, the flames having robbed them of the Reichstag building, and they gathered in the Kroll Opera House, an immense swastika forming the background for the proceedings, constant reminder of the new order.

No Communist members were present, and there were many gaps in the ranks of the Social Democrats, which could only have been filled had the gaolers released their political prisoners. The only purpose of the meeting was the passing of an Act of authorisation which should give the right of law to the powers which Chancellor Hitler had been despotically exercising. The autocratic purpose was somewhat disguised by the high-sounding title of the statute for the " Reduction of the Misery of the Nation and the Reich." It conferred upon the Government authority to pass laws, even though they might conflict with the letter of the Constitution.

There was some doubt as to whether the Government would obtain the necessary two-thirds majority necessary for these fundamental amendments of the Constitution to have legal effect, for they held a total of only 349 seats out of 647. After much hesitation the Catholic Centre Party at length braced itself up to acquiesce in these despotic powers being granted to the Government on the ground that the Party did not wish to obstruct the work of national renewal. Thereafter the Reichstag was suffered to pass into oblivion, for the Chancellor was consistent to a surprising degree. The truths he had enunciated in his autobiography nine years before were those which governed his present actions, and he had written :

" The National State must work untiringly to set all government, especially the highest, that is the political leadership, free from the principle of control by majorities —that is the multitude—so as to secure the undisputed authority of the individual in its stead. The best form of State and Constitution is that which with natural sureness of hand raises the best brains of the community to a position of leadership and predominant influence. There must be no majority-making decisions, but merely a body of responsible persons, and the word ' Council ' will revert to its ancient meaning. Every man shall have councillors at his side, but the decision shall be made by the one Man. The parliamentary principle of decision by majorities has not always governed the human race ; on the contrary it only appears during quite short periods of history, and those are always periods of decadence in nations and States."

In the autumn of the year the formality of electing a new Reichstag was observed, but it was an election on a new model, intended as a demonstration of Nazi ascendancy and not for the summoning of a body of legislators. Hitler had by then decided to withdraw from the League of Nations, as protest against the refusal of the Powers to grant Germany the principle of equality in armaments. He exploited the occasion to stage a national declaration of faith in his policy and ordered a plebiscite to be taken on the question. " Do you, German man, and you, German women, agree to this policy of your National Government, and are you ready to declare it to be the expression of your own opinion and your own will and to commit yourself solemnly to it ? " On a question such as this it would have been absurd to suppose that the German people would answer otherwise than in the affirmative. The only interest was in the figures, and these did testify to the extent to which Hitler had the nation behind him. No fewer than 96·3 per cent of the voters qualified went to the poll, and of these 95·1 per cent marked " ja " upon their ballots. Simultaneously on Germany's " Yes Day " a new Reichstag, 100 per cent Nazi, was appointed. The voter was given only the option of assent or dissent. All parties, excepting the National Socialist German Workers, were prohibited by law, and the ballot contained no more than the names of the Hitler Party and ten of its leading candidates. The votes cast numbered 95·2 per cent of the qualified electorate, of whom 92·2 per cent voted for Hitler. It was a stroke of political genius for Hitler to have seized this opportunity for a manifestation of national unanimity.

Even before the passing of the Bill for the creation of a dictator, Hitler had taken steps to secure control of the States forming the Federation known as the German Republic in a manner that Bismarck had never dared, by summarily extinguishing their rights of sovereign independence. The Nazi steam-roller flattened out everything throughout the length and breadth of the land. Seventeen States were sent entirely out of existence. Eleven were permitted to remain, and were placed under the authority of a Statthälter, or Governor, in whom was vested complete powers. The Governor was authorised to appoint or dismiss members of the State Cabinets to dissolve the State Diets, to publish the State laws, to appoint or dismiss State officials. The Statthälters were the dictators of the States and they were dictated to by the Dictator-in-Chief, their appointment or dismissal being determined on the advice of the Chancellor. Nazification, or political co-ordination, to use the euphemism officially employed, was completed throughout the whole of Germany in the civil service, municipal councils, economic and social organisations.

Side by side with these changes in the Constitution the Nazis proceeded with the enforcement of their " Aryan " policy. The historians of Hitlerism have devoted much thought to the elucidation of the origins of the pure-blood doctrines and the glorification of the Germanic, or Nordic, race whose God-given superiority in the Hitler concept entitles it to the overlordship of the world.[1] Hitler developed these notions of Teutonic supremacy and anti-Semitism to a degree which may seem exaggerated to English minds, but his convictions are patently sincere, as you may see from his autobiography. The book is inspired by belief in things German and hatred of things Jewish. There is the perpetual theme that the German Reich must

[1] The philosophical basis for his anti-Semitism has been traced back to a Frenchman named Gobineau, who held a minor appointment in the French Diplomatic Service, and who wrote on the inequality of the human race, arguing that the Germanic Aryans were descended from Odin and were superior to all men. His conclusions were pushed to fantastic lengths by an Englishman, H. S. Chamberlain, who made his home in Germany. He devoted himself to the theory that the world is the lawful inheritance of the Teutonic stock.

gather all Germans to itself, conserve the best of the racial elements and raise them to a position of dominance. Hitler shudders at the thought of the decay which he believes to be the doom awaiting races which permit themselves to degenerate by crossing. " It is," he declared, " the first duty of a National State to raise marriage from being a perpetual disgrace to the race and to consecrate it as an institution which is called to reproduce the Lord's image, and not monstrous beings, half-man, half-monkey." The application of his theories has led to the creation on the one hand of a militant-minded Germany, and on the other to the weeding out of the Jews from the State service.

The anti-Semitic notions have been applied even in the sphere of religion. Germans of a newly reformed Christianity have pronounced that Christ was not a Jew, but was of Aryan origin. The Nazification of the Evangelical Church as the " Church of Christians of the Aryan race " was to be carried out by Hitler's Primate, Bishop Müller, but the church-people of Germany have put up the resistance to the onslaught of Hitlerism which is so strangely lacking in the political sphere. In matters of religious faith the spirit of Luther is shown still to be alive. The Catholic Church in its ages-old conflict with the forces of secularism was brought into an unusual harmony with Protestant brethren. Nazi aggressiveness nullified the Concordat laboriously negotiated with the Vatican, and a Cardinal Archbishop in Hitler's own Munich denounced the racial prejudices which made war upon religion. Turning back the pages of history the Cardinal reminded Nazi Germany of the barbarism from which Christianity had redeemed its savage ancestors, offerers of human sacrifices to Teutonic gods. Nazi Germany looks back with reverence on its Teutonic origins, and the gospel of a new ancestor worship is the call to an old paganism. Strange are the reversions of history. In the past secular opinion had to fight for freedom against the oppressions of the Church. In the Germany of to-day, where politics, culture, scholarship, and even science itself, have failed to produce resistance to the Hegelian state monster, the Churches, refusing to bow down in the Nazi house of Rimmon, are the champions of freedom's cause. The Churches almost alone stand out against absorption in the totalitarian State.

The revival of Germany's national spirits and the dissipation of her national inferiority complex has been one of Hitler's achievements. Germany to-day has lost that sense which she had before the Hitler régime of being an outcast in the society of Europe. The transformation has been achieved by appeals to her national pride and the calling of the nation to high patriotic effort, to submit to martial discipline and training in arms. War has been glorified. The people have been taught to believe neither in the possibility nor in the utility of perpetual peace. Day after day through the medium of the wireless the German people have had to listen to militant harangues. The aim, doubtless, has been a psychological one to do away with the lassitude and despair of the years of disillusion, but the consequences abroad have been diplomatically unfortunate. Germany's neighbours who have heard the war talks have been conscious of Hitler's pan-German ambitions. They recalled his often-expressed intentions of bringing together in one national unity all the Germans of Austria, Czechoslovakia, Poland and the rest. Hitler's glorification of the Nordic race has led to a new orientation in Europe.[1]

The application of the anti-Semite principle to the German State service resulted in a new Test Act more vigorously applied than were those aimed at the English Nonconformists and Roman Catholics in the service of the Crown. As a consequence of this anti-Semite purge there has been much delving down into genealogies, for Civil Service officials not of Aryan descent were ordered to be placed on the retired

---

[1] As a result of the Nazi propaganda in Austria, Italy was alienated. In spite of the historic meeting of Hitler and Mussolini in Rome early in 1934, which was reported to have been most successful, the two dictators soon drifted apart, and Italy found occasion to come to better terms with France. On the other hand, following the death of M. Barthou, French Foreign Minister, and his succession by M. Laval, relations between France and Germany improved. The terms of the Saar Settlement, amicably reached in advance of the plebiscite, indicate a *rapprochement* which would have been impossible in Barthou's time. Hitler also gained a diplomatic success with Poland, concluding with her a pact of non-aggression, winning Poland's amity.

list, and the definition of non-Aryan went back to the grand-parents on either side.

Hitler also carried out a purge in the moral life of the country, stamping out undesirable activities in the cities and sweeping away pornographic literature.   The Nazis claim that by taking action against the Jews in the principal cities, they automatically achieved their purpose in this respect.   This particularly applies to the White Slave traffic.   A law was also passed providing on a national scale for the sterilisation of unfit men and women suffering from hereditary diseases—another step in the campaign for racial purity.   It was estimated that something approaching half a million men and women might come as a result before the Hereditary Health Courts which were con-stituted.

Apart from psychological and sociological measures, Hitler had to take steps in the economic and industrial sphere and here his policy has not been so clearly defined. The essential problem facing the rulers of Germany was to get the people back to work.   A considerable improvement has been effected in the employment situation, but it has not resulted from any drastic reorganisation of industry.   Pressure has been brought to bear upon employers to engage more workers, and posts have been found for large numbers of men as a result of the application of the Nazi principle that the place for women is the home.   As a result of the break-up of the Trades Unions, the German workpeople were left without the means for organisation.   Dr. Ley was accordingly instructed to enrol German workers in the Labour Front, a new organisation which was called into being to watch over the interests of the employers and employed.   Courts of Social Honour were set up to prevent employers, on the one hand, from exploiting, and to restrain employees, on the other, from being provocative.   Trustees of labour were established, district by district, to preserve industrial peace and in individual works Councils were formed to promote efficiency, secure co-operation and generally contribute to the maintenance of goodwill by the removal of causes of disagreement.

Hitler's policy is to develop a form of government by experts representing agriculture, the major industries and the professional classes.   The carrying out of this idea may be expected to proceed something on the lines of the Italian model, for the resemblance between Nazi Germany and Fascist Italy is a close one, and it is in the Italy of Mussolini that the form and machinery of the totalitarian State can best be observed.

9

A purge of another sort on the night of the Second Terror. Hitler, the avenger from the skies, descends upon his Chief of Staff. A chapter of intrigue and melodrama.

The night of June 30, 1934, will live long in German history as the occasion of Hitler's Purge. Tragedy and mystery alike envelop the events which are still to be seen as in a glass darkly.

Numbers of Germans, some holding positions of eminence in the State or in the Nazi organisation, were shot out of hand, without the formality of a trial. Their removal was justified on the ground that they had been guilty of plotting against the State. They were subject, indeed, to this treatment under their oaths of allegiance as Nazis. Nevertheless, the circumstances of their execution sent a shock through the civilised world. Death is the fate universally provided for the traitor, but we in England have not been accustomed to execution following upon arrest with such dispatch. Even in the days when Plantagenet and Tudor kings ordered off heads as lightly as we now order hats, there was a pause while the onlookers could be diverted by the spectacle of a State trial. On the night of the Hitler Purge the condemned had not the opportunity for their shriving.

The mystery which shrouds the circumstances of the Reichstag fire hangs over the Purge. Some of the circumstances have emerged, some disclosed by the authorities, some revealed despite official secrecy. Hitler has given his version of the affair, but the greater part remains still to be said. Hitler admitted to seventy-seven executions; there is a disposition to multiply the figures by ten. And even of the seventy-seven " admitted " deaths the names of only a few have been officially disclosed.   The identity of the most prominent we know.   They were :

Nazi Chief of Staff, Captain Ernst Röhm ;
General von Schleicher, Hitler's predecessor as Chancellor ;
Frau von Schleicher, who was shot in attempting to shield her husband ;
Gregor Strasser, one-time rival of the Left Wing for the leadership of the Nazi Party ;
Gustav von Kahr, the State Commissioner of Bavaria, who refused to join in Hitler's Munich *putsch ;*
Dr. Walter Lutgebrune, who defended Ludendorff at the trial following the *putsch ;*
Dr. Klausener, President of the Catholic Action, whose death led to a diplomatic protest by the Vatican ;
Dr. Beck, of the International Students' Exchange ;
Chief Group Leader Heines, who is alleged by the Left Wing critics to have been in charge of the Nazis who fired the Reichstag.
Chief Group Leader Ernst, who is similarly suspected of having played a part in the preliminaries for firing the Reichstag ;   his wife committed suicide.
Standard Leader Count Spretti ;
Standard Leader Uhl, who was stated to have admitted before death that he had agreed to take Hitler's life.

On the night of June 30–July 1 Hitler descended upon his old friend Röhm, now apparently turned traitor, like an avenger from the skies.

During the closing days of June the Chancellor had received reports from the secret police that a plot was brewing to overthrow his régime.   He resolved to take summary vengeance on the conspirators.   On the fatal night Hitler travelled by plane to Munich from a West German labour camp, where he had been carrying out a round of ceremonial duties in order to preserve the appearance that all was well, to lull the conspirators into a sense of false security.

We have the authority of an eyewitness for it that the bearing of the Leader was one of " extraordinary resolution " as he embarked after midnight on this flight.   Dr. Goebbels, with touches to be expected from a Minister of Propaganda, filled in the picture later when he broadcast a description of the events to the German people—the most melodramatic eyewitness story that has come over the radio.

" I can see the Leader standing on the terrace of his hotel. He looks seriously into the dark sky. Nobody yet knows what threatens ; the Leader is true to his own principles. He is full of determination to deal with the reactionary rebels who have cast the nation into unlimited disturbance. Reports came to him from Berlin and Munich. After only a few minutes' conference the decision is made not to wait until the morning, but to start at two in the night. At four we are at Munich. On the aerodrome the Leader receives reports. He interviews the rebels. He throws his anger into their pale faces and tears off their identification labels. Then he decides to go into the lion's den."

Into the lion's den meant, presumably, the country house of Röhm, which proved a den of another kind, according to the eyewitness' story. The Chief of Staff was on sick leave and was arrested in his bedroom by the Leader. Group Leader Heines, Troop Commander of Silesia, was also spending the night there and he, too, was arrested. The eyewitness' narrative states : " A shameless sight presented itself to the eyes of those who entered the bedroom. Heines lay in bed with a homosexual youth. The disgusting scene which took place on the arrest of Heines is not to be described. It throws a clear light on the state of affairs in the immediate entourage of the Chief of Staff."[1]

Leaving Röhm and the others under arrest, Hitler returned to the Brown House at Munich where he harangued

---

[1] The eye-witness' assumption of judicial ignorance concerning the habits of Röhm could not have imposed upon his German fellow-countrymen. Röhm was a notorious evil liver, against whom complaints had been made to Hitler, but the Leader nevertheless issued a categorical rebuttal of charges of homosexuality against the Chief of Staff as being " infamous lies and slanders." Röhm himself had put it on record that " I am not one of the morally upright, and do not wish to become one." It has been asserted that the name of van der Lubbe, executed for firing the Reichstag, was on the list of Röhm's young men.

the Storm Troop leaders. He had previously arrested two of the plotters and ordered their execution. The summer's day had now advanced, and milkmen at their morning deliveries, seeing armed soldiers, spread the report that a revolution had been threatened but had been averted. The good citizens, their curiosity overcoming their timidity, ventured diffidently from their homes to investigate. The streets were busy with soldiery and machine-guns covered strategic points for some hours, but there was no firing. Before noon came the soldiers had been ordered back to barracks. Peace reigned again at Munich. Only the curiosity of good citizens disturbed the stillness of the summer afternoon.

Meanwhile, in Berlin, General Göring had been playing his part in the suppression of the mutiny. Like Hitler, he had been going about his affairs in a manner to lull suspicions, except those arising from the eccentricity of his own conduct.[1] At an early hour on July 1 troops and police surrounded a number of buildings in Berlin, including the palatial official residence of Chief of Staff Röhm and the headquarters of Group Leader Ernst. Lorry-loads of the special police in full equipment, with steel helmets, drove through the streets, led by advance guards on motor-cycles. One contingent proceeded later to the villa at Potsdam where General von Schleicher and his wife lived.

The General had just sat down to lunch when there was a peremptory summons at the door and the click of heels in the hall. He had time to push his little stepdaughter into an inner room when the armed police entered. Von

[1] General Göring's fondness for spectacular uniforms has become proverbial, and in those days he had been indulging his fancy to such an extent as to inspire the following : " A few days before the ' clean up' General Göring, in the costumes of Parsifal and Lohengrin, at a garden party to which he had invited members of the Berlin Diplomatic Corps and their ladies, caused more than one foreign Government, to which his performances were confidentially reported, to wonder whether Germany were not in the hands of lunatics, for the garden party turned out to be something between the proceedings at a stud farm and a display of theatrical charioteering." In the light of after events the proceedings now appear to resemble diplomatic dust-throwing on Göring's part.

Schleicher made a hasty movement and the police in haste fired. The General fell, mortally wounded, and his wife, too, was struck dead by a bullet. She had attempted to throw herself at one of the execution squad in an effort to save her husband.

Von Schleicher was the first victim of the Purge which proceeded until late that night by the light of electric standards and continued the next day. Storm Troop leaders were hurried before courts-martial and driven straight to the parade ground to their doom. They died bravely, some weeping, but none asking for mercy. " I die for my Leader and Germany," " Heil Hitler," were the last words heard before the drums crashed out in the tragic roll to muffle the rifles of the execution squad.

Captain Röhm in his cell at Munich was given a revolver with which to die at his own hand, but he declined to anticipate the executioner. He must have expected to the last that the Leader would hesitate to sanction the extreme penalty against the man who had served him and the cause since the earliest days, by whose side he had stood on the day of the Munich *putsch*. Only six months previously Röhm had received a heartfelt expression of gratitude from the Leader, who felt " compelled to thank thee for the insurpassable services thou hast rendered to the movement and to the German people." Hitler then expressed his gratitude to Fate that such men had been called to be his friends and comrades. And now fate beckoned Röhm in another fashion.

. . . .

The cleaning up proceeded throughout Saturday and Sunday. On Monday it was announced it had been completed. The whole nation, it was solemnly averred, " stands in unprecedented enthusiasm behind the Führer." From his home at Neudeck the aged President sent Hitler his congratulations. " From reports made to me," ran the Presidential telegram, " I learn that by your prompt action and courageous personal initiative you have nipped the most treasonable machinations in the bud. You have rescued the people from grave danger." For Göring, too, there was gracious Presidential recognition of energetic and successful procedure in suppressing attempts at treason.

One further intimation was received from Neudeck—that the President had entrusted the safety of von Papen to the Reichswehr, for the Vice-Chancellor had been arrested in the course of the round-up and he had reason to be grateful to Presidential interest for his ultimate freedom and retention of office.

No official announcement was at that time vouchsafed to a wondering and startled world of the nature of the plot which had evoked so ruthless a purge. There were vague allegations concerning a far-reaching conspiracy in which the intermediary of a foreign Power was suggested to be involved. Beyond that the official announcement was concerned with disclosures of immorality. An order was immediately issued to the S.A. charging all leaders to set an example of simplicity, sobriety and decency " so that every mother may send her son into the S.A., the Party or the Hitler Youth Movement without misgiving that he will be morally ruined." S.A. leaders were called on to appear as men, not "ridiculous monkeys." A statement by Hitler to the Storm Troops, explaining why compassion had not been possible in the case of Röhm, left it indecisive whether the fate of the Chief of Staff had been determined by his "unfortunate proclivities" or by his plotting with von Schleicher. In fact this double motive appeared to have governed the executions.

On July 13 Chancellor Hitler summoned the Reichstag to hear his account of the Purge. The Deputies, assembled in the Kroll Opera House, were given a new and dramatic concept of the role that may be thrust upon the Leader at a moment of crisis. The head of the State had previously claimed the right of plenary powers, but he had never before asserted a claim he now advanced to constitute himself a Lord Supreme Chief Justice. "In that hour," he declared, "I was responsible for the fate of the German nation, and in those twenty-four hours I was therefore the Supreme Court of the nation in my own person."

The speech was couched in a melodramatic vein, in which Röhm and von Schleicher played the parts of double-dyed villains, and Hitler appeared Lohengrin-like, a knight in shining armour to save the State from the dangers menacing it. The plot, it is to be deduced, had its origin in the long-standing difference in principle between Röhm and Hitler regarding the proper role of the Nazi Storm Troops. Röhm once again had been agitating, as he had agitated consistently throughout his association with the Party, for the reconstitution of the S.A. on a purely militarist basis, distinct from politics. Hitler, as always, was opposed to any such change. Thereupon Röhm, through the office of a "corrupt swindler," Herr von A . . ., opened negotiations with von Schleicher.

The two conspirators reached agreement that the Storm Troops must be amalgamated with the Reichswehr under the control of one man, namely Röhm. In return for his support von Schleicher expected Röhm's assistance for his own installation in the Cabinet in the place of von Papen, to be removed. Hitler, at any rate for the time being, was to have been left in his post. In order to further his schemes, Hitler alleged, Röhm had made use of the assistance funds, fraudulently diverting a sum of nearly a million pounds towards the purpose of his plotting.

Hitler further described how the conspirators had cleverly contrived to give the semblance of the Leader's approval to their schemes by insinuating that it was his secret wish that the Reichswehr should dissolve the Storm Troops, a project that his own weak character would not allow him to carry out. "A number of Storm Troop leaders were informed that I was in agreement with the scheme, but in order to create the appearance of knowing nothing about it I wanted to be arrested for a couple of days so that abroad no blame could be placed upon me. At the same time a man was sought out, his name is Standard Leader Uhl, who admitted a few hours before his death that he agreed to take my life at a later date." Specially sworn-in "terror groups" were formed as the first step towards bringing about this "Night of the long knife."

"This," declared Hitler, "was mutiny. It was too late for any but ruthless action. In that hour I was responsible for the fate of the German nation and tens of thousands of innocent lives. I could not leave the young German Empire to its fate. I gave orders to shoot those who were guilty of this treachery. I gave orders to burn out the sore down to the raw flesh. I gave orders that anyone who attempted resistance should be mown down at once. The nation must know that its existence cannot be threatened with impunity. Let all take warning for the future that he who raises his hand against the State is doomed to certain death. I am ready before history to accept the responsibility for the twenty-four hours which contained the bitterest decisions of my life."

The effect of the speech upon the immediate hearers was electrical. Hitler on his arrival had been received almost in silence. When he sat down the Deputies rose and greeted him with a mighty " Heil." The effect of the apologia on the German people was not easily to be discovered. The effect abroad was plain. Plot or no plot, danger or no danger to the Government, it was universally agreed that Hitler had acted with unseemly haste, and that nothing he had said could be held to justify the deep damnation of the taking off. Once the conspirators were under lock and key—as they were before their execution—the danger to the State was no longer such as to have rendered it hazardous for them to have been put on trial.

By the Purge the Nazis in one night did more to bring discredit upon their movement than by all the other activities to which their critics point. Events in the tragic year of 1934 moved so fast, however, that men had no time to react to the full to one shock before the next was upon them. Before the month of July had run its course attention was diverted to Austria and the assassination of Chancellor Dollfuss.

10

The Corporal ascends to the Field-Marshal's seat, sole master of the German people after God.

A few more days went by and a new tragedy turned the thoughts of Europe to Germany once more. On August 2 the blue, white and red tricolor of the Hindenburgs and the Presidential standard were lowered to half-mast over the mansion at Neudeck. President von Hindenburg had breathed his last, not far from the spot of his victory of Tannenberg. As a soldier and a statesman Hindenburg might have been lacking in the supreme gifts of insight and sagacity, but no man could have exercised a more steadying influence upon the people of Germany during the difficult years of his Presidency.

Hitler stood forth at last sole master after God of the German people.

The flags had scarcely been lowered to half-mast in Berlin before the Chancellor had authorised the necessary legal formalities for the succession. A bill was promulgated for uniting the office of President with that of Chancellor, a national plebiscite being fixed a fortnight ahead. The Corporal was to follow in the seat of the Field-Marshal, but one self-denying ordinance Hitler placed upon himself— he would not assume the Presidential title. " The greatness of the departed soldier-statesman," Hitler wrote, " has given a unique meaning to the title of President which must inseparably be connected with the name of Hindenburg." He therefore requested that he should be known simply as the Führer and Chancellor. The vote on August 19 did not result in so conclusive a manifestation of national unanimity behind the Leader. In a poll of forty-three and a half millions, over four millions voted " No," and over three-quarters of a million electors spoiled their papers. Nevertheless, in a ballot in which more than 95 per cent of the qualified electorate of the country had participated, practically 90 per cent of the voters had testified their support for Hitler.

Opponents might dwell upon the five million dissentients, but even in the circumstances of the polling, the tremendous efforts which had been made to whip up support and the proscription of anything in the nature of organised opposition, Hitler could accept the verdict as a magnificent testimonial. It marked, as he said, the close of a fifteen years' struggle for power. Germany, from its highest pinnacle through the entire administration down to the smallest hamlet, was placed in the hands of the National Socialists.

Since Hitler succeeded Hindenburg as President, Germany's re-armament has been made plain to the world. Conscription has been re-introduced and the air force has been developed on a scale which has caused alarm among the Powers ; on the sea, Germany has advanced a claim (now conceded by Britain) for building up to 35 per cent of Britain's naval strength. These measures were explained, and justification attempted by Hitler in the historic speech which he made to the Reichstag in May, 1935. The full text of this is given in an Appendix.

BENITO MUSSOLINI

1

Mussolini is a psychological rather than a political or economic dictator. His personal greatness has inspired a nation, but the new machinery of State he has introduced has yet to prove its worth.

ALL the world over, from Japan to Jamaica, the mirage of Mussolini is seen in the Italian sky. It is a mirage of magnificence, as is to be expected from this new Il Magnifico of Rome, with his record of achievements and successes.

Mussolini is the greatest figure on the Italian stage since the days of Imperial Rome. But that does not disguise—though it may explain—the fact that the world looks upon a mirage. Greatness is a quality which so fires the imagination that the great man's greatness is magnified by a hero-worshipping world.

Mussolini's greatness has inspired the Mussolini mirage. He stands at the head of the Fascist State, and so necessarily appears as founder and creator of Fascism. His career leaps to mind as that of a man who, inspired by the needs of Italy, devoted himself to the formulation of a creed, the creation of a party which would bring his country salvation. To this end he consistently laboured, built up the edifice of Fascism, undermined Italy's democratic State and overthrew it by the March on Rome ; and finally reared up the Corporative State on the ruins.

Thus the mirage.

Mussolini of fact has been inspired by no such consistency of purpose. Nothing in his career has been on a grander scale than his inconsistency. He has been the greatest opportunist, the greatest empiricist, of all time.

The new Italy which has been built on the ruins of the old democracy stands also on the ruins of Mussolini's past. His old political theories have gone with Italy's old political

78

" Mussolini's Italy is a psychological creation. The people have been roused to a fervour of national enthusiasm to consecrate their lives to the State."

system into the pre-Fascist limbo. The Imperialist Dictator of to-day began his career as revolutionary Socialist. He was not the sole founder of the Party he has lead. Co-ordinator of Fascism he may be ; scarcely its creator.

Fascism as a system has been an improvisation. It is the resultant of reactionary and revolutionary forces. On the one hand were the theoretical revolutionaries, who wished to create a new Italy ; on the other were the adversaries of Socialism, who wished to secure Socialism's overthrow. Revolutionaries and reactionaries shared in common in the founding of Fasci. They came to acknowledge one chief adversary—the Government and the system the Government stood for. Hence Mussolini. His leadership in the early stages was concerned with the supreme problem of marching in step with political opposites and irreconcilables.

They marched to Rome. He followed by train. Fascism invested Mussolini with power ; he did not know to what end to employ it. You can mark the pause of his early years while he was at the head of affairs, maintaining with grand imperturbability the grandeur of the Mussolini front and the ferocity of the Mussolini scowl, creating the impression of a man of action, busied in affairs, and doing——? He was thinking it out.

It was a leader writer who came to power in Italy in 1922, after the March (so-called) on Rome. Leader writers, of course, are the glibbest of all critics, exceeding even a parliamentary opposition in fertility of criticism. Criticism from an editorial chair comes easy ; the art of government is not so easy. The leader writer, suddenly invested with political power, had to pause while he learned his new job. Fascist Italy is the result of his improvisations.

Fascist Italy is first and foremost a psychological creation. The people have been roused to a fervour of national enthusiasm to consecrate their lives to the sacred cause of their State. That is the main change which Mussolini has produced. Subsidiary to this is the new political Italy, and on a still lower level of importance, the new economy, which is called the Corporative State. The politics of Fascism have achieved one principal result—they have placed Mussolini securely in power by the letter of the new constitution. The economics of Fascism have inspired treatises

and admiration, but economically they count little as yet.
It is the driving force of the Dictator, and not the impressive
machinery—it may or may not function—that has produced
Fascist Italy.

Mussolini is the Fascist State—Mussolini and the mirage, a
psychological creation, the grandest of the creations of Il
Duce. Mussolini has not become the Dictator of Rome by
means of the politics of Fascism or the economics of the
Corporative State. He is a psychological, not a political or
economic dictator. He has ministered to the soul of the
Italian people.

2

*After being sent to prison for six months for Socialistic activities, Mus-
solini becomes an editor and pleads for Italy's participation in
the World War—" to-day it is war, to-morrow it will be the
revolution." As a corporal, he is blown up by a shell.*

The War was the turning-point in the career of Mussolini.
Before the War, Italy's Colossus of Imperialism was an
apostle of anarchy, extreme of the extremists, who
justified bomb-throwing and outrage. He was a man who
could say : " In normal times bombs do not belong to
Socialist methods, but when a Government, be it liberal
or Bourbon, gags you, and puts you beyond the pale of
humanity, then one cannot condemn violence in reply,
even if it makes some innocent victims." When the
anarchist Alba attacked the King of Italy, a group of
Socialists congratulated His Majesty on his escape.
Mussolini demanded the expulsion of these Socialists from
the Party. He quoted precedents for a mason firing his
revolver at Victor of Savoy, and proclaimed : " An attempt
on life is an accident which happens to kings, just as falling
off a bridge happens to masons. If we are to shed tears
let us shed them for the masons." " Down with the State
in all its forms and incarnations " was the Mussolini gospel.
The only faith for him was the " ever-consoling religion of
anarchy."

The history of Italy must have been different had
Mussolini remained true to his anarchical and Socialist

creed.   We may imagine that had he remained a Socialist leader a Soviet Republic would have been founded with its headquarters on the Tiber.   But the War took him from the ranks of the Left.

Socialism, revolution and anarchy were the creeds which inspired the youth of Benito Amilcare Andrea Mussolini. He was the son of a blacksmith whose family had been one of consequence in the Italy of a former age.   A street in Bologna bears the name Mussolini, and the family coat-of-arms remains to attest a former greatness.   The family patrimony had vanished prior to the generation of Alessandro Mussolini.   The creed of revolt was the only inheritance the blacksmith had to bequeath to his son—that and the gift of names of apostles of revolt—Benito Amilcare Andrea. Benito was conferred in memory of Juarez, a Mexican firebrand, Amilcare of a Romagna Socialist, Andrea of a Romagna revolutionary.   The child was born on the 29th day of July, 1883.   He and his school-teacher wife did not propose that little Benito Amilcare Andrea should carry on the smithy.   They trained him for a school teacher, and for a space young Benito played the decorous pedagogue, but his heritage of ideas would not suffer him to be retained by what he termed the " comfortable chains of bureaucratic employment."   He crossed to Switzerland to mix with the revolutionaries, who had found a refuge there when Russia became too hot to hold them.   Young Benito was an ardent disciple, and the Swiss deported him as a dangerous Radical.

Back in Italy he served his term as an Army conscript, a decisive stage in his development.   Socialism and anarchy, the discipline and national ardour of military service— these are the divergencies which have inspired Mussolini. By some strange mystery of human make-up his personality has bridged their gulf, responded to their seemingly opposite appeals.   Here is manifest some fundamental in the Mussolini character.   Back to this you must trace his capacity for co-ordination which has brought revolutionaries and reactionaries under the common black-shirt.

Mussolini was an admirable conscript.   His superiors had been warned against the dangerous Radical.   They found him to be the best soldier of his year, docile and efficient. His service was in a Bersaglieri regiment, the best Shock

Troops of Italy. When it was over he went back to agitation, this time in Austria. The result was the same as in Switzerland—expulsion. He continued his agitation in Italy, and they sent him to prison for six months for incitement to strikers.

By this time he had found his natural bent as a journalist. He founded the *Class War* at Forli and, remarkable to say, made it pay. He was invited to edit the *Avanti*, first among Italy's Socialist papers. And so he went to Milan.

When the War came Mussolini was one of the leading Socialists ; and Italian Socialism was ultra-Pacifist. Mussolini himself had been ultra-Pacifist at the time of the Tripoli conflict two years before, but when the World War began, following Serajevo, his Pacifism wavered. At first the editorials of the *Avanti* were firm against intervention, denouncing the Triple Alliance and insisting on absolute neutrality for Italy. Then for some reason the editor's Pacifism deserted him. He could not here bridge the divergencies. Socialist-Pacifism and the ardour of nationalism were rival and mutually exclusive loyalties. Pacifism had to yield ; step by step he was drawn towards the other camp. His editorials in the *Avanti* came to assume a tone which the Socialists regarded as a betrayal of the cause. The editor was called upon to resign, and his expulsion from the Party was decreed.

It was a courageous step for Mussolini to take, thus to wreck his career, to throw away the position he had built up for himself ; but no one has ever suggested that Mussolini lacks courage. He had courage enough to attend the Socialist Party meeting summoned to expel him, to stand up before his critics despite their boos and hisses in an attempt at justification. He made then a solemn declaration that in a few years the masses of Italy would follow and applaud him when they who were banishing him would no longer speak or have a following. The prophecy has been fulfilled, but scarcely in the sense that the prophet intended it. He did not regard his expulsion from the official Party as marking the end of his work as a Socialist. " You cannot," he declared, " forbid me my Socialist faith, or prevent me from continuing to work for the cause of Socialism and the revolution."

His banishment was decreed on November 25, 1914.

Before Christmas of that year he was back in an editorial chair as director of a new paper, *Il Popolo d'Italia,* in which he employed his powerful advocacy for Italy's entrance in the War on the side of the Allies. How he, virtually penniless, acquired the funds to launch this journalistic enterprise he has never explained. His critics have said that he was subsidised by France. He has been challenged to take action in the courts to rebut these accusations, but the charges stand, unsubstantiated but unrebutted.

The new newspaper was intended as an unofficial parallel to the Socialist *Avanti*—Socialist in all its ideas, except for advocacy of joining the nations at war. Mussolini's first editorial concluded with an appeal to the youth of Italy, and the cry of " War " was raised " without dissimulation but with a sure faith." Mussolini contrived to invest his arguments with a revolutionary appeal. A war to weaken Europe and humiliate Germany would be a war which must " necessarily create an atmosphere more propitious to the realisation of the demands of the working class. . . . To-day it is war ; to-morrow it will be the revolution."

Now were formed the first " Fasci " with which Mussolini was associated. The term was one with a considerable body of legend behind it in Italian political history. The growth of these Fasci—that is bands of patriots—who wished for war spread throughout Italy, and early in 1915 over one hundred of them had been formed. Their existence and the propaganda of Mussolini had a decisive influence in bringing about the change of public opinion in favour of the Government's ultimate decision to accept the inducements of the Allied Powers to come into the conflict on their side.

With the decision to fight, Mussolini joined up. The reputation of the conscript was confirmed. Mussolini was promoted corporal for his exemplary conduct, the Gazette pronouncing him to be first in any enterprise and in courage, regardless of discomfort, distinguished for zeal and devotion to duty. To what rank his zeal would have brought him, speculation alone is the guide. The bursting of a trench mortar cut short his military career. Five of his comrades were killed by the shell, which burst as he was directing its discharge. Corporal Mussolini was blown several yards, and forty-four pieces of metal were later removed from his body. As he lay wounded he received a visit from the

King, whom he, as an anarchist, had ridiculed not long before. Victor Emmanuel did not recall that, no less than kings and masons, soldiers were exposed to the accident of death. " I commend you, Corporal Mussolini," were His Majesty's words.

Mussolini went back on crutches to Milan to his editorial chair.

3

Italy, when on the brink of Bolshevism just after the War, fails to take the plunge owing to the timidity of the people's leaders. A Nationalist reaction sets in, and disconnected Fascist groups all over the country wage bitter war on the Socialists. Mussolini, in his newspaper, addresses the rival Fascists as though he were the acknowledged leader.

From the World War Mussolini returned with two major lessons learned—the value of discipline and contempt for democracy. Discipline and democracy came to assume a rigid antithesis in his mind. He was roused to disgust that the whole people were not mobilised for war ; that amusements, leisure, and even liberty itself, were not proscribed while the struggle lasted. He dwelt on the idea of the nation, under an iron discipline, consecrating its strength physically and morally to the supreme national cause. He was aroused to impatience by parliamentary tactics and delays, the partisan fights of little men. He pictured the weary soldier in the trenches asking himself : " Why should I suffer and die while at Rome they are debating ? "

When peace was concluded it was difficult for the editor of *Il Popolo d'Italia* to know which policy to support. By faith he was still of the Left Wing ; but he had no party, and had to play a lone political hand. No niche appeared to be awaiting him. He had to improvise a party and a programme. His improvisations were attuned to, and reflected, the fluctuations of Italian opinion.

In the first stage Mussolini sought, in common with the Left, to exploit Bolshevism. In the second phase he was anti-Bolshevik. Finally, he established himself as champion-in-chief against the Left Wing.

Italy's Bolshevik phase was the result of her post-war

disappointments. Before the War she had aspired to, but had not attained, the position of a major Power. After it, her voice was scarcely heeded at the Peace Conference. She had been induced to enter the War by promises of territories in Africa, which would rank her with the owners of empires, but the triumvirate of Versailles, in apportioning the spoils of victory, failed to fulfil Italian expectations. So brusquely were her claims dealt with, that her delegates withdrew in disgust from the Peace Conference. They had the mortification of witnessing the bestowal elsewhere of all Germany's colonial possessions. No part of Asia Minor was assigned to Rome, and even the extension permitted Italy to the north-west fell short of her aspirations.

The high hopes which arose in Allied countries when the War ended chilled nowhere more quickly than in Italy, giving way to resentment and the bitterness of frustration. A spirit of cynicism and defeatism spread. Economic hardships bred political unrest. Socialism flourished as discontent grew ; Communism found a readier response. The shadow of the Soviet was over the land of the Cæsars. " Evviva Lenin " was heard in the streets of Rome.

Bolshevism became the fashion. No one knew precisely what Bolshevism meant. Each advocate had his own interpretation. But there was general agreement that this was the creed for the moment when illusions had been shattered.

As the wind was blowing from the Left, so Mussolini set his sails. He enunciated a radical programme designed to appeal to Socialists and Trade Unionists. Its chief points were the dissolution of the monarchy and senate ; the abolition of all titles of nobility ; the confiscation of church property ; workers' control of factories and industries ; and the formation of a Constituent Assembly which should be the Italian section of an International Constituent Assembly of Peoples. Mussolini had gone extremist without reservation.

When the elections of 1919 were held, however, Mussolini received scant support, polling only 4000 votes out of a total poll of 346,000. The electors, it was clear, had no use for Mussolini's brand of Socialism. They wanted the genuine article, guaranteed by the Party. The Socialists scored an electoral success. The tide was running strongly in their favour. They had risen from a party of half a million to two millions. The Trade Unionists had similarly increased. No fewer than 150 Socialist Deputies were returned ; and in local affairs municipality after municipality fell under their control.

The elections resulted in a political deadlock. There were 250 deputies in the various groups from which the Ministry might look for support. They were balanced by 100 Christian Democrats and the 150 Socialists. The position was one which favoured party intrigue and corridor plotting as leaders of rival groups strove to exploit the turn of events to their own advantage. The Ministry, whatever Ministry it was in office, was at the mercy of the leaders of the rival factions. There were successive crises, and the prestige and authority of the Central Government were reduced in the eyes of the people.

It was particularly unfortunate that this should have been the case when the country was seething with unrest. The *morale* of the people was at its lowest ebb. Their country had won the War, but lost the peace. For Italy, the fruits of victory seemed to be scarcely distinguishable from the humiliations of defeat. As in other lands, the fall in the price of living had not kept pace with reduction in wages. There were successive strikes as the workers sought to preserve their wage rates. For political ends the Socialists encouraged and aggravated industrial dissensions. The Left Wingers, working under orders from Moscow, saw the day of Soviet Italy approaching.

Tension reached its climax. In the northern areas, the Black Country of Italy, the Labour leaders gave orders for the metal factories to be occupied. Red Guards were organised and Works Councils were appointed to take over business control. The country was on the brink of Communism. Had the Labour leaders dared to lead, the Socialist State would have been launched. At their call the workers would have taken over all national services. The call never came, but instead a summons to a conference.

While the workers were decking their machines with red rosettes their chiefs were passing resolutions inviting the Prime Minister to act as arbitrator in the dispute. Masters who had expected to forfeit their possessions, ministers who had waited for the call which would mean the end, at least, of their political existence, breathed again. Had Mussolini still been a member of the official Socialist Party the workers might have heard the summons, not to a congress, but to a revolt. The bourgeois State might have been summarily ended, and under Comrade Benito a Soviet established on the Russian model—might have been or might not ; for who can tell that Mussolini, taking power on behalf of the workers, might not, as Socialist Dictator, have created the system he has evolved as Fascist leader. Events did not show. They did prove that the Socialists had not the stomachs for revolt. The crisis fizzled out.

Mussolini from his editorial chair, watching the development of events, discovered how the failure of the older parties gave the opportunity for the new.

Italy's Bolshevist phase was passing. Mussolini, who had failed on the Left Wing, was shown how he might succeed on the Right by exploiting anti-Bolshevism and the new spirit of Nationalism and Imperialism. There came two events which plainly betokened the course of Italian opinion. The first was the incident of Fiume in the summer of 1919, when Gabriele D'Annunzio stood for a moment in the international limelight.

They hailed D'Annunzio at the time as a national hero, but his fame has faded. They called him nationalist, but remember him now as novelist ; called him romantic, and now re-write it eccentric. Fiume, former port of Austria on the Eastern Adriatic, was one of the prizes that Italy hoped to win at the Peace Conference, but the Council of Three decided against her claims and in favour of those of Serbia, which is now Yugoslavia. Italian opinion had been worked up to fever heat. Fiume had come to have an importance in Italian eyes far exceeding its commercial or strategic value. In September, 1919, D'Annunzio, in defiance of the Council, took the place by force as leader of a band of black-shirted Arditi—Shock Troops of the War.

Premier Nitti, who had succeeded Orlando, negotiated with Yugoslavia, and it was decided then that Fiume should be made into an independent city state ; but Nitti did not dare to give the order necessary to implement this decision by ejecting D'Annunzio and his rebel forces. Italian sympathies were on D'Annunzio's side, particularly the sympathies of the armed forces of the Crown. Disaffection was abroad. The loyalty of the officers was in doubt. The troops would be unlikely to obey orders if the officers thought fit to give them. So for nearly a year D'Annunzio lorded it in Fiume, until at last they plucked up courage to expel him.

The success of D'Annunzio was a lesson for Mussolini. There was an example of what a man of action could achieve ; and the passions evoked were the indication of the existence of a body of strongly Nationalist opinion. Mussolini and his neo-Fascists embraced the D'Annunzio creed and adopted the D'Annunzio symbols, the black shirt, the Roman salute and the old Roman fasces—the bundle of rods enclosing a battle-axe carried by the lictors to symbolise strength and power.

The other lesson Mussolini learned was from the Catholic People's Party, whose success in the 1919 elections showed what a new organisation could achieve if its appeal were attuned to the public ear. The Church had realised the dangers to its authority of secularist socialism and godless communism. The Pope removed his ban against political parties, and early in 1919 the Catholic People's Party was formed under Don Sturzo, a Sicilian priest. It was a party of mild Liberalism, the party of the little man, the minor official, the small shop-keeper, the small landowner and the peasant. In a few months Don Sturzo's supporters exceeded a million. Preservation from the Socialist menace was one of the principal planks in the platform of a party which nevertheless spoke with favour of a mild revolution within the existing state of society.

The success of D'Annunzio and Don Sturzo explain the origin of the new gospel according to Mussolini, who began to emerge as the leader of the forces against defeatism, the champion against the " beasts of decadence." Everywhere the discontented and disillusioned were forming into Fasci ; and the common title gave the illusion of motion towards a common goal. But what common goal could there be for industrialists and landowners, workers and landless peasants, shop-keepers and public servants, retired officials and pensioners, the soldiers and police, the ex-combatants of the War and patriots, the visionaries of youth and the disillusioned of age ? Such was the conglomerate of Fascism, the movement to which Mussolini contrived to impart

the semblance of purpose, and on behalf of which he spoke
with the voice of leader.

It is a concept in the saga of Fascism that the Party sprang
from the Fasci di Combattimento which Mussolini launched
at Milan in March, 1919, and that, fostered and marshalled
by Il Duce, the Fascists became organised throughout the
country, inspired by the vision which has now been brought
to life in the Corporative State. But there were Fascists
before Mussolini ; there were Fascist leaders who were not
disposed to yield him the authority to which he aspired, to
accept his version of Fascist faith or to pursue his style of
Fascist tactics.

In his " Autobiography " the co-ordinator of Fascism
puts the best gloss he can upon it ; but his account of the
origins of Fascism falls far short of the Mussolini myth. He
writes :

" I speak of Movement, and not of Party, because my
conception always was that Fascismo must assume the
characteristics of being anti-party. It was not to be tied
to old or new schools of any kind. The name of ' Italian
Fighting Fascisti ' was lucky. It was most appropriate
to a political action that had to face all the old parasites
and programmes that had tried to deprave Italy. I felt
that it was not only the anti-Socialist battle we had to
fight ; this was only a battle on the way. There was a
lot more to do. All the conceptions of the so-called his-
torical parties seemed to be dresses out of measure, shape,
style, usefulness. They had grown tawdry and insuffi-
cient, unable to keep pace with the rising tide of unexpected political exigencies, unable to adjust the formation
of new history and new conditions of modern life. It was
not sufficient to create an anti-altar to the altar of
Socialism. It was necessary to imagine a wholly new
political conception, adequate to the living reality of the
twentieth century—overcoming at the same time the
idealogical worship of Liberalism, the limited horizons of
various spent and exhausted democracies, and finally the
violently Utopian spirit of Bolshevism. It was necessary
to lay the foundation of a new Socialism."

Mussolini's Fasci di Combattimento of Milan consisted
at their inception in 1919 of a group of war veterans. Their

programme, as has been explained, was a revolutionary one, Mussolini's aim at that time having been the foundation of a producers' republic of a sort. The fighting title of " Combattimento " that he assumed was a political and intell ectual rather than a physical connotation. In other parts of the country Fascist groups sprang up—not under the inspiration or control of Milan—which did not assume the title of Combattimento, but which had a combative intention. These were the Squadristi, who set out to grapple with the Socialists.

Italy in the years after the War had a surplus population of young men who, after the excitement and adventures of the War, were not content to resume the dull routine of everyday life. After the English Civil Wars of the days of the Stuarts, similarly, there was a wave of banditry, when the soldiers who had lost their occupations took up the exciting life of gentlemen of the road. Thus it was in Italy after the World War, with the difference that the young adventurers, instead of becoming gentlemen of the road, joined the Fascist squads against Socialism.

In town and country, in highways and fields, Fascists and Socialists met in bloody and bitter strife. In Fascist homes votive lamps were soon burning in memory of the fallen. Fascists laid snares for Socialists and fell victims to Socialist ambushes. Such ferocity of outrage and murder in a civilised state shocked Europe.

Throughout Italy punitive expeditions were organised by the Fascists ; by train and lorry their forces were carried in organised masses against municipalities under Socialist control. Socialist headquarters were plundered and s et on fire. In the autumn of 1921, 3000 Fascists under arms invaded Ravenna. The police and military forces were quasi-spectators as the Fascists flung themselves upon their Socialist opponents. The conquest of Ravenna was the first conclusive demonstration of Fascist strength. In the following year they concentrated in Bologna to the number of 10,000 to compel the resignation of the Prefect. Then in the South Tyrol they gave another demonstration of their power, invading the Prefecture and compelling the Prefect to resign.

Milan, too, had its experience of Squadrism. Mussolini had to stand aside and watch the conflicts ; but as they proceeded he grew alarmed. This fighting organisation was not the Party he wished to lead ; but it was not in his power to control events. His paper was the Fascist organ, and that made him the most prominent of the Fascists, but there was no co-ordinated disciplined national party of which he was the leader.

Though he might seem to laugh at the " gypsies of Italian politics " who were not tied down to any fixed principles, Mussolini was acutely conscious of his lack of authority and set about creating an organisation. He sent out emissaries from Milan in an attempt to bring all Fascism under his unified control. Local bosses, however, were not content to surrender and accept his leadership.

In the elections of 1921 the first Fascists were returned to Parliament—thirty-five of them, including Mussolini himself. This success first brought the problem of leadership to a head. The Fascist deputies from the provinces would not accept the decrees of the leader from Milan. Mussolini concluded a pact with the Socialists, the Pact of Pacification, in an effort to bring to an end the bloody conflict. The Pact was not honoured in the country, the Squadristi wishing to finish off their opponents. At a provincial meeting the truce was repudiated, whereupon Mussolini announced his resignation, declaring that he was unable to guide an undisciplined and chaotic movement. The Milan Fascists, however, induced him to withdraw his resignation, and circumstances arose which enabled Mussolini to declare the Pact of Pacification to have been broken by the Socialists, and thus to have become a dead letter. And so the work of the Squadristi went on.

To the observer from outside, with no knowledge of events behind the Fascist façade, and no awareness of the rivalries amongst the Fascist leaders, the movement could have taken on the appearance of an organisation which was being systematically promoted throughout the country. To such an observer it would have appeared that Mussolini was at the head, the unchallenged chieftain of the Black Shirt legions. In the *Popolo d'Italia* he wrote in the manner of an acknowledged leader. He grouped all the Fascisti, all their aims and activities together, gave them a co-ordination which did not exist and spoke on their behalf with the voice of assurance and authority.

To the onlooker, particularly the onlooker interpreting events in the light of subsequent happenings, the events of 1920 and 1921 present the appearance of a struggle between Fascism and parliamentary democracy, culminating in the March on Rome. Looking behind the façade of Fascism, it is evident that not until a fairly late stage did the March on Rome come to be a definite objective. It was not an original aim which inspired the formation of a party to which all activities were subordinated. It was a master stroke of opportunism. In locality after locality the local Fascisti expelled their political adversaries from municipal control. The ease with which these successes were achieved prompted the suggestion : Why not eject the authority in chief ?— and so the March on Rome, the capture of parliamentary institutions, and after an attempt to work those institutions, the final overthrow of democracy. It was thus by slow degrees that Mussolini evolved co-ordination in the Fascist conglomerate.

4

A country contemptuous of governments that cannot govern and of parliamentary deadlocks rallies to Mussolini who puts the Fascist organisations on a military basis and arranges the March on Rome. In power he proceeds constitutionally and wins a great victory at the polls.

In the post-war years of Italy's distress, her parliamentary Government exhibited a sorry spectacle. Ministries were unstable because they lacked a substantial majority. They could command no authority in the Chamber ; they lacked prestige in the country ; they were powerless to cope with the succession of strikes which paralysed industry. When the Fascist squads campaigned against the Socialists, the Prime Minister, the Liberal Giolitti, decided as a matter of policy not to intervene. Let the Fascists work their will with the Socialists, and then, his principal enemies removed, Giolitti might be master of the situation. The Army was allowed to arm Fascisti, retired officers to command them. Police and magistrates took no account of complaints of Fascist violence. As the squads swarmed to the towns, looted chambers of workers and Trade Union head-

quarters, and man-handled Socialist leaders, the authorities turned a blind eye. Socialists might be liable to arrest
for violence ; Fascists, even when caught red-handed,
would be set free on the ground of lack of evidence.

A Government that does not govern, but stands aside
while civil strife proceeds, is moribund. The Italian
Parliamentary system itself was moribund. The rivalries
of the groups, who would not yield their independence
sufficiently to make one master of the situation, brought
democracy to its doom.

Here Mussolini's account of the passing of the old régime
is vivid and true. He draws a picture of a parliament
playing at political pea-shooting, the groups engaged in
cloak-room conspiracies, making and unmaking ministries
but never giving the nation a firm administration. Giolitti
fell, to give place to Bonomi, a Socialist. Bonomi fell, and
returned ; Bonomi fell again, and gave way to Facta, a
mediocrity. Facta fell, and they were hard put to it to find
a successor. Each of the veterans was suggested as the head
of a ministry—Orlando, Bonomi, Giolitti. Politics had
reached a deadlock. Group plotted against group, bringing
the Italian parliamentary system into complete disrepute.
There was general contempt for Governments which could
not govern, and for a system of politics which could not even
produce a ministry.

Figures, familiar and unfamiliar, came and went on the
screen of Italian politics. Each had the transient hour of a film
star, and as little influence on the course of events. There was
endless wrangling and crisis after crisis. Deputies played the
political game within. Without, Mussolini denounced and
fulminated. They approached him to take part in a coalition.
He consented, but only on condition that he was its head.
They refused. He warned them. He threatened Parliament
and the parliamentary system. The Deputies smiled, and
while they smiled and played their game, the Fascist
militia extended itself in the Provinces and tightened
its grip.

The Fascist organisation was perfected on a military basis.
The land of the Romans once again had its maniples,
centuries, cohorts and legions, with Mussolini over all as
Chief Honorary Colonel. The young men rallied in large
numbers to the Black Shirt militia, and took their oath

" in the name of God and Italy, in the name of all those who have fallen in battle, for the greatness of the Patria," to devote themselves exclusively and unceasingly to Italy's good, ready to meet the enemies of Italy on the basis of " an eye for an eye, a tooth for a tooth, hair for hair, fire for fire, wound for wound, bruise for bruise and life for life."

While the legions grew, the Duce del Fascismo grew bolder in his warnings to democracy, plainer in his promise of the coming of a dictator. " From government by many or by all, men will probably turn to government by a few or by one only. In economics the experiment of government by many or all has already failed. In Russia they are returning to dictators in the factories. Politics must inevitably follow economics. Before long universal suffrage and its proportion-istic amendments will be an old game. Men will, perhaps, long for a dictator." Deputies in Rome still smiled ; still they hinted that Mussolini might become a junior participant in a coalition ; but Mussolini told them that Fascism " would not come into the Government by the servants' entrance." Already the Fascist chief had received indi-cations from the Palace that when the time was ripe the main gates would not be closed in his face. Twice or thrice King Victor Emmanuel commanded Mussolini to an audience in the Quirinal.

As the summer of 1922 passed into autumn there were Fascist murmurings of a March on Rome. Fascist activities were speeded up. They seized the communal governments of Milan and Genoa. A drive was made on the remaining Socialist and Radical communes whose officials had not already been frightened into resigning. The Fascist militia was rounded up in readiness. Calls were sent out for more ex-soldiers. Special appeals were made for volunteers for parts of the Fascist service which were deficient. A supply department was built up and Red Cross contingents organised.

The second political convention of the Party met at Naples. It was not so much a convention as a mobilisation. The Duce del Fascismo held a final review of his forces. Here were the means to make smiling deputies cease their sneers—cavalry, uniformed and helmeted ; bicycle squad-rons ; the general staff and gold medallists ; the legions ;

the Boy Scout squads ; the principi and triari all in their
uniforms with their blankets and rations slung on their
backs.

Honourable gentlemen in Rome might smile, but the
hour of their destiny was now proclaimed by Mussolini.
" We are," he told his forces at Naples, " at the point at
which the arrow parts from the bow, or the cord too tightly
drawn is broken. By what right shall Fascism become the
State—legality or illegality, parliamentary conquest or
insurrection ? " In secret session the Fascist leaders read
final reports on the measure of Fascist preparedness.
Throughout Italy, above all in Tuscany, the key province,
effective steps had been taken to secure strategic points.
Some were guarded by Fascist forces ; others were weak
and easily to be taken. Prefectures and police headquarters they were masters of ; railroads and telegraph
offices were under guard. The word went forth. " On
to Rome."

The Naples Convention was dissolved. The Fascist
forces converged on Civita Vecchia, a little to the north
of Rome. Here was no smiling matter for honourable
gentlemen ; here were 50,000 armed men under military
formation and military law. A quadrumvirate was in
control of the hosts—Michele Bianchi, General de Bono,
an army officer on active service, Captain De Vecchi and
Lieutenant Italo Balbo. Mussolini himself marched not, but
awaited the outcome of events at the safe distance of Milan,
ready to play the conquering hero—or to fly as a refugee if
need be. That night, October 27, 1922, he attended the
theatre at Milan. The next day the Black Shirts poured
into Rome, heralded by the proclamation of the quadrumvirate that they were marching, not against King, army
or police, but against political weaklings who could not
give the country a Government.

    " Fascisti ! Italians !
    " The time for determined battle has come ! Four
years ago the National Army loosed at this season the
final offensive, which brought it to Victory. To-day the
army of the Black Shirts takes again possession of that
Victory, which has been mutilated, and going directly to
Rome brings Victory again to the glory of that Capital.

From now on principi and triari are mobilized. The martial law of Fascism now becomes a fact. By order of the Duce all the military, political and administrative functions of the Party management are taken over by a secret Quadrumvirate of Action with dictatorial powers.

" The Army, the reserve and safeguard of the nation, must not take part in this struggle. Fascism renews its highest homage given to the Army of Vittoria Veneto. Fascism, furthermore, does not march against the police, but against a political class both cowardly and imbecile, which in four long years has not been able to give a Government to the nation. Those who form the productive class must know that Fascism wants to impose nothing more than order and discipline upon the nation and to help to raise the strength which will renew progress and prosperity. The people who work in the fields and in the factories, those who work on the railroads or in offices, have nothing to fear from the Fascist Government. Their just rights will be protected. We will even be generous with unarmed adversaries.

" Fascism draws its sword to cut the multiple Gordian knots which tie and burden Italian life. We call God and the spirit of our five hundred thousand dead to witness that only one impulse sends us on, that only one passion burns within us—the impulse and the passion to contribute to the safety and greatness of our country.

" Fascisti of all Italy !

" Stretch forth like Romans your spirits and your fibres ! We must win. We will.

" Long live Italy ! Long live Fascism !

" The Quadrumvirate."

Here was the challenge to smiling deputies. Facta was at the head of affairs, genial and peace loving. What was he to do in the hour of crisis ? Genial Facta made an effort to bestir himself ; posted cavalry and machine-guns and issued his proclamation in reply to the Quadrumvirate, declaring a state of emergency and siege. Poor Facta ! In the hour of crisis he made ready to play a leading role, only to find that there was no room for him in the cast. His proclamation fell stillborn, countermanded by the King, and so Facta fades away. The March on Rome is accomplished.

It was not so much a march as a pleasant excursion, and the marchers found that they held only week-end return tickets. The man from Milan advanced upon the stage, and ordered, as leading actors do, that it should be emptied of the crowd, to be graced by him alone. Mussolini arrived by train on October 29, and received the command to form a government. Almost his first thought was to order the legions out of the city. The Fascist Chief of Staff was embarrassed by the peremptory instruction to get his men away within twenty-four hours.

Such was the March on Rome. No opposition ; no bloodshed ; no fighting. The peaceful entrance of 50,000 men and their swift departure.

Il Duce del Fascismo reigned as Il Capo del Governo, but it was a restrained Mussolini who took up the reins of government. No furious Jehu this, but a man ready to pick his way slowly ; no aggressive dictator, but an almost conciliatory Parliamentarian. The Cabinet was announced. In a Cabinet of fifteen only five portfolios fell to the Fascists and two of these, Foreign Affairs and the Interior, were held by the Duce himself. Of the junior Ministers, fifteen were Fascists, and fifteen from other parties. This was not the Fascist Government that the Fascist forces had expected, that Liberal Deputies had feared. Honourable gentlemen might almost smile again. But there was no smiling on the morrow after the Duce had thundered at them. They were left feeling that they were scarcely worth the bother of his attention. " With 30,000 youths fully armed, fully determined, and almost mystically ready to act on any command of mine, I could have made this grey hall a bivouac of squads. I could have kicked out Parliament—I could have—but I did not want to, at least for the present." And then, having thus reduced their self-importance, he bade them not to prattle too much. After the scolding, the Deputies voted their lecturer plenary powers for the space of twelve months, and only the Socialists dared go into the division lobby against him.

Mussolini for a space played the parliamentary game. He had only thirty-five Fascist Deputies, and, as the keynote of his policy was to act within the Constitution, he had been forced to form a coalition. The Popular Party, Liberals, Nationals and Democrats, all of whom had suffered his taunts, many of whom had had experience of Fascist violence, forgot the past sufficiently to permit themselves to co-operate with him. But he was in no doubt as to their hopes. They were older hands in politics than he. They had visions that they would worst him at the game, and that he would have to withdraw discredited. He was determined to beat them, but to beat them within the terms of the Constitution, even if the Constitution had to be altered. A majority in the Chamber was essential. Under the system of proportional representation it could not be hoped for, and so proportional representation must be swept aside as a means of ending the deadlocks and squabbles. Honourable gentlemen were invited to vote their own political suicide.

The formalities were observed by the appointment of a commission of all parties to draw up a system of reform, but it was a Fascist, Acerbo, who produced the necessary rabbit out of the hat—a Bill to provide that whichever party obtained the greatest number of votes at a general election should automatically become entitled to two-thirds of the total seats in the Chamber, the remainder to be divided between the other parties. It was a Fascist Bill, sponsored for Fascist ends ; for the Duce made no secret of his aspirations, declaring his wish to see a " panorama of ruins " about him, the ruins of other political forces, so that Fascism could stand alone. There was a show of opposition, but in the end the measure was carried by a two-to-one majority.

It was a political gamble for a man with only thirty-five supporters in the Chamber to stake his existence on the hazard of the election. When the elections were held, local Fascisti took action to ensure that the risk their leader ran was minimised. Officially Mussolini frowned upon the practices, but he benefited from the results. The campaign was characterised by an orgy of intimidation and worse. Opponents were harassed. The distribution of their literature was stopped. Their meetings were broken up, castor oil was forced down many throats to promote political conversions, and one Socialist candidate, Piccinini, was kidnapped and shot. On election day the Fascist militia was organised—there were always enough incidents to permit of the pretext that the legions were needed to assist in the maintenance of law and order. The result of the poll exceeded even Mussolini's hopes, giving him a two million majority over any other single party, and a clear majority over all others combined. There voted :

Fascist	4,800,000
Socialist	1,000,000
Others	1,200,000

5

Fascism survives the Matteotti scandal, but is wracked with personal feuds and internal dissensions. After thorough-going reforms Mussolini is invested with complete autocracy.

When the Chamber met, there was an immediate and loud outcry from the ranks of the defeated at the manner in which the Fascists had bludgeoned their way to success. From this arose the Matteotti murder, which shook the Fascist régime.

Giacombo Matteotti came of a well-to-do family, who were owners of land. His sympathies were Socialist, and he became a Trade Union organiser, working among agricultural labourers. He was recognised as a zealous and tenacious opponent, a man of courage in the face of personal danger. He took a prominent part in the exposure of Fascist election methods, following up his disclosures in the Chamber with a book exposing Fascism. This contained a damaging enumeration of graft, outrage and murder, with promise of further revelations to follow. One of the Fascist members of the ministry, Finzi, Under-Secretary to Mussolini at the Ministry of Interior, was deeply implicated in the charges. Matteotti undertook to produce the evidence in support of his accusations, but before he could do so he was spirited away, kidnapped in broad daylight by Fascists. They bore him off to a motor-car, and as he struggled and cried for help, one of the gang struck him with a dagger. Two months later his body was found in the river.

There was a wave of disgust and indignation when the crime became known. Mussolini was charged with moral responsibility for the murder, in that he had failed to exercise

control over his wild gangsters.   His opponents quoted a
passage from the *Popolo d'Italia*, a passage the Duce himself
had written, declaring that Matteotti for his outrageously
provocative speech deserved some more concrete reply than
the epithet of scoundrel.   The Duce's personal complicity
was not seriously credited, but the crime shook his popularity.
He feared that the Nationalists would withdraw their
support, and took hurried steps to placate opinion, dismissing from office all who were under suspicion of complicity,
including Finzi.   He introduced more Nationalists into the
Ministry and promised reorganisation of the Fascist Party,
and the suppression of violence, but in the bringing of the
murderers to justice, he acted with less dispatch.   Two
years passed before they were put on their trial.   Three of
the accused were sentenced to six years' imprisonment, but
were set free two months later.   The assassin Dumini, a
gangster from America, had to serve three years, but in his
case the circumstances supported the suggestion that he
was penalised as much for threatening to make accusations
against the chief Fascist, as for his part in the murder.

Nothing attests the political ineptitude of the opponents of
Fascism more than their conduct after the Matteotti murder.
The crime had shaken the foundations of Fascism.   Had
the advantage been properly exploited, the edifice might
have been reduced to the ruins its architect-in-chief had
designed for other parties.   A rallying-point for the dis-
affected had been provided, but instead of ramming home
their advantage, the opposition left the Chamber.   They
withdrew to the Aventine Hill, classical home of the dis-
affected in Rome, hallowed by Plebeian memories.   This
political gesture was a political mistake.   Secession might
be eloquent testimony of the moral indignation of the
secessionists, but it left the other fellows in undisputed
control of the parliamentary machine.

Mussolini affected to be embarrassed by the purge, but
he was shortly entertaining the faithful rump of the Chamber
with a lively dissertation on the grotesque anti-Fascist
Army of the Aventine Secession, representing Anarchists,
Communists, Maximalists, Unitary Socialists, Republicans,
Popularists, Social Democrats, Constitutional Democrats,
Peasant Party, the Sardinian and Lucan Party of action,
the groups of Free Italy for Country and for Liberty,

the Liberal Revolution, the hosts of Freemasonry, and the dissident more-or-less Fascisti.

The Matteotti storm died down in course of time as the Fascisti and their chief passed from strength to strength, but Mussolini was given a shock which finds its expression, despite his assumption of serenity, in his " Autobiography." The Duce, pitching the tone of a leader of a much calumniated party, reproaches his opponents with having made Party capital out of Matteotti's death, " an ignoble game started not from any love of the poor victim, but solely from hate for Fascism." Contrasted with this is the Central Government faithfully and energetically searching for the authors of the crime, taking the sternest proceedings without limit or reservation, but with such severity that some of the measures turned out to be excessive. In denouncing the calumnies cast on Fascism the Duce is moved to long and vigorous protest :

" It was a shame and a mark of infamy which would dishonour any political group. The Press, the meetings, the subversive and anti-Fascist parties of any quality, the false intellectuals, the defeated candidates, the brain-soft cowards, the rabble, the parasites, threw themselves like ravens on a corpse. The arrest of the guilty was not enough. The discovery of the corpse and the sworn verification of surgeons which stated that the death was not due to a crime, but was produced by trauma, was not enough.

" Instead, the discovery of the corpse in a hedge near Rome, called the Quartarella, unstopped an orgiastic research of details, which is remembered by us with the ignominious name of ' Quartarellismo.'

" On the Matteotti tragedy there were built fortunes ; they speculated on portraits, on medals, on commemorative dates, on electric signs ; a subscription was opened by subversive newspapers and even now the accounts are still open. I did not have a moment of doubt or discouragement. I knew the attitudes, postures and poses of these adversaries. I knew they would have ignobly used the corpse of the Socialist Deputy, to make of it if they could an anti-Fascist symbol and flag. But their ghoulish politics ᐧpassed my imagination. Besides these

speculators there were the timid and flabby fringes of
Fascism.   They let themselves be wheedled by the
political atmosphere.   They did not perceive that an
episode is not the stuff of which history should be made.
In the name of a so-called sentimental morality, they
wanted to kill a great moral and political probity and
knife the welfare of an entire nation.

" There were also in this circumstance many repented
Magdalenes, and many—drawn by the sad habit of many
Italians to consider as pure gold the acts and the work
of any oppositions—hid their Fascist insignia and,
trembling, they abandoned the Fascist nation, already
made red-hot by a thousand attacks and counter-attacks
of the adversaries.

" We were going back into the depths of a revolutionary
period, with all the excesses of such abnormal times with
spites, troubles, explosions.   An atmosphere was formed
in which many magistrates, often under Masonic influence,
could certainly not give equitable and faultless judgments.
Various parties beyond the borders gave help to the
Socialists at home.   It was then clear how anti-Fascism
was still abroad in some international zones where
democracy, Socialism and Liberalism had consolidated
their weight of patronage, blackmail and parasitism.

" All this could have given for a moment, in some
political atmospheres, the illusion that the Government
had weakened.   In December, 1924, at the end of that
painful three months, some calculated the days of life of
our Ministry.   A great hope sprang upon the hearts of
the politically hungry.   There was, in fact, a miserable
manœuvre on the part of the three former Presidents of
the Council ; they were able to delude themselves and
others.   But these professional political men have so little
practical sense that they could not understand that it
would have been enough for me with one breath to give
an order to the Black Shirts to overturn once for all their
fancies and dreams.

" The swelled frogs waited for their triumph.   The
corrupt Press gave the maximum of publicity to the
calumnies, to incitation to commit crimes and to spread
defamation.   The Crown, supreme element of equilibrium,
was violently menaced with blackmail and worse.   As

ever, there were adventurers who wanted to speculate on
any turn in the tide of events to create again for themselves
a political rebirth. This base and pernicious crew I, for
my part, have always eliminated from the sphere of
activity and position controlled by me.

"The contemptible game lasted six months. The
weak consciences had sunk under the surface, the singers
of the doleful tunes felt their throats parched. The
speculators were now disgusted with themselves.

"In all that time I credit myself with the fact that I
never lost my calm nor my sense of balance and justice.
Because of serene judgment that I endeavour to summon
for every act of mine, I ordered the guilty to be arrested.
I desired justice to follow its unwavering course. Now
I had fulfilled my task and my duty as a just man. So I
now could have against the adversaries, my own game—
in the open."

The Matteotti affair must indeed have given Mussolini
a shock to have inspired such an outburst six years
later.

The very success of Fascism brought its problems and
difficulties in its train. Even before the March on Rome,
Fascism, in the snowball fashion that belongs to a political
cause which is succeeding, had gained an abundance of
recruits. The waverers and hangers-on in political life
flocked to the Fascist standard. The seekers of office who
looked for reward, the holders of office who needed to be
confirmed in their authorities, swelled the roll of recruits,
but as the Party grew so did dissensions multiply. It was
not possible to satisfy both the office-holder and the office-
seeker.

Fascism had been a movement with vague aspirations
rather than a programme. Men of varying faiths had seen
in it the means to the fulfilment of mutually contradictory
aims. Fascismo had developed as a fighting force. Its object
achieved, the day of fighting over, the organisation had to
pass through a transition stage to become a political
machine ; but there were many anxious days before the
transition was accomplished. Personal strife between
the leaders of the various groups grew bitter, threatening the
very existence of the Party. There were the Squadristi and

the politicians, the pre-march veterans and the post-march recruits, Socialists and syndicalists ; young students from the university and young aristocrats ; democrats, anti-democrats, monarchists, gunmen adventurers and Liberals who deplored violence and aggression.

There was a succession of ugly incidents. There was Misuri, a Deputy who launched a scathing attack, despite the Duce's warning, on some of the Party leaders. He was treated to a dose of Fascist medicine, beaten until he was unconscious. The leader of the squad responsible was promptly locked up, but only for a few hours, and it was noticed that he was always received in the Duce's entourage.

Sala and Forni were two organisers of dissentient Fascism. They dared so far as to appear as candidates at the elections. Instructions were issued by the Party directorate that life must be made unbearable for any dissentient candidate. The following day Sala and Forni were attacked at Milan and beaten, Forni barely escaping with his life.

The organisation of Fascismo was the cause of dissension which endangered Party unity. There were those who favoured one-man control from above ; there were critics who wanted democratic control from within. Massimo Rocca, a dabbler in philosophy, brought about a crisis. He was a friend of Mussolini and a champion of syndicalism. He maintained that the revolution had been made by the Fascisti for Italy, and not for the Fascisti themselves, and went on to argue that Italy stood for Mussolini, who was less Fascist every day. The ultra-Fascisti at once leapt to the defence of the Party, and a pretty quarrel was soon in progress. The Party executive proposed to expel Rocca for indiscipline, and when Mussolini objected they handed in their resignations. The Grand Council then intervened. It ordered Rocca to abstain from politics for four months and abolished the Executive board, which was replaced by a national directorate. The directorate was no more successful than the Executive, and was deposed by Mussolini after the 1924 elections. A quadrumvirate was thereupon appointed to the head of the Party, a step which was unpopular on all sides. Then came the Matteotti murder and the quadrumvirate was deposed. Thereafter a new directorate was set up.

Discipline in the Party was not achieved until in 1926 the Grand Council instituted thoroughgoing reforms. This resulted in a definitely hierarchical Constitution, involving strict obedience. Mussolini was invested with complete autocracy.

It is from this point that the final enthronement of Mussolini the Dictator dates. Before then he had contrived, sometimes precariously, to occupy the pinnacle. Thereafter he was by the letter of the Constitution " on top." The Party was entrusted to the rule of the Grand Council, and the Grand Council was placed in charge of the Duce. He became paramount in Party and State. As Prime Minister he was made responsible to the King alone, freed of control of Cabinet, Senate, Chamber of Deputies or Fascist Grand Council. The Cabinet was degraded to a board of advisers for the Prime Minister when he should seek advice. Ministers were made responsible to him ; their appointment or dismissal was vested in his hands. It was for him to summon them as he wished, to take their advice or overrule them.

In no modern civilised state is there as complete a merging of executive and legislative authority. The head of the State can find a counterpart only in the Mikado. At one period in 1929 the Italian Pooh-Bah was President of the Council, Minister of the Interior, Minister of Foreign Affairs, of War, of the Navy, of Aviation, of the Guilds and of Colonies. The Duce is a very jealous leader, suffering no star to appear in the Fascist firmament of a magnitude comparable with his own. Everything in the State is done in his name ; his is the power and assuredly his the glory. It is an instruction to the Press that regulations issued by under-secretaries of State shall be published as orders from the Duce. No man in Italy is allowed to reach a position in which he might stand as possible rival to Mussolini. To gain eminence is the signal for demotion. Thus Balbo led the massed flight of Italian planes across the Atlantic ; his signal success cost him his post as Minister of Air and he was sent to virtual exile as Colonial Governor.

Parliament was reduced to a machine for registering the Dictator's wishes, confirming his decrees as he thought necessary. Side by side with the relics of Italian parliamentay democracy is the Fascist Grand Council. It is formed out of the high Party officials and Ministers of chief rank. The list of its duties is impressive. Its tasks are to draft new legislation, name the successor to King and Premier, deliberate on international treaties and appoint the National Directory, the Executive of the Fascist Party.

The Grand Council is clearly at the head of affairs ; but equally clearly the Dictator is at the head of the Council. By virtue of his Presidency of the Council, he alone has the authority to call it together, to decide on the subject of the discussions. Membership of the august body is terminable at will by the Prime Minister, who also has the right to appoint new members. In the Fascist Party no less than in the State the power of the Grand Council is supreme. It is charged with defining political objectives, deciding the nomination and retirement of all officials.

By means of the Grand Council the ultimate control of the Fascist State and the Fascist Party is thus vested in the Dictator. His position is inviolable. The subordination of Parliament is proclaimed by law by which it is illegal for any subject to be placed on the agenda of either House without the consent of the head of the Government being first obtained. Deputies are bound to be of good behaviour, for anyone ejected from the Fascist Party is automatically expelled from the Chamber.

The appointment—it would be a misuse of the term to say election—of the House of Deputies is the prerogative of the Fascist Grand Council. The people vote, but it is only the total of their suffrages that the poll can affect ; they cannot add or detract from the list of candidates submitted to them. The Council is supreme. Suggestions may be made to the Council by employers' or employees' organisations and certain other bodies, but this is a formality which is not binding, for the thousand names submitted may be all erased by the Council, or may not. All that the Council is required to perform is to produce a list of four hundred candidates for endorsement by the electorate.

The voter has three choices—endorsement of the list (yes) ; rejection of the list (no), or abstention. Not by one initial can he alter the list as it is submitted to him. The Council's choice is unchallengeable, except by the Master of the Council. Thus is it arranged that, to a Chamber devoid even of the semblance of power or authority, none but the chosen of the Dictator can be returned.

Only if the approved list of candidates failed to secure half of the votes cast would the events of election day have any influence on the constitution of the Chamber. In that case the Grand Council would need to submit alternative lists and the list gaining a majority of votes would be entitled to three-quarters of the seats—but why mention the proviso ?

The rejection of the official list could only be expected on an election day on which the Fascisti went off duty. As it is, the election arrangements are contrived so that two requirements may be satisfied—the official assurance that no pressure is exercised on electors and the official concern that the result shall be satisfactory. What more simple means of achieving this than the employment of different coloured voting papers ? The endorsement of the official list is given on a paper in the colours of the Italian tricolour ; rejection on a white paper. And there is the assurance of an observer that at the last election most of the electors testified their loyalty by ostentatiously dropping the white slip upon the floor so that it was plain for all to see. Out of ten million voting slips deposited in the urns, only fifteen thousand were not of the predominate tricolour.

6

Mussolini muzzles his political opponents and takes stringent measures to protect the Fascist Party and its leaders. Attempts are made on his life, but "the bullets pass, Mussolini remains."

Once he had weathered the Matteotti crisis, Mussolini set about the business of suppressing his political opponents, their parties and their Press. Political journalists in Italy had never been used to wearing kid gloves. Mussolini himself had assailed the governments of democracy in language of virulent invective which has long passed out of fashion in English public life. His critics returned abuse for abuse, but he was not prepared to give them the licence he had enjoyed. At first the more extreme and violently partisan organs were suppressed, and then gradually the muzzling was extended to the Liberal newspapers. A body of censors was set up to enforce the censorship, all matter dealing with politics having to be submitted to them. As this did not silence criticism, opposition papers were suppressed entirely or Fascisticised.

After the Press the parties themselves suffered suppression, the Liberals and Socialists first, and then all the others. Finally, the members of the Aventine Secession were dealt with, the faithful Rump of Chamber passing a law depriving one hundred and twenty-five of them of their seats. Mussolini could look around and see the panorama he had wished for— the ruins of all other political forces, with Fascism standing alone. The Chamber no longer afforded the spectacle which had nauseated him. Parliamentarianism had been subdued.

From the Central Government, Fascist authority was made complete amongst the local authorities by the appointment of Fascist prefects and sub-prefects to the provinces. Local Government was reformed to bring the provinces under direct control of Rome.

Restriction on party organisations other than the Fascist Party has for some years been absolute. Restriction on the Press other than the Fascist Press, has been equally complete. The profession of journalism is limited to persons on the official list and to this the Fascist passport is essential. It is frankly avowed that in the totalitarian State the Press must be the servant of the régime ; the only freedom permitted is freedom to serve the national cause. Nor is control limited to restrictions ; political injunctions are issued to editors concerning the prominence to be assigned to various items of news. " Publish the announcement in grand style on the front page " is the command issued from time to time by the ex-leader-writer, who now edits on occasion the entire Italian Press. Other instructions are such as these : " The Duce's speech to appear on the front page—in italics " ; " Publish in grand style on the front page the news of the vast repercussions caused by the Duce's article on Germany " ; " The Duce's Rome speech must be printed in heavy type or in italics."

The Italian lives to-day in a political hot-house, scrupulously nurtured in Fascist air, screened from the chill blasts of non-Fascist opinion. The older generation has been deprived of free speech and writing, which was its birthright. The younger generation has been indoctrinated in Fascism from its youth. A nation which hears no other gospel but the one which is perpetually recommended by every intellectual agency, must ultimately become 100 per cent converted. And where all the nation is one way of thinking politically, political contentment should be the result. Mussolini and Lenin point one way to a cynical realisation in the brave new world of the greatest happiness of the greatest number. Fascist and Communist may look with arrogant self-satisfaction on lesser tribes without the law who preserve their liberties at the price of the political divisions and discontent which free speech and free thought produce.

Side by side with the restriction of anti-Fascist thought, proceeds the positive campaign for the inculcation of Fascist principles. The schools, no less than the Press, have been enlisted in support. No educational institution, from the elementary school to the university, is exempt from the duty of forming the Fascist conscience. Elementary schools are required to glorify the personality of the Duce ; secondary schools are instructed to promote recruitment of Fascist youth organisations. A new Test Act has been imposed upon university professors, imposing on them an oath of loyalty to the Fascist régime.

The inclusion of the youth of the nation in the Fascist ranks is sought at the earliest age. The call to service invites them to step into the army of the Duce and be the best soldiers—and army here means an essentially militarist organisation, though its recruits are only on the point of emerging from childhood. In the training of the younger generation of Italy Fascism and militarism go hand in hand. Joined with the cardinal axiom that Mussolini can do no wrong are the commandments that Fascisti may not believe in everlasting peace and that the rifle has been entrusted to the recruit not to be damaged, but to be kept ready for the purpose of war. From the age of seven children of Italy are enrolled in Black Shirt organisations. The boys become members of the Opera Nazionale Ballilla, the girls of the Piccole Italiane ; at fourteen they pass into the Avanguardia and Giovani Italiane and remain until they come of age in Fascism in their eighteenth year. The organisations for both boys and girls are on the ancient Roman model, with squadrons, cohorts and legions. The boys are trained so that on passing out of the Avanguardia at seventeen the complete Fascist is already a perfect soldier—or seaman, or airman. Rifles and machine-guns are provided so that the Avanguardists may have practical as well as theoretical knowledge. In the naval divisions there is opportunity to become proficient in naval warfare, and for the air divisions there is training both in theory and practice. Even girls are organised in semi-military fashion and are taught martial songs. In the schools training is professedly Fascist in politics and patriotically militaristic.

The penal code has been rewritten to further the needs of the totalitarian State. No form of opposition to Fascism can escape the net widely stretched against persons who may be " dangerous to the State," a definition subject to vastly extensive interpretation. Police surveillance, which involves virtual ostracism, is a mild penalty for offenders. Deportation to the islands—Lipari is the best known of these places of exile—is the more stringent measure. To strengthen the forces for the preservation of duty, there has been created a Special Tribunal for the Defence of the State, before which offenders may be brought. This Special Tribunal is composed not of professional judges, but of officers of the militia. It is vested with powers of life and death.

In the stiffening of the penal code to suppress and penalise activities which are considered to be dangerous to the State, energetic measures were taken to afford protection to the Fascist Party and its leaders. A penalty of imprisonment up to six years is provided for the crime of vilifying the Party's emblems. The Grand Council of Fascism is similarly protected from vilification. The penalty of death is enforceable against those who make any attempt upon the life, safety or personal liberty of the Dictator. In this respect the head of the State is placed in the same position as the King and Queen and heir to the throne. This provision is the sequel to the various attempts which have been made on Mussolini's life, of which he himself gives the following account in his " Autobiography."

" I could repeat, as I said one day, after an attempt against my life : ' The bullets pass, Mussolini remains.' Zaniboni initiated the series of attempts against my life.

One was a vulgar Socialist, who received two cheques of 150,000 francs each from the Czechoslovakian Socialists to lead an anti-Fascist struggle. Naturally, Zaniboni, a drug addict, used the 300,000 to prepare with devilish ability his attempt against me. He chose the sacred day of the commemoration of the Victory. He ambushed himself in a room of the Hotel Dragoni just in front of Palazzo Chigi, from the balcony of which I usually review the processions which pass on the way to the altar of the Unknown Soldier to place their flowers, their vows and their homage. Having an Austrian rifle with fine sights, the fellow could not miss his aim. Zaniboni, to avoid being suspected, dressed in the uniform of a major of the Army, and got ready in the morning to accomplish his crime. He was discovered. He had been followed for a long time. A few days before, General Capello had generously given him money and advice. Masonry had made of him its ensign. But with a simultaneous action, Zaniboni, General Capello and various less important personages of the plot were arrested one hour before they planned the attempt. So closed the first chapter.

" In 1926, in the month of April, when I inaugurated the International Congress of Medicine, a crazy and megalo-maniac woman, of English nationality,[1] exalted by fanatic-ism, came near my motor car and fired at close range a shot that perforated my nostrils. A centimetre of differ-ence and the shot might have been fatal. It was, as I said, a mad, hysterical woman, led on by elements and persons never clearly identified. I abandoned her to her destiny by putting her beyond the frontier, where she could meditate on her failure and her folly.

"Just after the occasion, before my nose was out of its dressings, I was speaking to a meeting of officials from all parts of Italy. I felt impelled to say, ' If I go forward, follow me ; if I recoil, kill me ; if I die, avenge me.'

"Another attempt, which might have had grave results, was that of an Anarchist, a so-called Lucetti, who had come back from France with his soul full of hate and envy against Fascism and against me. He waited for me in the light and large Via Nomentana, in front of Porta

[1] She was an Irishwoman named Gibson. It was discovered that her act had no political significance.

Pia. He was able to meditate his crime in silence. He had been eight days in Rome and carried powerful bombs. Lucetti recognised my car, while I was going to Palazzo Chigi, and as soon as he saw it he hurled at me the infernal machine, which hit an angle of the car and bounced back on the ground, exploding there after I had passed. I was not wounded, but innocent people were hit and taken to the hospital. When arrested, the miserable man could justify his crazy act only by his anti-Fascist hate. I did not give a great importance to the episode. Having to meet the English Ambassador, I went directly to Palazzo Chigi and the conversation with the foreign diplomat continued calmly enough until a great popular manifestation in the streets interrupted us. Only then the English Ambassador, somewhat amazed, learned of the attempt against my life.

" The last attempt was on October 31, 1926. It was in Bologna, after I had lived a day full of life, enthusiasm and pride. A young Anarchist, egged on by the secret plotters, at a moment when the whole population was lined up for the salute, came out from the ranks and fired at my car with a gun. I was sitting near the ' Podesta ' of Bologna, Arpinati. The shot burned my coat, but again I was quite safe. The crowd, in the meanwhile, seized by an impulse of exasperated fury, could not be restrained. It gave summary justice to the man."

7

The Corporate State machine as a whole has not yet been set in motion. The future will show whether Mussolini has worked as well as the Italians already imagine he has.

Since the year 1926 Mussolini has been the Dictator of Italy in the Party and in the State, supreme, unchallenged, his position made impregnable. He has been Dictator *de facto* and *de jure*. So firmly established is he by the letter of the Constitution of Party and of State that his removal is impossible, except by revolution. He can be in a minority of one and yet by constitutional right override the combined wishes of all other members of the Italian community, for by his consent alone would it be possible to diminish the sovereign prerogatives that he exercises.

The term of his dictatorship has seen the birth of a new Italy. The Risorgimento of 1870 has been completed. The Risorgimento created a unified State. Mussolini has created an Italian people working in unity of purpose. He has replaced old defeatism by new enthusiasm. *Dolce far niente* is one of the tags which used to convey the spirit of Italy, but it applies no longer. At Mussolini's call a new spirit of discipline and militarism has sprung into being. Italy has now been advanced to take the place that she thought was her due amongst the Powers.

The transformation is Mussolini's personal achievement. He, and he alone, is the creator of the new Italy. Will he be remembered also apart from his personal achievements and his statesmanship as a political innovator, founder of a new order of society—the Corporate State ? The answer cannot yet be made. He is the author of a great experiment, but until the experiment has stood the test of experience it cannot be said whether the Corporate State stands as a new form and order of national society.

There is much talk of the Corporate State of Italy, based on the assumption that the Corporate State is in being and is functioning. The transformation in Italy is attributed to the Corporate system and hailed as an indication of the system's triumphant success, but this is a wrong identification of cause and effect. The transformation in Italy has been the result of Mussolini's magnetic influence and drive, produced irrespective of the political and economic order of Italian society. Coincident with his work of transformation the evolution has proceeded at his direction of the machinery for the working of the Corporate State. But this machinery is not yet functioning. The constitution for the new society is there. Some of its parts are in working order. But the machine as a whole has not yet been set in motion.

The Corporate State is a syndicalist organisation. Georges Sorel, the Frenchman, is the man to whom credit is given for this conception of society. Sorel, disgusted by the scandals in the public life of the France of his day, advocated the reconstruction of the French State on an economic rather than a political basis. This idea has attracted many minds

in different countries since his day, and has had its advocates
in England. Other Italians besides Mussolini were attracted
to it ; but although the Duce may be indebted to Sorel for
the principles, the mechanism is his own invention.   Sur-
veying the Italian scene , he has improvised an organisation
which he believes to be best suited to the character and
needs of the Italian people. He goes further, and claims
that his system is the best for the conduct of affairs in the
highly industralised modern world.

The aim Mussolini has had in calling the Corporate
State into being is to reorganise production and distribution
on the lines of national economic planning. It is a half-way
house to Communism. The control of a nation's productive
industries is sought without the final taking over of ownership. Mussolini and Lenin are alike in believing in the
Totalitarian State. In their concept everything within the
State should be performed in the name of the State,
and the State should be concerned in the performance of
everything that is done within it. Their views diverge
on the principle of the rights of the individual. Lenin and
Communism stand for the equality of all. Mussolini and
the Corporate State postulate the fundamental inequality
of man. Lenin led a revolution to bring about equality on
the basis of the masses. Mussolini is directing evolution on
the basis of the acceptance of existing classes.

Mussolini's ultimate design is the evolution of an Italian
parliament which shall be representative of the different
sections of Italian industrial life. This instrument of the
collective wisdom of producers will regulate production
throughout the country in the interests of the State, stimulating or restricting output in accordance with current
needs, regulating wages and hours of work and giving the
national Government the information and guidance necessary for the formation and carrying out of a national
industrial policy. To this end the Corporations and the
Council of Corporations have been instituted.

The foundations of the Corporate system were laid by an
Act of 1926. This provided for the regularisation of industrial syndicates. As soon as a syndicate includes 10 per cent
of those engaged in a particular trade, it is given the
authority to represent the entire trade, industry or profession. Syndicates are federated into confederations of groups

of employers and employees, and above the federations stand six major Corporations—the Corporations of Agriculture, of Industry, of Commerce, of Internal Transport, of Sea and Air Transport and of Banking and Insurance with the National Confederation of Professional Men and Artists.

This organisation was carried a step further in 1930 by the establishment of a National Council of Corporations, of which Mussolini himself became the first minister. By this machinery it is intended ultimately to regulate the entire field of Italian industry—but that day is yet to come. The regimentation which has been effected so far has been attained by sporadic interventions by the Duce and his advisers in a manner which is paralleled in other countries which lack the Corporate State's machinery.

Italy to-day is proud of her Dictator. There are many reasons for her pride. Chaos has passed away and order reigns. Distress has not ended, but has been reduced. There is a new efficiency and a glory in work. Above all there is a great national uplifting of spirit. A great, psychologist has played a master stroke. A national inferiority complex has been dissolved, and a feeling of national superiority reigns. There is a spirit which has not been abroad since the days of Imperial Rome. Italy feels herself to be a Power, *the* Power in Europe. Mussolini has beaten the national drum and has aroused the martial spirit. He has appealed in the sacred name of the Totalitarian State, and has been answered by the nation. Youth has responded with fervour. The ideal of service and of discipline has been adopted with enthusiasm. Such is the success of Mussolini, the psychologist. He has secured the people's acceptance of the burdens and sacrifices imposed by Mussolini the politician—the loss, or severe restriction of their political liberties, the right of free speech and free action.

One day, if Mussolini is able to carry his intentions into operation, we shall see a Parliament of Industry regulating the affairs of Italy. Until that day is reached it must remain a matter for argument whether a country's affairs are best guided by the collective wisdom of the industries or whether the professional politicians, experts in the machinery of statecraft, are better agents for the execution

of the difficult and delicate task of government.   Supporters
of the democratic and parliamentary system will note that
the Mussolini who has created the new Italy developed as a
politician and leader-writer, a survivor of the old political
order which it is his purpose to destroy.

II

THE MARTYR DICTATORS

Κing alexander of Yugoslavia and Engelbert Dollfuss, Chancellor of Austria, will be remembered by their people as the martyr dictators. They fell victims of assassination within a few weeks of each other during the year 1934. Europe had barely recovered from the shock of the passing of the Little Chancellor of Austria before the ruler of Yugoslavia was dead.

Their careers had more in common than the coincidence of martyrdom which brought them to a close. The circumstances which led the constitutional King to play the role of dictator were paralleled by those which made the constitutional Chancellor become an autocrat in Austria. Neither had intended to suppress and supersede democratic institutions. Each had acted a constitutional part at the head of affairs until circumstances arose which led to the establishment of a dictatorship. Each could have argued that the assumption of dictatorial power was necessary because democratic institutions were failing to provide a strong government.

In neither case, however, can it be claimed that the dictatorship led to a solution of the difficulties. The King, who had assumed dictatorial powers as a temporary expedient, did not find that circumstances were working towards a return to the political normal. The Chancellor re-wrote his country's constitution, but without appearing thereby to advance towards a solution of his country's problems.

In Yugoslavia it was the contending and intense rivalries of the different peoples forming the State which led to the overthrow of parliamentary government. In Austria it was the uncompromising hostility of Socialists and anti-Socialists which brought into existence armed and rival political forces, and showed the way to democracy's undoing.

ENGELBERT DOLLFUSS

1

Dollfuss, far rom being the leader of a revolt, has his dictatorship forced upon him by political necessity. He lacked the ruthlessness of other dictators.

T HERE has been nothing more pathetic in the post-war history of Europe than the story of Engelbert Dollfuss, the Little Chancellor of Austria. It was the tragedy of his political career that he was called upon to become a dictator. The supreme tragedy of his death was that his assassination was an accident which neither the assassin nor his leaders had intended.

Dictator by force of political necessity, victim of an accidental assassination—the career of Engelbert Dollfuss is one of those which makes the gods laugh.

There was something pathetic about the assassins as well as their victim. They raided the Chancellery on the fatal day in July, 1934, imagining that they were taking part in a well-organised revolt, which, according to their account, had the backing of the President himself. They carried out orders successfully and captured the Chancellery. Then there was a double tragedy—there were no leaders to instruct them how to proceed and in the course of the raid Chancellor Dollfuss received the shots which cost him his life. "We did not know what to do : our leaders had left us in the lurch," was the confession of the assassins.

It was a tragic futility that Engelbert Dollfuss died to no better purpose. The Little Chancellor had won the sympathy of the world by his courageous efforts to fulfil the role that his country's needs had forced upon him. Among the dictators his place is unique—he was the Reluctant Dictator.

A democratic statesman, he would have been happy had

" It was the tragedy of Dollfuss's political career that he was
called upon to become a dictator."

he been left leader of a democratic party. But it was his destiny to assume dictatorial powers, to expunge the democratic republican constitution and to found a Corporative State on the Italian model. But these things he did reluctantly, wherein lies the difference between him and the rulers of Nazi Germany and Fascist Italy.

Dollfuss did not take the dictator's path to power. His position in its origin was similar to that of the men whom Hitler and Mussolini supplanted. Dollfuss rose to become head of an Austrian Ministry, and it was according to the principles of the democracy that he sought to rule. When at length circumstances would no longer permit him to govern democratically he would have preferred to resign from his position, but was called upon to remain at the head of the Government. Unwillingly, in compliance with the request of President Miklas, he consented to stick to his place at the helm. Inevitably, because of the weakness of his parliamentary position, he had to resort to rule by decree—the first step on the path to dictatorship. He was driven to the inevitable, for only by assuming complete dictatorial powers could he maintain himself precariously against opponents within and without the State.

If a man is going to play the part of dictator it is better perhaps that he should do it without misgivings. In their 100 per cent efficiency and ruthlessness lie the reasons for the success of Hitler, Mussolini and the Ghazi Kemal Ataturk. Doubts and hesitations are misplaced in a dictator. Dollfuss had not the capacity for this extreme ruthlessness, which you may gather from the fact that it was with reluctance that he took on the job at all. Ruthlessness at the first may save bloodshed afterwards. Hitler, Mussolini and the Ghazi, ruthless men all, have survived to continue to serve the States to whose existence they believe, in common with every statesman at the head of affairs, that their own existence is essential. Dollfuss, the reluctant dictator, has perished.

His one act of supreme ruthlessness, the suppression of the Socialists, does not suggest that he could be wise in his ruthlessness. But it was, perhaps, at the suggestion of Mussolini that Dollfuss extinguished his opponents on the Left, the one act in his career that, in the eyes of the admirers of the Pocket Chancellor, detracted from the magnificence of his struggle against foes on either side.

2

Austria recoils from friendship with Germany with the coming of Hitlerism. Dollfuss seeks the protection of Mussolini, and to safeguard his position has to accept the support of the Heimwehr.

In stature Dr. Dollfuss was the smallest man to play a leading role in Europe since Napoleon. He was an inch less than five feet in height—curious that destiny should have chosen his small figure to bear the burden of all the troubles of Austria. The disproportion is equalled by the contrast between his size and the robustness of his energy, the vitality of his spirit, the reach of his courage.

One thing he had in common with the dictators of Rome, Berlin and Angora—the humbleness of his origin. He was the son of a peasant. He married a peasant girl, and his brother remained in his village home at Texing in Lower Austria to carry on as a peasant farmer. Dollfuss's bravery was made manifest during the World War, and he was promoted to lieutenant for the valour he displayed in service on the Italian Front. The War ended, he studied law and economics in Vienna and Berlin, and entered upon a political career by forming the small farmers into a Peasants' Union. He gained the reputation of being the leading agricultural authority, and as such was invited to take Cabinet office as Minister of Agriculture. He showed himself, though unskilled in affairs, to be possessed of considerable political talent, and was called upon to succeed his chief, Dr. Buresch, in the Chancellorship.

When Dollfuss took office in May, 1932, the outlook for Austria was conspicuously black, even in the gloomy history of that country since the War. National bankruptcy appeared to be imminent, civil strife to be the inevitable outcome of the rivalries between Social Democrats, Austrian Fascists and Austrian Nazis. The history of his Chancellorship is the record of his attempts to guide Austria to safety by rallying to his aid the forces which were anti-Socialist and anti-Nazi. His own party of Christian Socialists was

not strong enough on its own to afford him the strength he
needed. Allies he had to choose, and reluctantly—there
was reluctance in the adoption of almost all the expedients
to which he was driven—he had to accept the aid of the
Heimwehr. An ally, too, he needed abroad. Austria had
to choose. Italy or Germany, which? The Chancellor's
solution was to seek the protection of Mussolini to save
himself from absorption by Hitler.

Mark the Austrian *volte face* which was caused by Hitlerism
in Germany. Previously Austria and Germany had only
been kept apart by the continuous opposition of the
Powers. Austria's first constituent assembly had in 1919
declared the country to be an integral part of Germany, but
the Allied Powers placed their caveat on the proposed
Anschluss. In the distress of 1921, when the League of
Nations was appealed to for loans to feed the starving
populace, the Austrian Government proposed holding a
plebiscite on the question of incorporation of the Austrian
Republic in that of Germany. Again the Allied Powers
intervened. In 1925 distress again made Austrians look to
union with Germany as the only means of economic salvation. Italy and the Little Entente Powers warned the
Austrian Government to stifle the Anschluss Movement.

When in 1931 the world depression intensified—its herald
was the collapse of the Austrian Kredit Anstalt—Austria
again looked towards Germany. A protocol was signed
for an Austro-German customs union to promote trade
between the two countries. But though it was explicitly
provided that the political independence of the two States
would be maintained, the opponents of the Anschluss were
immediately aroused to violent protest. A customs pact
was suspected as the precursor to a political alliance.
Financial and diplomatic pressure was brought to bear.
The authority of the Hague Court of Justice was invoked,
and the customs union was judicially prevented by the
finding that it would involve the violation of the pledge
Austria gave in 1922 not to imperil her independence.

With the advent of Hitler to power and the Nazi terror
in Germany there was a sweeping reversal of Austrian
opinion. There had always been a body of opposition to
incorporation with Germany and now the minority became
the majority view.

The Austrians are a proud and independent race. The majority no longer wished for union with Germany, lest Austrian individuality be crushed under the iron heel of Hitler. The Austrian Socialists did not wish to share the fate of their German fellows. Austrian Catholics grew increasingly uneasy over the treatment meted out to the Catholic Church in Bavaria. Austria drew back, and every step away from Berlin was one nearer to Rome. Italy had protested time and again against the Anschluss. Her strategic interests required the existence of a buffer State between herself and the Germany which was becoming more militantly minded. How better to prevent the Dictator of Berlin from extending his influence to the Tyrol than for the Dictator of Rome to extend his influence over Austria? Mussolini reciprocated the advances of Dollfuss.

The Little Chancellor was shown, internally and externally, that the new policy had vigorous opponents. The Austrian Nazis declared their enmity ; the Germans began an offensive of frightfulness, a campaign of propaganda and of bombs. The more aggressive Germany became, the more heavily Dollfuss leaned on the powerful shoulders of Mussolini. In the extinction of the Austrian Socialists, as a prelude to the creation of an Austrian Corporate State on the Italian model, you may see the price the Duce exacted for his support. In choosing Mussolini in preference to Hitler, Dollfuss made it inevitable that the Socialist Schutzbund would be handed over to the mercy of the Heimwehr.

Post-war Austria has been the land of irreconcilables. The industrial workers of Vienna and the Eastern Plain are Socialists and anti-clerical. The rural workers are Conservative and religious. The Social Democrats held control of Vienna throughout the years following the War, and they carried out Socialist schemes on a large scale, taking over control of passenger transport, water and lighting systems, establishing a municipal brewery, bakery, and even a municipal crematorium. They launched an extensive programme of municipal house construction, and the Karl Marx Hof which they constructed was the largest boarding-house in Europe, being more than three-quarters of a mile long. These activities antagonised anti-Marxists.

Each party developed its defence force—the Socialist Schutzbund of nearly 100,000 armed men, and the Heimwehr of the Fascists (as much anti-Nazi as anti-Socialist) of some 60,000. Both forces were possessed of considerable quantities of munitions and war supplies, which had been handed out at the time when the Communists at the end of the War threatened to turn Vienna " red." The Socialist munitions were stored in secret hiding-places. The municipal flats in Vienna were strongholds from which they would issue to the attack, or in which they would take refuge against Heimwehr assaults. Clashes between the two forces became frequent. The Heimwehr threatened to march on Vienna as the Fascists had marched on Rome. Chancellor Dollfuss was at length driven by the insecurity of his position to accept the Heimwehr support he had repeatedly rejected.

The danger in which the Chancellor stood, and the intensity of feeling existing among the Austrian Nazis, were attested by an attempt made on his life in October, 1933. With another Minister and his personal detective he was passing through a vestibule in the Parliament building when a young man approached under the pretext of delivering two letters, drew a small pearl-handled revolver and fired two shots. Dollfuss cried out, " I have been hit," and flung open his coat to show his linen, already bloodstained. One of the shots had entered his chest two inches above the heart. Its course had been deflected by a waistcoat button, to which the Chancellor owed his life. The assailant, who was overpowered by the Chancellor's colleague, was Rudolf Dentil, a young man of twenty-two who had been enrolled in a Nazi Storm detachment.

3

The Heimwehr, permitted to arm on account of Austrian Nazis, make an onslaught on the Socialists and shell them into submission. The civil war. Dollfuss looks on while democracy in Austria is knocked on the head by Starhemberg and Fey.

When Dollfuss accepted office in May, 1932, he had a majority of but one in the Nationalrat. Twice he escaped defeat in the Chamber by the providential death of an opponent. Then, as a consequence of a dispute concerning procedure, the Speaker and two of the Government supporters resigned. The Chancellor's position was thereby made impossible in the existing Chamber, and he dared not ask for a dissolution. He accordingly proffered his resignation, but President Miklas would not release him. Strict constitutional government being impossible, Dollfuss had perforce to resort to expedients. He reorganised his Cabinet, taking five portfolios himself in the manner of Mussolini, and then announced that he proposed further Fascist experiments. " We will," he said, " build up a Catholic German State, which will be thoroughly Austrian upon a corporative (Fascist) basis. It will be an authoritarian State based on corporations formed on occupational lines."

While he was thus engaged the Chancellor had to meet the growing menace of Nazi propaganda and terrorism from inside the country and from outside. Germany declared an economic boycott and placed tourist traffic under an interdict, both damaging blows at Austria's economy. It was a continual struggle to hold the Nazis within Austria at bay, and Dollfuss had at length to arm a section of the Heimwehr against them. He took the decision with reluctance. The Heimwehr accepted the invitation with alacrity. Now under Government auspices they would be able finally to dispose of Social Democrats.

In the early days of 1934 there was activity on the part of Heimwehr leaders in the Tyrol. They reported a Socialist rising to be imminent, and carried out searches of Socialist headquarters. In Upper Austria next, and then in other quarters, the Heimwehr mobilised, and raided Socialist quarters in the network which spread round Vienna. The final struggle was foreshadowed on February 11 by Major Fey, Vice-Chancellor and Austria's strong man. Addressing his Heimwehr troops on parade, he declared that during the last two days he had made certain that Dollfuss was with them. " To-morrow," he added, " we are going to clean up Austria." His words were spread abroad over the radio, but though their meaning was apparent, the Socialist leaders hesitated to give the call to resistance. They could scarcely credit that at the critical juncture in his affairs Chancellor Dollfuss would jeopardise his position by permitting the Heimwehr to make their onslaught. Instead of a call to action, the leaders gave a warning to their followers.

On the last night of peace a messenger came to the Vienna Socialist G.H.Q. with the tidings that the Socialists at Linz were certain that a Fascist coup was pending. He urged that it would be folly for them to submit to being disarmed by the Heimwehr. However, a message was immediately sent to Linz that whatever the provocation no pretext must be given for a Heimwehr offensive. Despite the warning, when the Workers' Club at Linz was raided on the Monday morning, the Socialists refused to submit to the indignity of being searched. Firing broke out, some of the Linz Radicals were wounded and a few killed. It was the signal for the onslaught. The Socialists throughout the country took up arms, feeling no doubt that their existence as a party was at stake. Either they must fight to maintain their liberties, or submit to extinction—the fate of their comrades in Germany.

Again the Linz Socialists sent a warning to Vienna, and from the Viennese headquarters the orders for an immediate general strike throughout the country were decided upon. But the necessary instructions could not be conveyed. Local commanders of the Socialist Defence Corps had been arrested. Heavily armed police and troops already occupied important buildings in Vienna. The Socialist Mayor was dismissed ; the Vienna Diet was dissolved ; the Heimwehr flag of green and white was hoisted over the Town Hall.

Nevertheless, the Socialists were not intimidated and the initial moves to bring about a national stoppage of work were made. The Viennese power stations were put out of action. Within their strongholds of the municipal flats the Socialists with rifles and machine-guns stood in their last defence, formidable opponents. That night Vienna was a city of battle. In industrial centres throughout the country the Socialists took to arms—in Upper Austria, in Styria and the Tyrol. Workers at Steyr stormed one of the armament factories, and then took control of the town, posting armed forces with guns in strategic points on the hills around.

Socialist resistance was stronger than their opponents had expected. For four days Vienna was a battle ground and civil war swept the country. The Government represented that their forces were suppressing an armed revolt ; the Socialists that they were fighting to save their political existence. Of the two claims the latter is borne out.

All along the line the Socialists found their movements forestalled. Their summons to the workers to down tools throughout the country in a last effort to preserve their liberties met with meagre response, for the reason that it could not be effectively circulated. The Socialist lines of communication had been cut.

In Vienna the Socialists might put the power stations out of action, but the authorities otherwise had control. When the Heimwehr flag was run up over the Rathaus, the inner city was cut off by a cordon of troops, and barbed-wire knife-rests across the streets. Martial law had been proclaimed.

The Socialists took refuge in the municipal dwellings, then virtually armed fortresses. Heimwehr troops surrounded these strongholds. On either side snipers' bullets whistled across the streets and there were desultory bursts of machine-gun fire. But the besieged were safe against these attacks and artillery had to be called for. Then howitzer shells were sent crashing into the Karl Marx Hof, and under cover of the bombardment steel helmeted troops advanced.

As the shelling ceased the Socialists emerged from their cellar refuges. The bayonet attackers were repulsed and had to fall back. Howitzers had again to be brought into action. For two days the Socialists kept the attackers at bay, but one by one their refuges were shelled and they had to hoist the white flag. Ambulances and motor hearses were kept busy removing wounded and dying. Block after block of flats was in ruins, their stucco fronts pitted with the marks of hundreds of bullets and rent with jagged holes where shells had torn a way through.

In provincial centres the resistance continued longer. At Linz there was ding-dong fighting, attack and counter-attack ranging over several days. Prince Starhemberg, the Heimwehr leader, himself took control of the offensive, but so well entrenched were the Socialists, so well armed, that repeated assaults failed. Taking the offensive themselves, the Socialists destroyed part of the railway and set the station alight. The conflict was prolonged at Graz, where the Socialists took up the paving stones to form barricades ; at Pernegg, where they tore up the railway track ; at Woergl, where they seized the railway junctions ; and at a dozen other industrial centres. But it was in vain. The Socialists had been taken at a disadvantage. They might struggle hard, but there could be only one ending.

Before the last shots had been fired, courts martial had begun to deal with the leaders, and the hangman was there to carry out the courts' decisions. Dr. Julius Deutsch and Dr. Bauer, who organised resistance in Vienna, were lucky to escape across the frontier. Deutsch, commander-in chief of the Socialist Defence Corps, lost the sight of an eye, hit by a stray bullet, and the other eye was damaged. Partially blind, he made off through woods and fields. Once he was challenged by a Heimwehr patrol, but in the darkness played the part of a drunken peasant, and so got across into Czechoslovakia.

Many other leaders, less fortunate than these two, met their end at the hangman's hands, for the Heimwehr were allowed their vengeance. Many Socialists were imprisoned ; their property was confiscated ; their organisations were disbanded. And before the firing was over, Prince Starhemberg announced the foundation of the new Fascist State.

Austro-Fascism was differentiated by its authors from Italian Fascism and German Hitlerism. But though Heimwehr Fascists might stand for an independent Austria and for the Catholic Church against German absorption and German State Paganism, it was the death of Austrian democracy, deliberately intended by men who despised democracy as intensely as Hitler or Mussolini.

4

By a ruse Nazis gain admittance to the Chancellery, intending to kidnap the Ministry while their comrades take command of the country. Dollfuss is assassinated and Dr. Schuschnigg succeeds.

With the Socialists crushed out of existence, or reduced so that their activities had to be carried on underground, the Little Chancellor had now to fight on one front only, against the Austrian Nazis, who, inspired and abetted from over the German border, intensified their campaign with bomb, bullet and propaganda. The Nazis sought to secure the overthrow of Dollfuss as the first step towards the absorption of Austria by Germany. Had Dollfuss been a dictator-born, like Hitler or Mussolini, or Mustapha Kemal, there would have been short shrift for the Nazis, who in their turn would have been wiped off the political map ; but Dollfuss's misgivings made him pause before advancing to final ruthlessness, and while he hesitated the Nazis struck.

It would be hard to find a parallel in the history of Europe for the state of affairs in Austria, where political movement against the Government was financed and fomented by the Government of a neighbouring and ostensibly friendly State. The Austrian National Socialist Party was incorporated in the National Socialist Party of Germany. An Austrian Legion was trained in Germany and supplied with arms for purposes of terrorism. Nightly over the wireless the German Commissioner for Justice made appeals from Munich to his comrades in Austria, denouncing Dr. Dollfuss and his Government.

There was a supreme act of Nazi impertinence when Dr. Franck, as Hitler's representative, made a triumphal progress through Vienna, delivering violent speeches against Chancellor and Government. He was expelled. Dollfuss was not to be turned from his purpose by propaganda or plots. He issued a decree dissolving the Nazi Party in Austria, and the Nazi Storm Troopers.

As the summer of 1934 advanced it became apparent that the Chancellor must stem by force the rising flood of terrorism or be swept away by it. Reports to the Cabinet showed that the Nazis were completing their plans for armed revolt. Each day the Chancellor received threatening letters as numerous as the " fan " mail of a Hollywood star. Every member of the Government carried his life in his hands. As a precautionary measure Frau Dollfuss was sent to Italy to remain at a safe distance until the crisis had passed.

On July 18 Dollfuss threw down the gauntlet by introducing a law to make political acts of violence punishable by death and imposing Draconian penalties for the possession of arms and explosives. The Nazis were alarmed and infuriated. Hitherto the extreme penalty of the law had been reserved for Socialist terrorists. Would the Chancellor dare to inflict it on Nazis ? If so, wholesale executions were in prospect. They were not left long in doubt. Under the new ordinance a Socialist was hanged, and the judges were ordered by proclamation to bestow the same sentence on any of the Nazi conspirators in custody or awaiting trial who should be found guilty on the same charge. As a means of saving their comrades in custody the Nazis decided to strike during the final days of July.

An elaborate plot had been prepared, complete with all the paraphernalia of international spy drama from the pages of William Le Queux. There were secret codes, whispered messages from unknown intriguers, meetings behind closed doors, pledges of secrecy, and hanging over all, the spell of danger. Despite the precautions the Cabinet learned that trouble was afoot, but precise information was lacking as to the quarter from which the blow was to fall. The Socialists, rather than the Nazis, were suspected, and a round-up was ordered of such agitators of the Left as remained at large. Then numbers of young Nazis were brought into the concentration camps. Still mysterious hints came from the underworld. Police and troops were ordered to stand by. A heavy consignment of explosives from Germany to Austria was captured. It was a plain indication that the Nazis were at last to make a bid to seize power by force. Such preparations as were possible were taken by the authorities.

On the morning of Wednesday, July 25, there was yet another meeting of the Cabinet to discuss the latest reports concerning the imminent insurrection. About the same hour a body of young men met in a gymnasium hall in Vienna. They arrived in ordinary clothes, and changed into the uniform of the regiment on duty at the Chancellery. By some means the police got to learn of this meeting of Nazi conspirators and four detectives were sent hurrying to the hall. They were in time to see four lorries drive away with uniformed men, and the detectives assumed that troops were carrying off conspirators.

A message had been sent through to the Cabinet then in session, and Ministers dispersed. Some left the Chancellery, including the Minister of War, who gave instructions for new precautionary measures to be taken and for additional guards to do duty around the departments of the Ministers of State. A few minutes later four lorries drove up to the Chancellery with the men in the uniform of the reinforcements of the guard that were expected. The first lorry drove into the courtyard, having paused for a moment so that the gates could not be slammed against the three lorries behind. The precaution was needless for no suspicion had been aroused. From the four vehicles the Nazis made their way within. In a few moments the guards on duty had been overpowered and the building was in the hands of the raiders.

Dollfuss received the first alarm by the clatter of armed men in the corridors. The Chancellor's door-keeper had heard the shout of " Hands up." He set off to find his master, who was unarmed. He hurried the Chancellor through the rooms to the famous Congress Hall, the hall with eight doors, originally constructed so that the representatives of the eight Powers attending the Congress of Vienna might not be troubled over claims of precedence. The Chancellor and his servant were about to leave when one of the doors was flung open and a party of desperadoes burst into the room. One of them without warning raised a revolver and discharged two shots. He was five yards away from the Chancellor, and this time the shots did not go wide.

Dollfuss fell, and there was a loud crack as his head struck the floor. Dropping his pistol, the assailant knelt beside the Chancellor and partially raised him, asking him whether he was wounded. " I do not know," Dollfuss replied. He was then told to stand up, but said : " I cannot walk." He was lifted on to a sofa. There was blood on his face. It was apparent that he was wounded, and examination showed that both bullets had taken effect. There was a severe gash in the throat from which the blood began to pour. The crimson stream spread over the sofa, and someone fetched a basin to receive it. It was the Chancellor's life blood.

In other rooms in the building the officials were rounded up by the raiders, who made a comb-out of the Chancellery, breaking down any doors that were locked. Only two other Ministers were in the place, Major Fey and Herr Karwinsky,

Under-Secretary for Defence. The two Ministers, officials, women clerks and foreign visitors were driven under threat of revolver through the corridors into an inner courtyard. The men were searched for arms. In the courtyard were the guards, who had been disarmed, standing in a corner with rifles trained on them by other of the Nazi raiders. Officials were ordered to remove from their buttonholes badges of the Patriotic Front. Most of them refused and the badges were roughly torn off. One official, a Jew, was struck with a rifle butt.

The two Ministers after being searched for arms were removed to a small room and a strong guard was mounted over them. They were valuable hostages.

Consternation was plain on the face of the raiders when, on the completion of the search of the Chancellery, it was apparent that besides Dollfuss only two members of the Government had been trapped. Their plans had been laid on the supposition that the entire Cabinet would have been made prisoner, in which event there would have been no person of responsibility at large to take control of events and order the steps necessary for the suppression of the rising. The telephone message of warning to the police had frustrated the scheme at the outset. Within an hour the raiding party in the Chancellery realised that the plot had failed. From the windows as they looked out they saw a double ring of armed men cutting off their escape. The inner ring held rifles directed towards the Nazis ; the outer pointed rifles at whomsoever approached.

Another raiding party had captured the Ravag head-quarters of the Viennese Broadcasting Company. A contingent of fourteen young men carried out this coup. They shot down a policeman who opposed them. Inside, one of the directors offered resistance, and he was shot. Some of the party entered the studio in which a broadcast was in progress. Revolvers were levelled at the announcer, who, under threat of death, was ordered to announce that the Dollfuss Cabinet had been deposed and that President Miklas had entrusted the government to Dr. Rintelen.

The announcement was heard throughout Austria, causing surprise and consternation. It was heard by Heimwehr forces, who interpreted it as a warning to report to local headquarters. It was heard by the Nazis, who recognised the signal for revolt, for so stringent had been the need for secrecy that no summons had been sent out throughout the country. The message was heard, too, by the members of the Government, who had escaped the trap in the Chancellery, and who knew it to be untrue. They gave prompt orders for action. The first step was to prevent the rebels from making further use of the wireless to call for a general Nazi mobilisation. To forestall this, the cable connecting the studio with the transmitting station was cut. It was the second blow at Nazi hopes.

The laconic message which had been sent out concerning the fall of Dollfuss and his replacement by Rintelen was not the ample instruction which the conspirators had reckoned on being able to give. But the fourteen raiders in the Ravag had other matters to think about than the failure of their plans. Within a few minutes policemen, revolvers in their hands, came hurrying to the scene. Revolver shots shattered the windows and were answered from within. Then by lorry and motor-coach steel-helmeted troops with rifles and bayonets were brought to the scene. There were fourteen youths in the station. Without were a force of one thousand attackers, armed with machine-guns, and for three hours the fourteen kept the thousand at bay. At length their ammunition was exhausted. There was a final furious bombardment ; hand-grenades burst open the doors, and the troops charged into the building. There was silence, and then one by one the young desperadoes, most of them with blood telling of their wounds, were marched out of the building. Twelve of them were driven away in lorries, two of them were borne off by motor-hearse—the first prisoners and the first Nazi victims of the revolt.

In the Ministry of War, Ministers were in permanent session. Their chief was a prisoner in the hands of the enemy, and so, too, was the strong man, Major Fey. The Vice-Chancellor, Prince Starhemberg, was out of the country. In the moment of crisis, Dr. Schuschnigg, Minister of Education, and leader of the Catholic Storm Battalion, was elected to temporary charge of affairs. In the hour of crisis he proved himself.

From the Chancellery came a telephone call. The insurgents wished to speak with a Minister. Dr. Schuschnigg took the receiver. He was informed that Dr. Rintelen was

now in charge of Austria, and that all who opposed the
Nazis in the execution of Rintelen's orders would suffer for
it.   In Rintelen's name the voice demanded the removal of
the troops from around the Chancellery.   It was a desperate
bluff.   Threats grew more extreme as the level voice of
Dr. Schuschnigg ridiculed the suggestion that he should
abandon his post of duty.   The raiders were told to look out
of the windows and see the massing of the Government
forces, troops, auxiliaries and armoured cars.   They were
given a time limit of fifteen minutes in which to evacuate the
building.   If they did not, it would be stormed, and no
mercy would be shown to its occupants.

At this threat the voice told Dr. Schuschnigg that the
blood of the hostage Ministers would be upon the man who
ordered an attack.   Dr. Schuschnigg was in a dilemma.   To
take action against the raiders would be to imperil the lives
he wished to save.

Meanwhile, within the Chancellery, Dollfuss was
breathing his last.   During the afternoon he recovered
consciousness.   There was talk with his captors, who gave
the Chancellor the same false report about Rintelen that
had been broadcast to the country.   The Chancellor's
faculties were fading ;   he seemed almost to credit that
Rintelen had been nominated to succeed him.

Death was now upon him.   A Nazi had tried to stem the
loss of blood with a bandage applied by clumsy, inexpert
hands.   Dollfuss asked for a doctor, but in vain.   Then he
expressed his wish that a priest should be summoned to him,
but again without avail.   He was told that his was only a
surface wound, but the Chancellor felt the weakness of death
upon him.   Seeing that priest and doctor were refused him,
he asked for Fey, having been informed that the Major was
also a prisoner.

A patrol brought Major Fey to the room, and he
approached the sofa.   Dollfuss was almost too weak to move,
and spoke with difficulty.   He appealed to the Major to
stop the shedding of unnecessary blood.   " I resign," he
said, " that there may be peace and Rintelen shall take over.
I believe that bloodshed in Austria can be avoided."   He
then asked that should anything happen to him his wife
and children should be looked after.

Major Fey was then ordered from the room.   He had time

to press the hand of his dying chief before he was hurried out.

There was only a short space before Dollfuss lapsed finally into unconsciousness. " I only wished for peace. May God forgive the others," he said as death came upon him.

There were agonising hours for Major Fey. He and the more important prisoners were several times threatened with death by their guards. But in their lives and safety lay the only hope of salvation for the raiders, who, as the game had plainly gone against them, now thought only of evading the penalty which awaited them as traitors and assassins.

Parleys proceeded throughout the afternoon. Major Fey was then led on to the balcony of the Chancellery and made to declare that Dollfuss had been gravely wounded and, wishing to avert bloodshed, had decided to stand down in favour of Rintelen. The Heimwehr troops within range of his voice were amazed at his words. Another hour passed and the Major reappeared on the balcony to tell the troops not to attack without his orders, for he had been informed by his guards that he and his fellow-prisoners would be shot if any attack were launched.

Then a member of the Government, Herr Neustädter-Stürmer, advanced with a final offer. If the Chancellery were evacuated there would be a safe conduct for the rebels, otherwise the place would be stormed and all taken alive would be shot. The rebels, with the knowledge that the Chancellor was dead, wished for an independent witness to the agreement. Dr. Rieth, the German Ambassador, was summoned. He was understood to give an assurance that the Nazis should be guaranteed free entry to Germany.

At length the raiders were satisfied. Troops were allowed to approach, and under the welcome guard, for they feared they would be lynched, they were removed to barracks. Major Fey rejoined his fellow-Ministers. Dollfuss, alone, was dead. His body lay half-naked on the sofa, a piece of news-paper flung over it. It was borne reverently, for Dollfuss was loved, to the room where in his life he had worked for the peace of Austria to which his thoughts had turned in his last moments.

There was some criticism afterwards that the life of Dollfuss might have been saved had the Chancellery been stormed and had he received the medical attention denied him by the rebels. This view was negatived by the doctors. The Chancellor's death had, indeed, been hastened by the unchecked loss of blood, but death would have been inevitable. The bullet which broke a blood vessel in his neck had also damaged his spine.

5

The Nazi rising is quelled. Hitler disowns the rebels and makes friendly gestures towards Austria, while Mussolini as a precaution sends troops to the Austro-Italian frontier.

The hours of the day that remained were spent by Ministers in repairing the Patriotic Front, and directing measures throughout the country to deal with the rising of the Nazis on the morrow. The radio proved an invaluable aid to the Government, as it had done to the British Government during the critical hours of the General Strike of 1926. The Austrian nation were informed that the Chancellor had been slain, but it was added that the Government, with Dr. Schuschnigg at its head, had taken steps for the maintenance of public order. Major Fey himself went to the microphone to give an account of the tragic events in the Chancellery. Dr. Schuschnigg followed with the reassuring announcement that the *coup d'état* could definitely be stated to have failed.

So far as Vienna was concerned the announcement accurately conveyed the position, but in the provinces there was no such certainty. Reports had been received from many centres that the false wireless announcement representing Rintelen to have been appointed successor to Dollfuss had been the signal for Nazi action. District prefectures had been stormed, and at Munich, over the border, three or four thousand Austrian Brown Shirts were known to be ready to move across the frontier.

Having come through the peril of the first hours when taken by surprise, Dr. Schuschnigg could look with more confidence to the future, but he was uneasy until Styria was safe. Over that province Anton Rintelen had been governor for several years, and he had been allowed such independence that he was known as King Anton of Styria when he left to take up his appointment as Minister in Rome.

When the first announcement containing Rintelen's name was made over the wireless, the Ministers were inclined to exempt him from complicity, but later information caused them to revise their views. Dr. Rintelen was found to be in Vienna, and Dr. Schuschnigg himself went to the hotel where he was staying, to enquire why, without authority, Rintelen was absent from his duty in Rome. The Ambassador made no reply. Thereupon Dr. Schuschnigg ordered his arrest. His rooms were searched, and incriminating documents were found, including a memorandum with the names of a new Cabinet. The list was headed by the name of Anton Rintelen.

Throughout the evening of that tragic Wednesday there were discussions regarding the fate of the desperadoes at whose hands Dollfuss had met his death. A pledge of safe conduct had been given, but were the terms binding when it was given in ignorance of the circumstances in which the Chancellor, himself unarmed, was shot down? Would public opinion tolerate the liberation of the murderers? It was a difficult problem, and it was after midnight before the final decision was reached. At 1.30 in the morning the last wireless announcement of the day was made— that the rebels were to be brought before a military court. The safe conduct, it was announced, had been granted on the condition that no Minister lost his life, but at that very time the Chancellor was lying dead, and the promise, therefore, was not valid.

Throughout the night troops were moved to the areas where Nazi risings had already broken out, or were to be expected. On the Thursday, Austria, for the second time within six months, was in the throes of civil war. There was hot fighting in Styria throughout the day, and Carinthia, too, was the scene of conflict. Casualties on both sides were considerable and fighting continued for several days. But at an early stage it became apparent that the Government troops were in the ascendancy, and the rebels were forced to fall back on the Yugoslavian frontier. Admission to Germany was barred.

For the Nazi rebels this was the final shattering blow. Hitler, to whom they looked as their leader in chief, had disowned them. The Führer had indeed acted with precipitancy in the hope of escaping public odium for complicity in the rising in which Dollfuss perished. He was anxious that his name should not be associated with the assassins. He learned with disgust that his Ambassador in Vienna had been party to the agreement that the raiders on the Chancellery should have a safe conduct into Germany. For his indiscretion Dr. Rieth was recalled from his post, and his action was disowned. Far from offering refuge, the German Government bolted and barred their frontier to Austrian Nazis, who had to look elsewhere for a retreat.

Orders were sent from Berlin to Munich calling a halt to the plans of the exiled Austrian Nazis for a dash across the frontier. At one o'clock in the morning, two thousand men had been waiting at Munich barracks, with lorries and equipment, for the word to start. In other towns several thousand more were prepared for the order to attack. Instead of the expected signal there came instructions for them to return to barracks and camps. Steel helmets and rifles were removed and guards were posted to prevent any indiscretions. Later in the day, Herr Habicht, Nazi Inspector for Austria, was removed from his post, on the ground that he had been involved in the events in Vienna. A ban was placed on the Commissioner for Justice, who had been conducting the wireless campaign from Munich against Dollfuss.

By these means Hitler sought to dissociate himself from the assassination. One further gesture was made—Hitler appointed von Papen to undertake a special mission as German Minister in Vienna in succession to the recalled Rieth, in consequence, as Hitler explained, of his wish to contribute to the relief of the general situation, and to bring Austro-German relations once again into normal and friendly channels.

Hitler's gestures brought relief, if not friendship, in Vienna. The Austrian Government were relieved of the chief anxiety by the knowledge that while their troops were dealing with the insurgents there would be no stab in the back from across the Bavarian frontier. Prince Starhemberg returned from Venice, and as Vice-Chancellor quickly got busy. He called out the Heimwehr and the reserves throughout the whole of Austria.

In Vienna investigation into the plot proceeded, and each hour brought new disclosures to light. On a German who was captured attempting to cross the frontier were discovered plans, complete to the last detail, for the course of the insurrection when the Dollfuss Government had been forced to leave office. The Storm Troops were to have marched through the streets as if for the innocent purpose of propaganda, but in reality to seize public buildings. There were instructions for the capture of the prisons and the freeing of their occupants, including the Communists, to add to the general disturbance. It was learned, too, how the S.S. squad of the Nazis who raided the Chancellery formed the spearhead of the revolt. The secret signal for the meeting in the gymnasium had been given by means of small pellets of paper dropped into the letter-boxes in their homes, naming the time and place of the assembly.

The unhappy Dr. Rintelen made an unsuccessful attempt to take his own life. A revolver had been provided in the room at the Ministry of War where he was under arrest, doubtless intended as a hint. He made use of it, and was taken to hospital in a critical condition, but the doctors were able to save his life.

During these days the rulers of Austria were encouraged and heartened by the messages of support which they received from the Powers. From Rome came an expression of sympathy in which the Duce paid tribute to the probity, simplicity and great courage of his personal friend, Dr. Dollfuss, and condemned those responsible for his death, both by that direct action and " from afar "—the latter words pointing at least to Munich, and perhaps further to Berlin. The Duce followed up his message by dispatching 40,000 troops to the Italo-Austrian frontier—an action which caused a certain anxiety in the Chancelleries of Europe. Any interference from without in the domestic affairs of Austria was held to be a step attended with the utmost hazard to the peace of the world. Austria was the powder magazine of Central Europe. The crossing of her frontier by the troops of any one power was likely to be the signal for intervention by other foreign armies. Expressions of horror at the murder received from Great Britain and France were coupled with expressions of the duty to maintain Austrian independence.

6

The leader of the rebels and Dollfuss's assassin are put on their trial and state that they were told that the head of the new Government would be waiting in the Chancellery. They die with the cry " Heil Hitler ! " upon their lips.

By the week-end the Austrian Government had crushed the last remnants of rebellion, but with the passing of one danger, another peril seemed to grow. Alarm was renewed in Vienna at reports that the Heimwehr, victorious over the Nazis, were planning a coup to seize power throughout the land. Police were again called upon to stand by in full strength ready for any emergency. The rumours proved to be without foundation, and the reconstruction of the ministry was completed.

It had been generally anticipated that Prince Starhemberg would be promoted from deputy rank to Chancellor. The choice, however, fell upon Dr. Schuschnigg, who had proved himself in the hour of crisis, and who, as a Catholic, maintained the balance of power in the ministry which had existed prior to the assassination. This principle governed the filling of the other posts. It was a wise solution. There was a spirit of rivalry between the Heimwehr and Catholics, and though the leaders worked harmoniously together, the rank and file were not so readily prepared to forget their animosities in the interests of the preservation of the National Front.

There remained the duty of bringing to trial the murderers of Chancellor Dollfuss. A court was constituted of three army officers with a judge as legal adviser. The two men singled out to make the first appearance were Franz Holzweber, leader of the rebels who raided the Chancellery, and Otto Planetta, who fired the fatal shots. The first was charged with high treason, the second with murder. Both pleaded not guilty, but their only line of defence was that they were entitled to liberty under the promise of safe conduct. Both were ex-soldiers who had been dismissed from the army because of their Nazi activities.

Planetta submitted that he had not fired with any intent

to kill. The orders given to the raiders were, indeed, that violence was to be avoided, and no life must be taken except in extreme emergency. The questioning of the accused showed again the precautions for secrecy which had been taken in the carrying out of the initial revolt. Planetta stated :

"On the Tuesday and the Wednesday I made myself ready. At daybreak on Wednesday morning a tiny sheet of paper was slipped into my place giving me written orders to present myself at the gymnasium, there to await further instructions. It is not permissible for me to disclose the identity of the man whose signature was attached to the instruction. I was informed that perfect legality would attach to all the steps which were to be taken. It was my duty to pass on the instructions to the other members of my group. At the gymnasium I was supplied with a revolver and ammunition and the uniform of a lieutenant. After putting on the uniform I got into a lorry which was driven to the Chancellery. We drove into the courtyard."

The President : "How can you say that you could suppose that what you were doing was legal?"

Planetta : "I had been told that officials of State had sanctioned what we were to do. More than that I cannot say. When I got to the Chancellery I acted on my own initiative. I ran up the stairs into a large apartment, and went from room to room. As I opened one door I discovered a big man with his back to me, and I shouted 'Hands up.' Two other men were there, but who they were I did not realise in the scurry. As I was talking to the big man one of the others ran past me. I was afraid. I suppose I jerked the trigger of my gun, which fired."

The President : "You, a man with long service in the army, afraid of a shadow?"

Planetta : "I was. I was excited. The pistol went off in my hand while I was talking with the big man. Not until he collapsed did I see the little chap. Then as he dropped to the floor I recognised him as Dr. Dollfuss. I wish the court to understand that I am very sorry that Dollfuss was struck by my shot."

The President remarked that a second shot was fired. Planetta replied that this was fired automatically.

The President pointed out that the pistol was not one which would have fired automatically a second after the first shot. To this Planetta had nothing to say.

Holzweber said that he had received orders on the Wednesday morning to the effect that the Government was to be arrested and forced to resign at the wish of President Miklas, who would himself appear when the Chancellery had been taken and announce the appointment of Dr. Rintelen. There had been no intention to do personal violence to the Chancellor. " We were shocked," declared Holzweber, " when Planetta told us he had had bad luck and had fired at the Chancellor." The rising, he said, had been poorly organised. " We completed our task, but our leader did not appear. I telephoned to a café in Vienna, hoping to get in touch with the leader." Holzweber averred that he did not know the leader's real name—he had known of him only under various aliases.

The Court pronounced the inevitable verdict and sentence of death. Before he was removed Planetta again expressed his regret, declaring that he was no cowardly murderer, and had no intention to kill, and begging the forgiveness of Frau Dollfuss. Holzweber made a declaration of protest at the manner in which he had been left in the lurch by his leaders. He had been informed before he set out that Rintelen would be at the Chancellery, the new Government having already been formed. When he realised the situation he had not known what to do ; he had taken over the leadership of the raiders because no other leader was there. And so they went to their death, which they met bravely, both with " Heil Hitler ! " upon their lips.

KING ALEXANDER OF YUGOSLAVIA

1

King Alexander was a reversion to the age of absolute monarchy. Not until his death did it become generally realised that he was one of the ten statesmen who were shaping Europe's destinies.

ON October 9, of the year 1934, King Alexander of Yugoslavia perished by the assassin's bullet. M. Barthou, Foreign Minister of France, lost his life while gallantly attempting to shelter the King.

It was established forthwith that the King was the victim of political vengeance. Europe was horrified by this act of barbarism ; terrified as well, for the parallel with the crime of Seraievo sprang inevitably to the mind. An assassination in the Balkans set the world at war in 1914. Was the precarious peace to be terminated by this shooting of a Balkan King at Marseilles?

The assassin's act was a link between the underworld of crime and the world of diplomacy. The contrast was at once sordid and vivid. The assassin was of the type that makes politics the excuse for indulging in gangster crimes. The incitement of petty intrigue and of café plots, the paraphernalia of secret societies, are attractions for this type of mind.

A notable life was forfeit to a ruffian on the quayside at Marseilles. A man from the underworld fired his shot, and thereby set in motion world machinery of politics and diplomacy. A tremor went through the Balkans. There was apprehension in the lands of the dictators, only recently recovering from the shock of Dollfuss's murder. The French Government rocked uneasily, and shortly afterwards fell. Complaint was lodged before the Tribunal of the Nations at Geneva.

King Alexander was an outstanding figure in the post-war

" Alexander of Yugoslavia was at once the King and Dictator of his
country—something of a political anachronism."

world. He had a mind of great political astuteness and sagacity. He was at once the King and Dictator of his country—something of a political anachronism. The age of the dictator kings of Europe was supposed to have passed with the coming of democracy. The dictators of Italy and Germany are dictators of a new style. Alexander was of the old style, a reversion to the absolute monarch that Charles I of England sought to be. Alexander might fittingly have adopted the French king's motto : " L'état, c'est moi." He did not rise to power by creating a party to overthrow all other parties. With patience he tolerated democratic politicians playing the party game. They placed party interests above the interests of the State ; personal ambitions and the pride and profit of place were their motives to which the interests of Yugoslavia had to be made subordinate. Patiently, Alexander submitted to their manœuvrings. There were twenty-five Cabinet crises in less than ten years. Then, with a wave of his hand, he swept them aside. The game of politics was put away, and the King-Dictator became ruler of Yugoslavia.

The affairs of the distant Balkans are not followed in England except when an upheaval is threatened in the Near East. Until his death, the British public did not realise that the King of Yugoslavia was one of the ten men who counted in the shaping of the destinies of Europe. Only with his death did the skill of his statecraft stand revealed to us. There have been few kings in Europe like Alexander. In his capacity for work he resembled Albert, Prince Consort of Victoria. Both gave themselves up like permanent Secretaries of State in home and foreign affairs, devoting the major portion of their day to the task of gaining from advisers and dispatches the accumulated and detailed knowledge necessary for the man who rules a modern State. But Alexander had experiences unknown to Albert. Like another Albert, King of the Belgians, Alexander of Yugoslavia led his troops in war, suffered heart-breaking reverses, was an exile in arms from his country, and finally returned victorious. He lived to see his international policy crowned with success. Little Serbia became the Kingdom of Serbs, Croats and Slovenes, the predominant partner in the Little Entente.

Alexander was a benevolent despot. His people recognised his benevolence, but were not prepared to acquiesce

gladly in his despotism. He was above parties, but never
succeeded in composing party differences. To a people who
are governed by a dictator it is not a matter of particular
consequence whether the dictator rules with a wisdom which
is appreciably the greater or appreciably the less than their
own. To the extent to which he is wiser or less wise, his
policy will be unacceptable. King Amanulla of Afghanistan
lost his throne because he was wiser than his people ; sought
to push them along the road of Western culture quicker than
they wished to travel. Alexander was never in danger of
arousing such national antagonism, but his dictatorship was
the cause of resentment. He looked upon the affairs of
Yugoslavia from the detached standpoint of a man who was a
player on the European stage.

2

*After the World War the newly reconstructed country is made uneasy
by the differences between Serbs and Croats. Alexander stands
aside while political crises occur with unfailing regularity.
He becomes Dictator in 1928.*

Alexander was the most courageous, as well as one of the
most sagacious, of monarchs. Throughout his life as King
he lived under the shadow of assassination. No ruler of
Serbia before him had died in his bed whilst still in power.
His predecessors who were not deposed met violent deaths
in battle or at a murderer's hand.

He was a Karageorgevitch. The first of his line, who had
fought for Serbian independence against the Balkans, was
killed as he slept. His successor, an Obrenovitch, was
assassinated half a century later by Karageorgian partisans.
The return of the Karageorgian line in 1903 was preceded
by a double murder at the Palace of Belgrade, the King and
Queen being the victims. They had fled through the Royal
apartments, pursued by a band of rebel officers. They took
refuge in a tiny dressing-room with a secret door. A bullet
fired at random penetrated their hiding-place, wounding
the Queen, who cried out in pain. She and her husband
were dragged forth and butchered.

Peter, father of the late King Alexander, then succeeded to the Serbian throne. At the age of nineteen Alexander became Crown Prince in succession to his elder brother George, who was forced to relinquish his rights of succession because of scandals in which he was involved. Prince Alexander led his troops to victory in the Balkan Wars, and in June, 1914, was appointed Regent of the country, the health of his father having failed. Four days later came the Serajevo murders, and in a month the world was at war.

The Serbian capital, Belgrade, was the first to receive the enemy shells. Austria's opening attacks were repulsed, but when Bulgaria joined the Central Powers, Serbia was overrun. Then the Prince Regent and his troops had to retire across the mountains of Albania to seek refuge at Corfu. Having refitted themselves, they rejoined the campaign as part of the Allied Army operating from Salonika. The Serbian forces had the satisfaction of taking part in the fighting which led to the first armistice of the War on the collapse of Bulgarian resistance. After four years of exile, Alexander led home his victorious troops, and then secured for Serbia recompense for her sacrifices.

The Kingdom of Serbia, by reason of her two principal accessions, became the Kingdom of Serbs, Croats and Slovenes, in which were incorporated, in the fashion of a United States of the Balkans, Montenegro, Bosnia-Herzegovina, Croatia, Slavonia and Dalmatia and parts of Styria, Carniola, the Banat of Temesvar and Western Bulgaria. The Serbs formed the strongest section numerically of the new kingdom, a little less than half; Croats and Slovenes over a third; the remaining 17 per cent of the population consisted of Rumanians, Germans and Magyars.

It was a proud Prince Alexander who, in his father's name, began to rule over these extended dominions. But, alas for the vanity of human triumphs, the extension of his domains served but to make a burden of the ruler's task. This mingling of peoples who have yet to fuse into a nation produced the circumstances which led to Alexander's dictatorship and the assassin's shot on the French quayside. The rivalry of Croat and Serb brought political confusion to the kingdom, and again we see the vanity that attends the fulfilment of human wishes. Croats and Serbs many centuries ago were members of the same

race. They passed under the dominion of different conquerors. The Serbs, as we have explained, gained their
freedom from the Turk under a Karageorgic king. The
Croats, when the World War broke out, were subjects of
Austria, partly self-autonomous, but striving to be entirely
free. When the defeat of the Central Powers brought about
the realisation of their dreams of a thousand years, the
Croats decided to seek amalgamation with the Serbs,
resolving to forgo complete independence, which was
fraught, they feared, with the peril of absorption by a powerful neighbour—and Croat eyes turned uneasily to Rome.
Thus they entered as willing partners into union with Serbia.

The marriage of the peoples was founded on affection, but
between nations, no less than between individuals, affection
alone cannot assure success in matrimony. To this end tact
is, at least, as necessary as love, and the politicians of
Serbia and Croatia, in the first flush of success of their
common cause, were distinguished by enthusiasm rather
than by tact. The initial spirit of goodwill was dissipated by
the sparrings of the partners. To Serbian conception, the
rule of the new State was to be centralised in Belgrade. The
Croatian aspiration was a federal kingdom with wide powers
of autonomy for the individual partners. Belgrade was
insistent—Zagreb sensitive. Serbia, fresh from the humiliation and catastrophe of foreign occupation, concentrated on
the creation of a closely bound national unit, which would
be a guarantee of national strength. The Croats, free at last
from foreign rule, could see only the virtues of a loose alliance
which would permit them self-government within the new
kingdom. So feelings changed ; the newly married partners
began to quarrel fiercely.

Alexander stood aside while the Serbian Premier, Pashitch,
and the Croatian peasant leader, Raditch, passed from
argument to abuse in the manner that disputes progress in
the domestic sphere. For some time the Croats, like Irish
politicians, boycotted the Parliament at Belgrade. Then,
again in the Irish parliamentary fashion, they attended
to play the game of obstruction. Their numbers gave them
the power to force Pashitch out of office and thereafter to
stultify parliamentary proceedings. Ministries were formed
with difficulty ; lived precariously for a few weeks ; then
fell. In ten years there were 25 Cabinets and 130 Ministers.

The bitterness and antagonism was extended from Parliament to the streets. There was a succession of riots and outrage.

In 1928 came the climax. Raditch, from his seat in Parliament, launched an outrageously virulent attack on the Government. A ministerial back-bencher drew his revolver and emptied it among the opposition. Two deputies were killed and several others were wounded, among them Raditch, who succumbed to his injuries. He was canonised as a Croatian martyr. The Croats withdrew from the Parliament of Belgrade, threatening to set up their own independent legislature.

At length King Alexander—he had succeeded to the throne on the death of his father in 1921—was forced to intervene. His talent for diplomacy was never more strikingly evidenced or employed to greater advantage for his country. He visited the wounded Raditch on his death-bed, which did something to mollify Croatian opinion, and by his tactful handling of the situation, averted the threat of civil war. Such was his statesmanship then that it appeared the more regrettable that he had not intervened when disputes first threw a shadow across the union of his peoples. His gift of tact might have brought about an understanding years before, but by 1928 the time for tact had passed. Strong measures were needed and Alexander showed that strength was his no less than tact. Parliament by his order was dismissed, the Constitution abolished, political parties suppressed, the holding of political meetings made illegal. A Royal dictatorship was established.

Alexander became the most powerful King in Europe, combining in his person the role of sovereign, executive and legislature. His intention was that his despotism should last no longer than the state of national emergency. He set to work to devise measures to give peace, order and security to his people. As a means of emphasising the essential unity of his dominions, he superseded the title of Kingdom of Serbs, Croats and Slovenes, with its federal implications, and replaced it with the simpler name of Yugoslavia, a symbol of unity. He extinguished the old territorial divisions by means of which the administration had been carried on, creating nine districts in place of the former thirty-three.

Finally he promulgated a new constitution and a new Parliament was elected under a system founded on the

Fascist model. But despite the changes, the King had to remain Dictator, and despite his efforts at appeasement, Croat discontent grew.

3

By a tragic irony King Alexander is killed when landing in France on a mission of peace—namely, a general rapprochement between Paris, Rome and Belgrade. The boy king Peter succeeds to the throne.

It was fantastically ironic that King Alexander should have been assassinated when he walked ashore at Marseilles in October, 1934, for he was journeying to France on a mission of peace, the promotion of good relations between France and Italy. Alexander's diplomacy in the Balkans had been rewarded by the strengthening of the ties between the States of the Little Entente. Even with Bulgaria he had succeeded in coming to terms.

The two countries, close neighbours, and linked by ties of common blood and language, had been separated by two bitter wars. In the autumn of 1933 King Alexander met King Boris of Bulgaria, their first personal contact for twenty years. Exchange of visits followed this reconciliation, and there were demonstrations of national enthusiasm on either side at this *rapprochement*. The Balkan Pacts co-ordinated Czechoslovakia, Rumania and Yugoslavia into an Entente whose massed forces constituted a power to be reckoned with. The agreements bound together as a single unit in the pursuit of a joint foreign policy states whose peoples exceeded forty-five millions, and whose armed forces aggregated nearly half a million.

Side by side with the growth of this alliance had proceeded the growth of friendlier feelings between France and Italy, a re-orientation of policy produced by the militancy of Nazi Germany. The interests of Yugoslavia were affected by the new relations between Rome and Paris. Yugoslavia, in common with other Balkan States, had been encouraged to regard France as her patron. Relations between Italy and Yugoslavia had been more correct than cordial since the War, and at times scarcely even correct.

The visit King Alexander paid to France in October, 1934,

was intended to promote a general *rapprochement* between Paris, Rome and Belgrade. The ultimate hope was that Czechoslovakia and Rumania might be brought into accord with Italy. It was a grim irony that this mission of peace should end in bloodshed and result in a setback to the friendliness it had been designed to promote.

The circumstances of the murder of King Alexander at Marseilles on October 9 are well known. They have been recorded for ever in the most tragic film of real-life drama. The King had been barely five minutes upon French soil. He was not more than one hundred yards away from the quayside where he had landed, when the assassin, extricating himself from the crowd, jumped on to the running-board of the slowly moving car. There he shot at point-blank range. The King received two wounds and fell, never to regain consciousness. M. Barthou, the French Foreign Minister, who was in the car at his side, tried to shield the King. He, too, was gravely wounded, and bled to death before he could receive medical attention. The assassin was struck down by a lieutenant of a French infantry regiment, his skull cleft to a depth of three or four inches. As he lay on the ground he received a bullet in the face from a police revolver. The crowd swarmed upon him and began to tear him to pieces. There was scarcely any clothing left on his body when the police succeeded in driving off the frenzied crowd.

Queen Marie of Yugoslavia would have been with her husband on the tragic journey but for the boisterous weather at sea, which caused her to change her plans at the last minute and travel to France by train from Italy. At his school in Surrey King Alexander's heir, his eleven-year-old son, Prince Peter, was awakened on the following morning to be told that he had succeeded to the Yugoslavian Crown. He was taken by his grandmother, Queen Marie of Rumania, to join his widowed mother in Paris.

A proclamation was issued in Belgrade announcing that the martyred King had sealed with his blood the work of peace for which he had entered on his journey to allied France. The succession of the Boy King was announced, and the proclamation concluded with a moving appeal to the loyalty of the people. " The last word which the King was able to speak before his last breath was, in his great patriotism, the most precious inheritance he left to his

nation, ' Watch over Yugoslavia.' The Government appeal
to the whole Yugoslav nation to guard the inheritance loyally
and with dignity." In accordance with the Constitution, the
King had nominated a Council of Regency for the minority
of his boy son, a triumvirate consisting of Prince Paul, Dr.
Stankovitch and Dr. Perovitch. Under their guidance the
State passed safely through the first dangerous days of unrest
caused by the assassination, with nothing more serious than
anti-Italian demonstrations.

There was criticism of the French authorities that stricter
measures had not been taken to safeguard the person of the
King. These criticisms were echoed in France, and led to a
political crisis that ended in the overthrow of the Doumergue
coalition. Europe had begun to consider the unsettling
consequences of the assassination to be passed, when international anxiety was renewed by the submission to the League
of Nations of a formal complaint on the part of Yugoslavia
against Hungary for the harbouring of the gang of assassins
responsible for the murder.

4

*The assassin of King Alexander was a notorious terrorist twice sentenced
to death for murder. The fact that he took refuge, while preparing for the crime, in Hungary leads to a grave situation
between that country and Yugoslavia. After Britain intervenes
the dispute is settled.*

Secret societies and terrorism are ages-old methods of
politics in the Balkans. They have survived as relics of the
times when the Balkan peoples lived in servitude, ruled by
foreign oppressors. The foreign oppressor has gone, but the
terrorist and gunman still remain. To be left-handed is a
byword in the Balkans, meaning that the person concerned
uses his left hand because his right is always in his pocket
gripping a revolver.

The assassin of Marseilles was first identified in the name
of Kalemen, a name that conveyed nothing of his associates
or antecedents, but tattooed on his left forearm was a death's
head, surmounted by the letters V.R.M.O. These are the
initials of an organisation well known in the annals of
Balkan terrorism, which passes otherwise as the I.M.R.O.—

that is to say, Internal Macedonian Revolutionary Organisation. The V.R.M.O. is the organisation with the worst
record among the societies which employ the dagger, the
revolver and the bomb as a means of enforcing its arguments.

As the police of France and the Balkans proceeded with
their enquiries and the circumstances of the murder plot
were unravelled, the personality of the murderer took on a
more concrete and notorious identity. It was established
that he was Vlada Georgieff (or Chernozemsky), a terrorist
with a known record of murder. Georgieff was the former
chauffeur and henchman of Ivan Mihailoff, leader of the
V.R.M.O., and Georgieff was known to have joined the
Oustava, society of the Croat terrorist, Pavelitch. The
V.R.M.O. and the Oustava had recently joined forces, and
their headquarters were supposed to be on the Hungarian
side of the Yugoslav frontier. The Oustava had been founded
since the War, but the V.R.M.O. had a much longer record
of crime and murder behind it. It was founded back in the
'70's of last century by Bulgars in defiance of the Turks, and
in furtherance of the promotion of independence for Mace-
donians. After the War, under the leadership of Mihailoff,
the society's aims were directed against Yugoslavia as
successor to Turkey in Macedonian hate.

The reconciliation between King Boris of Bulgaria and
King Alexander of Yugoslavia fanned the flames of V.R.M.O
fanaticism against the Yugoslavian King. As a result of the
rapprochement between the two countries, King Boris
agreed to suppress the V.R.M.O., whose headquarters were
seized and whose leaders were either arrested or had to take
flight. Mihailoff and Georgieff were among those who fled.
Losing their refuge in Bulgaria, the V.R.M.O. leaders
decided to merge their organisation with the Oustava, who
were organising and training in their camp in Hungary so
that one day they could realise Croat dreams of vengeance
against the Yugoslavian King. The Croat desperadoes were
ready to give a warm welcome to Georgieff, the man with a
notorious record as a gunman. Twice he had been sentenced
to death—in 1924 for the murder of a Communist deputy,
and in 1930, for the killing of a Macedonian leader. On the
latter occasion a life sentence was passed on him, but he was
released under an amnesty. The Croat conspirators had

established themselves on a farm at Junkapuszta. Here terrorists were trained, one of the courses of instruction arranged for new members being target practice on a life-size dummy of King Alexander.

Yugoslavia's complaint to the League of Nations against Hungary for the harbouring of the assassins brought deep anxiety to Europe. There followed two dramatic interventions which saved a conflict. When Prince Paul returned to his country after attending the wedding in London of the Duke and Duchess of Kent, he brought wise counsel with him. At his order the expulsion of Hungarians from Yugoslavia ceased. Then at Geneva Britain intervened in the dispute and Mr. Anthony Eden played a conspicuous part in the negotiation of a resolution acceptable to both disputants. This intervention was hailed by Mr. Lloyd George and others as a pattern for the " bold, decisive and firm lead " which Britain should give in the world situation. Thus was another Serajevo avoided after a shot had killed a Balkan King.

III

THE MILITARY DICTATORS

THE Ghazi Kemal Ataturk, creator of the New Turkey, and the late Marshal Pilsudski, saviour of Poland, saw their power originate with the army. Their position is thus in contrast with that of the two constitutional dictators who came to power in Italy and Germany. Pilsudski and Mustapha Kemal rose to prominence as commanders of armies, and both exploited their position as military leaders to dictate the destinies of their countries. Without Mustapha Kemal a very different Turkey—if it could be called that—would have emerged from the War, a Turkey partitioned almost out of existence. Pilsudski was the leader of the struggle for Poland's liberation.

Their careers as dictator, however, are in striking contrast. Mustapha Kemal has presided, a warrior-pedagogue, over the birth and infancy of the new Turkey which he has fashioned. Pilsudski was an aloof dictator. For some years he lived a life apart, withdrawn from Poland's affairs, looking with detached scorn upon the parliamentarians, and then he made a dramatic return to politics. They speak of Mussolini's march on Rome—an unopposed and bloodless entry of Fascist forces. Pilsudski's was a march on Warsaw, with a three days' battle as a prelude to his dictatorship.

Mustapha Kemal is a constitutional ruler in the sense that he has been appointed President of the Turkish Republic, elected by the Grand National Assembly on a wide democratic franchise. He has built up a party, the People's Party, which gives a political basis to his despotism, but the despotism is not to be disguised by any political cloak. The People's Party is the Ghazi's own creation. He has been even more ruthless in the suppression of opposition than the Nazis. In Turkey, as in Italy, Germany and Russia, one party alone is permitted to exist, the Party of the Dictator.

When growing pains beset the new Turkey, Mustapha Kemal suppressed his opponents who would have given the country a parliamentary constitution with parliamentary government and parliamentary opposition, upon the lines of a Western State. He intended that his country should be westernised, but there was to be no westernisation in a democratic sense of the machinery of government. Unity, in his view, is essential, and he has no tolerance for rival theories or rival parties. His Liberal opponents were hanged, shot, imprisoned or banished. The Ghazi was constitutionally elected to the head of the Turkish Republic by the Assembly, but it should be borne in mind that the Constitution also provides that he has the right to name all candidates for the Assembly, and that the President is not placed above party. The Turkish Constitution, indeed, repeats the Italian provisions for ensuring that the pretension of democratic machinery shall not tend to conflict with dictatorial views.

KEMAL ATATURK

1

Observers in the western world have watched Mustapha Kemal develop from the intransigent of the Anatolian wilds into a statesman who has transformed a country of 13,000,000 inhabitants.

THE whole effort of every sincere man, said Remy de Gourmont, is to convert his personal impressions into universal laws. Few now can doubt Mustapha Kemal's sincerity; everyone must be astounded at the completeness of his autocracy and at the comparative ease with which he has converted his personal beliefs into universal laws.

Slowly, very slowly, the popular notion of Mustapha Kemal in European minds has undergone a change. When, after the World War, he first emerged as a national figure, men speculated on the length of time that must elapse before this Anatolian adventurer was overwhelmed by some other Anatolian adventurer. Surprisingly, he consolidated his position, became master of Turkey and overlord of 13,000,000 souls. When his photograph began to appear in British newspapers many were astonished at this Turk who wore a silk hat and a tail coat. Westernisation of Turkey, they reflected, might be his professed policy; but who could have faith in one whose plans for westernisation omitted the most important point of all, namely, liberty for the individual. How was it, the Anglo-Saxon later pondered, that a man who professed reforming ideals could be so ruthless with foe and friend alike? Had he not permitted the extermination of thousands of Greeks since the Græco-Turkish war of 1921-22? Had he not held "bloody assizes" and hanged many of the intimates who had been at his side through his early struggles? Was he not a mere large-scale gangster holding a country in subjection with revolver rule? Now in these later days of the dictators we can look with less misgiving upon the Ghazi Kemal Ataturk and concede that he has justified himself as an excellent Dictator—for Turkey.

Undoubtedly he has mellowed with the years. The revolutionary of yesterday has by no means become the reactionary of to-day. Yet he has celebrated the eleventh anniversary of his accession to power in an atmosphere of calm, even of respectability, fitting for one who has established himself as the saviour of his country.

His first known occupation was scaring birds in a bean-field. There is something attractively appropriate about this. For, thirty years later was he not scaring carrion birds from the prostrate body of Turkey ? The achievement of Musta-pha Kemal can be summarised simply : the boy from the bean-field became a soldier ; the soldier became a revolu-tionary and worked to overthrow the Red Sultan ; the conspirator developed into the general who helped to wreck the hopes of the Allies at Gallipoli, smashed an invading Greek army and became a national hero ; the national hero made a new and vigorous nation out of an old and dying one. In all he has launched eleven successful revolutions—military, political, religious, social.

2

As a young man Mustapha Kemal witnesses the death struggles of the old Turkey, culminating in the overthrow of the Red Sultan by the Army. A new Sultan is enthroned to rule as the revolutionists wish.

Sultan Abdul Hamid II was the Red Sultan so fiercely denounced by Gladstone for the Armenian atrocities, the " Abdul the Damned " of Sir William Watson's poem. In 1908, from his palace on the Bosphorus, he ruled a Turkey many centuries behind the times.

His Sublimity, short-sighted, shuffling, hook-nosed, main-tained a thousand servants and ten thousand spies. At his palace of Yildiz, that treasure house and torture chamber as fantastic as anything in the *Arabian Nights*, he kept

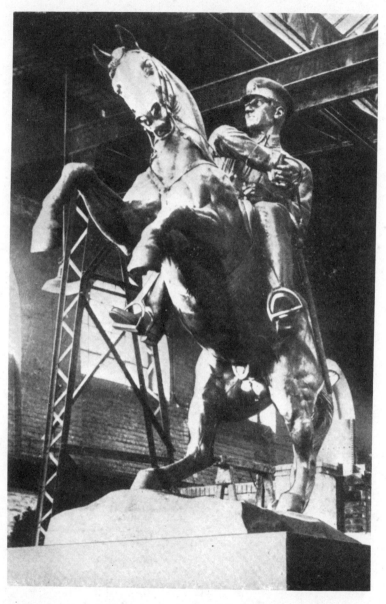

" In all Kemal Ataturk has launched eleven successful revolutions—
military, political, religious, social."

*An equestrian statue of the President of Turkey erected at Samsun,
the Black Sea port.*

millions of " djournals," or spy reports. When he was over-thrown and Yildiz was ransacked a haul of them sufficiently large to occupy a whole building in the War Office was made. " Djournalism " was the Sultan's passion. Seventeen out of thirty-four previous rulers of Turkey had died violent deaths —by strangling, impalement, poison ; Abdul Hamid be-lieved in all things traditional except that old Turkish custom. But numerous and industrious—not to say imagi-native—as his spies were, the Young Turks, the " Party of Progress," flourished and expanded. Soon the rumblings of revolt could be heard throughout the vast Ottoman Empire.

Mid-way through 1908 the Third Army Corps in Mace-donia, inspired by the revolutionary society called the Committee of Union and Progress, revolted, and the Sultan received an ultimatum. The Constitution of 1876 must be restored : Parliamentary Government must be the first step to universal reforms.

Thus it was that in July, 1908, a form of democracy came to Turkey. Faced with the prospect of a nation-wide revolt, Abdul Hamid, " the Shadow of God upon Earth," promised to abandon intrigue and become a constitutional ruler. After which he doubtless hurried to the palace of Yildiz and took his equivalent of a stiff whisky and soda—the latest batch of " djournals."

The action of the Third Army Corps brought the sem-blance of freedom to Turkey, but not the reality. When, five months later, the Third Army went to Constantinople for the opening of Abdul Hamid's first Parliament, a twenty-seven-year-old officer named Mustapha Kemal went with it. Since adolescence this young man—correct in dress, precise in word and action, brusque in manner—had been working with an intellectual passion for the overthrow of the Sultan's autocracy. Yet there was no joy and little satisfaction in him.

The soldiers at the head of the victorious Committee of Union and Progress—Enver Bey, Talaat Bey, Djemal Bey—did not consider Mustapha Kemal a person of any import-ance. He had failed to impress his personality on them, but in his self-confidence he assured himself that the fault was theirs. Towards Enver, the adventurer, he already felt something approaching hatred. During the next ten years each was to work unceasingly for the other's fall—with Enver holding all the cards all the time. But the last laugh was with Mustapha Kemal.

The young officer who was convinced of his superiority, but denied a means of showing it, could console himself with contemning Enver, but that was poor consolation in Enver's hour of triumph over the Sultan. The majority of his comrades Mustapha Kemal despised. His relations with a handful were friendly, but that was due more to forbearance on their part than amiability on his.

At this period he could have had no conception of his goal. Discontent with the present and anxiety about the future ; warring ideals and restless ambition ; a bitter sense of injustice with life because he had been rejected while inferior persons were occupying the important posts—these things were galling in the extreme. No conception of his goal ? One cannot be certain. Some things that keen brain must have divined. He must certainly have realised that the Red Sultan was too accustomed to tortuous paths to become a constitutional ruler and abandon intrigue. That was demanding too much of an aged autocrat whose misdeeds had shocked the civilised world. Turkey was disintegrating, slowly dying. Intellectual Turks of a century before had perceived that the Sultanate and the Caliphate were stifling the country. It is not unlikely that Mustapha Kemal saw more clearly than they that there could be no regeneration for his country, the " Sick Man of Europe," until the rule of the Sultan and the priests was abolished.

To the discontented soldier walking the streets of Constantinople, with Western ideals already fermenting within him, the feudal atmosphere of the capital must have been disheartening. Without faith himself, he could see everywhere evidence of obsolete religions and age-old superstitions. It was a city so religious that to wrap up parcels with newspaper was an irreverent act—the name of Allah might be printed somewhere on it. The Mohammedan religion, for Mustapha Kemal and the Young Turks, was the dead hand, the source of half Turkey's troubles. Europe was unified under Christianity. Turkey, in Europe, but not of it, appeared to be doomed because of its attachment to Islam. As Mr. H. E. Wortham expresses the matter in an admirable philosophical examination of New Turkey:[1]

" The Turk, though he has made some substantial ripples in the pond of history, has been unlucky—and he knows it. By a geographical accident he has missed his career amongst the European peoples. Had the Mongol pressure which originally forced him from his central Asian homelands driven him west, instead of south, he would, like his cousins, the Hungarians, have entered Europe through the plains of Russia, and in consequence have adopted Christianity, the necessary passport to Western culture. It happened that the first peoples less barbaric than himself whom he met with in his migration were Moslems, and so he became a convert to Islam, as a result being shut out, when at last he took Constantinople, from the full inheritance of Byzantine civilisation. His military virtues secured him the privileges of a ruling race, but he was unable to absorb the spiritual qualities that give an underlying identity to the European peoples. As Christians the Turks might have been the Normans of Eastern Europe. In professing Islam they hitched their waggon to the wrong star and became the protagonists of a losing cause, the issue of which, unbeknown to them, had been decided centuries before by Charles Martel on the plains of Poitiers."

Well, Mustapha Kemal the Dictator has frowned on Islam. Saint Sophia, Sultan Ahmed and the other great mosques are little frequented to-day. A people with centuries of religious tradition have turned their backs on public worship. The mosques remain to bear witness, but the light has been withdrawn from them.

The measure of the social changes that Mustapha Kemal has wrought in Turkey could not be more strikingly illustrated than by contrasting glimpses of Constantinople when Abdul Hamid opened Parliament in 1908 with the industrialised city of to-day.

On that December day the streets of Constantinople were thronged with a mass of nationalities strangely mixed. Representatives of races from which came the Talmud, the

[1] *Mustapha Kemal of Turkey.* (Holme Press.)

Bible and the Koran had gathered in force. The Galata Bridge across the Golden Horn presented a spectacle that would have astonished any European unacquainted with the diverse elements that went to make up the Ottoman Empire. With the slowly moving Turks, wearing their customary fezes, were gorgeously robed Arabs from the Yemen, Jews, Greeks, Tartars, Kurds, Druses, Kirghiz, Kutzovalaks : in short a representative pageant from the thirty kingdoms that offered up prayers for the Sultan. But barely a handful of women would you have seen among that slowly moving crowd, and those veiled.

By the Imperial edict certain words had been expunged from the vocabulary of the Turk for political reasons. Now the enthusiastic crowds, ignoring the law, were bringing them into their conversation. One of the words was dynamo, which the Censor, who was a trifle unfamiliar with these new-fangled terms, had confused with dynamite. Others which were held to have an inflammatory effect were progress, hero, arms, bloodshed, tyranny and—not surprisingly—Armenia.

So the crowds, 95 per cent of whom could not read or write, counted their beads while they waited for the Imperial procession and a glimpse of the Padishah and his harem.

At noon the White Lancers of Yildiz thundered through the streets before the carriage of the Sultan, who had dyed his beard and rouged his cheeks. He wore a mail waistcoat for fear of the assassin's bullet. Behind his victoria came the favourites of the harem—six coaches of them—escorted by eunuchs on horseback.

In a sense that day was the last spectacle of old Turkey. And the man who was to transform the country was there to look on.

The route to Parliament House was lined with green-turbaned giant Zouaves from Syria, with the khaki-clad troops from Macedonia (Mustapha Kemal was here) with the picked troops of the Sultan carrying the black silken banners of the Prophet.

Abdul Hamid was called the Red Sultan ; similarly Constantinople might be called the Red City, for the massacre of tens of thousands has taken place there. This Turkish heritage of bloodshed is not without bearing on

Mustapha Kemal's fortunes. It may be held to explain one of the paradoxes in his career. He, who has divorced Turkey from the East and turned her eyes towards the West and freed her from superstition and useless tradition, has in his time been guilty of acts which might have occurred in the Dark Ages. The hanging of the Opposition in 1926 is in the tradition of those Sultans of Turkey who marked their accession with the massacre of their brothers (the most ruthless of them all was Mohammed III, who is said to have removed nineteen brothers from his path at one swoop, including infants in arms). Resort to the sword is the heritage of the Turk.

The civil war which came to Turkey four months after the opening of Parliament by Abdul Hamid was remarkable not for its savagery, but for its civility. Abdul made his bow as a constitutional ruler on December 17, 1908, and the batteries of the Bosphorus fired a salute of 101 guns— the same number as when he became sovereign. The crowds thought that democracy—that blessed word—had come to their country, and that a most glorious era had opened in the history of Turkey. Alas ! In April, 1909, another enthusiastic crowd gathered in St. Sophia's Square —an army of 30,000 reactionaries, prepared to do battle for the Sultan and the Sacred Law and to cut off the heads of infidels who had tried to impose reforms on the country. The old " djournalist " had been unable to resist intrigue.

When the Hamidian counter-revolution was declared the Third Army Corps took its orders from the Committee of Union and Progress. Twenty-three thousand men under Mahmud Shevket Pasha left Macedonia and advanced on Constantinople—the army of Liberation. In attendance on the victorious General was Mustapha Kemal ; the day for his own victorious entry into Constantinople was not yet.

The city was taken without disorder. Abdul Hamid was deposed and packed off to Salonika, muttering that his domestic pets at Yildiz would die if he were not permitted to remain. A new Sultan, Mehmed Reschad, succeeded to the throne, a Sultan under the control of the Committee of Union and Progress.

We have glimpsed Turkey as she was a few years before the War—a theocratic State perhaps ten centuries behind other

European countries. Now all is changed. In ten years Mustapha Kemal swept away the accretions of ten centuries. His achievement has no parallel, but it should be remembered that many of the liberal principles associated with his name had been current in Turkey for close on a hundred years. The Young Turks of the first decade of this century were turning to the ideas and culture of the West. Even Abdul Hamid is said to have drawn up a memorandum on the desirability of introducing monogamy, the Gregorian Calendar and the Latin Alphabet. The Dictator of Turkey inherited his ideas ; but it was his genius that imposed them on his people.

3

Mustapha Kemal, contemptuous of the men who are in the limelight discovers wherein the secret of greatness lies—" The Leader must remain aloof from the many."

One night a short time before the 1908 Revolution, Mustapha Kemal sat in a Salonika café with some comrades in the Third Army Corps. As it grew late the talk became more vainglorious and vehement. The young men remodelled Turkey according to their hearts' desire, each braggingly casting himself for the role of destroyer of the Sultan and the priests. Kemal—we have it on his own authority—said nothing and listened to the unguarded conversation. Eventually the talk turned to heroes. There was one hero and true patriot, it appeared, in the Third Army. The soldiers were agreed on that. His name was Djemal. He was one of the leaders of the " Union and Progress," and Kemal's immediate superior. Djemal was toasted by every voice save one.

Mustapha Kemal sat in silence, while the eyes of the party turned towards him. Had he no opinion about Djemal ? Were the company not right in applauding a hero ? From beneath bristling brows the blue eyes of Kemal glared at one flushed face after another. Then with a contemptuous movement of the lips he signified his opinion of the hero-worshippers and their hero. They stared back at him, indignant at his cool insolence.

On Kemal's testimony that night's experience marked a

stage in his development. Before he had had little opinion
of the hero-worshippers. Where they thought him self-
opinionated, he thought them men of papier mâché. He
had no cause to alter his opinion now, but he perceived
something that had previously escaped him : that men
who talked vaingloriously of their own powers and then
were suddenly swept away by a wave of hero-worship were
men of straw and sawdust. The discovery hardly possesses
the quality of revelation. But it led him henceforth to
weigh every word of praise before he spoke, and confirmed
him in distrust of facile talkers.

Next morning, he tells us, he encountered Djemal himself,
and delivered a brisk homily on true greatness. Liberal
principles certainly had a firm hold in the Turkish army
when a subordinate could tell his superior that he should
regard himself not as a great man, but as a weak, insignifi-
cant one. Greatness, said Kemal, consisted in flattering
none, in deceiving none, and in seeing and following the
true and only ideal for one's country. And, most important
of all, the leader must remain aloof from the many ; he
must plough his furrow in solitude, shunning all easy
popularity.

Again, hardly a revelation. But worth mentioning because
Mustapha Kemal has put these principles into practice and
reaped the reward. The lonely furrow has led him to the
heights.

That evening in the café, then, opened a new chapter in
Mustapha Kemal's life. What had gone before, whence
had appeared this leader in the making ? Like Hitler, like
Mussolini, like Stalin, he was of the people, the son of undistinguished parents. The actual date of his birth is uncertain, but it is presumed to have been in the Turkish civil
year 1296—that is, 1881. His father, Ali Riza, was (like
Hitler's) a minor customs official in Salonika, where his
son was born. Little is known about Ali Riza except
that he had the initiative to throw over his job and strike
out for himself as a merchant. He had two children by
his wife Zubeida—Mustapha and a girl named Makboula.
The family was still very poor when Ali Riza died, leaving
his widow with the silent, obstinate, brown-haired little boy
and the docile girl on her hands. Zubeida had to take them
to live with her brother, who farmed land in a village outside

Salonika.   Here Mustapha was set tasks which he grew to like—the hard life of odd-job boy on a farm.

Zubeida's " difficult " son constantly occupied her attention, and as he grew stronger and acquired vitality from his work in the fields, so his stubbornness and fierceness increased.   When he was ten years of age Zubeida decided that he must go back to Salonika to live with his aunt and attend a small day school.   From here the boy moved to a higher elementary school.   With pupils and masters alike he was on bad terms, and after being involved in a fight with another hot-head, he was bastinadoed as a warning.   That was too much for one who was a natural rebel.   He ran away from school back to his mother, sullenly informing her that he had no intention of returning.

His next step was made without asking her advice.   The only life for him, he decided, was the soldier's.   He sat for the examination at the Junior Military College at Salonika, passed in, and not till then made Zubeida acquainted with his choice of career.   Soon he had reason to congratulate himself, for his flair for the work rapidly attracted attention. One of the masters, a Captain Mustapha, singled him out for approval, and a curious friendship sprang up between boy and man.

To avoid confusion the master bestowed the name Kemal which signifies " perfection " on the pupil, who enjoyed his favoured position and lorded it over his fellows with enormous gusto.   One can imagine what a tyrant the sixteen-year-old boy proved when, in the absences of Captain Mustapha, he was given charge of a class.   The boy is father to the man, and it is a safe guess that the President who has made a speech lasting six days and ordered the lives of his people down to the smallest detail, was not lost for verbosity and moral exhortation when he stood up to harangue his resentful contemporaries.   A year later he went to the Senior Army School at Monastir.

Voltaire, Rousseau, Hobbes, John Stuart Mill—these were forbidden authors in Turkey.   Mustapha Kemal read them.   He wrote fiery verses.   And while he was absorbing revolutionary and nationalist ideas, acquired a valuable command of literary technique.   He passed out of Monastir labelled " a brilliant, difficult youth with whom it is impossible to be intimate," was gazetted sub-lieutenant, and went to the War College at Constantinople. Here were picked young men of ability who were destined for the best positions on the Turkish General Staff. Mustapha Kemal was not long in discovering that his comrades were revolutionists almost to a man. Ever eager to impose his personality on others and demonstrate his superior abilities, he organised a revolutionary " cell " with a paper of its own.

Its members swore to depose the Sultan and replace his despotism by constitutional government ; to release Turkey from the grip of Islam ; to abolish the veil and the harem. The Commandant of the College realised what was proceeding but did nothing. The Sultan's men too realised what was afoot, but not clearly enough to lay the young conspirators by the heels. The authorities, however, were warned that trouble would follow if the cadets' revolutionary activities were not restrained. So the " Vatan," or Fatherland, Society was carried on outside the walls of the college and widened its scope in consequence.

Mustapha Kemal passed out in January, 1905, a Captain on the General Staff. Shortly afterwards the police raided the premises of the " Vatan " and took off to prison a batch of revolutionaries, Kemal among them. A Commission of Enquiry was held at Yildiz, and for some months Kemal, who was rightly adjudged to be the most dangerous man among the arrested members, was detained in the Red Prison at Stambul. His guilt was not in doubt and death might easily have been his fate. It was his youth that saved him. When he was released with a severe censure he was gazetted to a cavalry regiment at Damascus—an appointment to exile intended as a cautionary measure.

Punitive measures against the Druses should have been his sole occupation, but exile did not check the conspirator. Soon he had a network of secret societies running from Damascus to Beyrut, Jaffa and Jerusalem. Obtaining leave of absence, he went to Egypt and added another " cell." Then, daringly, he took French leave and visited Salonika in disguise.

Salonika, as ever, was the fountain-head of the rebels, and the only place for a young man with ideals, ambition and a taste for excitement. His mother had married again and was comfortably off. He made her house his headquarters while he diligently spied the land. Discontent and

disorder were in every corner of the Ottoman Empire.   In
Salonika there were discontent and disorder, too, yet with
something more—hope, ardour, confidence.   The doom
of the Sultan was sealed, the army believed, and a host of
police and spies could not save him from his fate.   Narrowly
escaping arrest, Mustapha Kemal slipped back to Jaffa and
from there was sent to a desert outpost by a commandant
who had gone over completely to the revolutionaries.

For a year Mustapha Kemal went to earth, until he succeeded in getting transferred to Salonika.   In his imagination he had seen himself as the leader of the revolution once
there, but actually things turned out very differently.   The
revolutionary spirit throughout Macedonia had been well
organised and the formidable Committee of Union and
Progress needed no advice from that highly critical personality, Mustapha Kemal.   The man who had been a leader
in Syria was to become a subordinate in Salonika.   He was
mortified to see Enver, that man of straw and seeker of easy
popularity, in the limelight, while the brilliant Mustapha
Kemal had to pass his time in the outer darkness.   Dis-
gruntled, he made himself as unpleasant as possible to his
comrades and withdrew from the secret meetings.   He
would play second fiddle to no man.   He had his night of
revelation in the café and supported himself in his despon-
dency with his vision of true greatness.

Then, in 1908, came the Revolution of the Third Army
Corps and the capitulation of the Sultan.   Nursing a forlorn
hope of political preferment, he conducted himself like a
good soldier through the counter-Revolution and the
deposition of the Sultan.   It was of no use.   Enver and the
other chiefs of the " Union and Progress," now a political
party, had marked him down as a carping, if clever, fellow,
who was not on any account to be encouraged.

In an access of unrighteous indignation he told himself that
the army's obsession with politics was a scandal.   He could
tolerate it no longer.   Enver might be the idol of the
Constantinople mob ; but Mustapha Kemal would return
to soldiering and prepare for the day when these papier
mâché men fell like Lucifer, never to rise again.

Accordingly, he went back to his place as soldier and put
his heart into his work.   In 1910, as Chief of Staff to the
Macedonian Army, he was sent to the French military

manœuvres. Back in Turkey again he added to his reputation by his command of the Officers' Training School at
Salonika. The younger officers began to look on him as a
coming man, and his confidence expanded under this influence. Again he looked towards the politicians. A " strong "
Turkey was a necessity, he told them. No one could assure
it so well as their servant Mustapha Kemal. His following
was growing, when, in 1911, Italy invaded Tripoli, having
assured himself of the neutrality of the Powers, and Mustapha
Kemal hurried off to the war.

Another chapter in his life had closed. Before him lay
ten years of fighting, of bitter back-to-the-wall struggles,
of chequered fortunes, and at last, of world renown. Somehow he emerged from the cataclysm ; somehow he got a
grip on a country swept by anarchism and never let go. He
built upon the ruins. And what he built has endured.

By 1912 his character was formed. He had served his
apprenticeship in the art of war and to some of his countrymen he seemed destined for the highest military honours.
As a politician he had been given little opportunity to show
his mettle, but the rebuffs he experienced helped him to
formulate the creed from which he has never seriously
swerved : the leader must be alone, feared, set high on a
pinnacle to look down on those inferior souls who have
to be governed.

4

*At the Dardanelles Mustapha Kemal scores a great success. In 1918
he accompanies the Turkish heir-apparent on a State visit to
Germany and perceives that a crisis must soon come.*

When the Great War broke out Mustapha Kemal was
military attaché at Sofia. The Minister was his boyhood
friend Fethi, now Turkish Ambassador in London. Between
the years 1911 and 1914 there had been momentous and
tragic happenings for Turkey. In the first Balkan War,
Montenegro, Serbia, Greece and Bulgaria had suddenly risen
up while Turkish attention was concentrated on Tripoli, battered the Turks everywhere, and demanded as the price of
victory all Turkey in Europe with the exception of Constantinople. Mustapha Kemal and Enver arrived back from

Tripoli, where a hasty peace was patched up with Italy, to find Constantinople panic-stricken after this lightning blow. Enver, backed by the " Union and Progress," stepped into the breach with the blessing of the weak Sultan, instituting revolver rule and becoming virtual dictator of Constantinople. Then, when the allies in the first Balkan War quarrelled among themselves over the spoils of victory and the second Balkan War opened with Greece, Serbia and Rumania ranged against Bulgaria, Enver earned the plaudits of his countrymen by snatching Adrianople back from the divided enemy. As Minister of War he was the man of the hour in Turkey ; with Talaat and Djemal he ruled the country.

Yet the triumvirate held to their original view of Mustapha Kemal—he was a carping fellow who should not be encouraged, and, specifically, he was too vehemently critical of their decision to reorganise the army with the help of a German Military Mission, headed by General Liman von Sandars. Mustapha Kemal (a lieutenant-colonel now) would be safer out of Constantinople ; at Sofia, for example, with his friend Fethi. So to Sofia Mustapha Kemal had to go. When the World War began—Bulgaria was then neutral —he was there in quasi-banishment, kicking his heels by day and acting the gallant to Bulgarian women by night.

From the first he was no believer in the invincibility of the Central Powers. The view he held was that Turkey should have stood aloof until she saw more clearly on which side of the fence it would be wise to come down. But, a soldier by instinct and choice, he was sick at heart that, though a war was being fought, he was debarred from taking part in it. He appealed again and again to Enver for employment and was ignored. So in February, 1915, he packed his bags, determined to thwart Enver by the only means in his power—enlistment as a private soldier. But Enver at that moment was discouraged and tired by his defeat at Sarikamish and could afford to neglect Kemal no longer. The military attaché was appointed to the command of the 19th Division.

It was a reversal of fortune ; somewhat shorn of its promise it is true, when he discovered that owing to the complete dislocation of the Turkish army no 19th Division now existed. However, he hastened to Constantinople to discover that Enver had gone to the Caucasus to grapple with the Russians,

The man of importance was the German reorganiser of the
army, General Liman von Sandars, who was working at
furious speed to organise an army to meet the threat of the
Allies at the Dardanelles. The two men, formed in the same
mould, respected each other from their first meetings, but
never at any time were their relations cordial. " Go to the
Dardanelles," said von Sandars. Alas, for the Allied hopes
of the Dardanelles assault. Mustapha Kemal went to the
Dardanelles as a dark horse ; he returned with a tremendous
military reputation, the hero of Anafarta and the best soldier
Turkey had produced for generations.

Success, if it did not go to his head, certainly intensified his
faith in himself, and convinced him in his low opinion of his
superiors. In Constantinople, a conquering hero, he had no
intention of assuming the role of strong, silent soldier. One
personality with whom he clashed was the Minister of
Foreign Affairs, Nessim, who reported him to the Cabinet
for insolence and angrily demanded that he should be
punished. Enver, at the head of a country already undermined by defeatism, wanted to strike at his rival, but dared
not. A way out was found by appointing Mustapha Kemal
to the command of the 16th Army Corps on the Caucasus
front, far from a Constantinople seething with intrigue and
discontent. The Turks had neglected the Caucasus since
the failure at Erzerum, when close on 90,000 Turkish troops
perished in the mountain passes. Now that the Russians
were preparing a great offensive under the Grand Duke
Nicholas, Mustapha Kemal must have realised that only
luck could save the starved, discouraged, demoralised troops
under him. Desperately he attempted a general reorganisation—yet it was luck that saved him. The Russian Revolution broke out ; the Turks' opponents crumpled up.

Again he had emerged victorious. But in Syria and Meso-
potamia a serious menace to Turkey was developing and he
was recalled to command the 7th Army. The lifelong apostle
of Turkey for the Turks became enraged when he found that
Enver had called in General von Falkenhayn, another
German, to organise a " lightning " force of Turks with a
backbone of German officers and men. Kemal began a
policy of obstruction and, after the German general tried to
bribe him and failed, brought things to a head by refusing to
return to his old command in the Caucasus. Enver again

yearned to strike—but dared not. His enemy now had a big following and, moreover, Germany's stock was so low in Turkey that a blow at Mustapha Kemal might have caused a nation-wide storm. It was Mustapha Kemal's round. Convinced that the old gang and their German backing must soon collapse, that before long his day must dawn, he returned to Constantinople with an order in his pocket granting him indefinite sick leave.

In the spring of 1918, however, Enver thought of yet another means to get this dangerous man out of the capital. The Turkish Crown Prince, Wahid-ed-Din, soon afterwards Sultan Mohammed VI, was to pay a State visit to Germany. Mustapha Kemal should accompany him as the representative of the Turkish General Staff.

In Germany, Mustapha Kemal found himself among men of his own mental stature. He disconcerted Hindenburg and Ludendorff with searching questions on military policy. Having quickly obtained the ear of the aged, degenerate Crown Prince—who was soon to demonstrate, however, that he possessed all the Osmanli passion for intrigue—he primed him with awkward interrogations, which were persisted in even in the presence of the Kaiser himself. Kemal, in fact, proved a Tartar at the German Court. He left more than ever convinced that a German collapse could not be long delayed, and his thoughts turned to that day when, amidst the crash of nations, a strong man might seize power in Turkey. Meanwhile another opportunity lay close to hand—the Crown Prince himself. He asked Wahid-ed-Din one day if he could talk frankly, and on being told to go on, whispered : " I wish to propose something that, if you agree, will link my life to yours."

The Turkish Crown Prince, suggested Kemal, like the German princes, should have command of an army. He must demand it of Enver as a right, and then—then his servant, Mustapha Kemal, could become his Royal Highness's Chief of Staff.

" Which army ? "

Mustapha Kemal had the answer pat. Before he could smash his way to power he needed an army at his back—the army nearest Constantinople.

" The Fifth Army."

The Crown Prince was non-committal in his reply. He

would, he said, think about the idea when he got
home.

5

*Turkey collapses and an armistice is signed, whereupon Mustapha Kemal
defies the British.   With the idea of Nationalism in his head
he is sent to Anatolia, where national feeling is strong and a
defence association has been formed.*

In July, 1918, Wahid-ed-Din succeeded to the throne, at a
moment when Mustapha Kemal was out of Turkey. Serious
kidney trouble had temporarily disabled him, and he was in
Carlsbad taking a cure. He heard without emotion that in
a clash with Enver the new Sultan had emerged with the
honours. Still ill, he dragged himself to Constantinople.
An interview with the Sultan revitalised him. He secured
another interview and yet another. At this last his soaring
hopes were completely deflated. The Sultan, who a few
months before had agreed with him about the worthlessness
of Enver and Talaat, said softly that he had made his plans
for the future with them. It was Enver's round, undoubtedly,
and there was worse to come. Again that apprehensive
dictator decided that Mustapha Kemal must be removed
from Constantinople ; and again Enver thought of the way.
The military situation in Syria was black enough in all
conscience. Kemal must be sent there, and, so that he
could not refuse, the Sultan himself must give the order.
And this the Sultan did.
    The task in Syria was hopeless. On September 20, 1918,
Lord Allenby drove the Turks from Nablous, and the rout
began. At Damascus, Mustapha Kemal conferred with his
generals, Ismet Pasha and Ali Fouad Pasha. Then, with his
kidney trouble upon him again, he began a retreat to Aleppo,
determined to protect all roads into Turkey by the formation
of a new line in the north. Despite his military preoccupa-
tions he found time to wire to the Sultan demanding the
ejection of Enver, Talaat and Djemal and the appointment
of himself as Minister of War in a crisis government. No
answer came from the Sultan ; but Mustapha Kemal's eyes
must have gleamed when the news came that Enver and
the two others had fled the country in the hour of crisis.

October ran out and the humiliation of the Ottoman Empire was complete. On October 30, 1918, a new Turkish Government signed an armistice with the British at Mudros.

The ideas of the soldier who had always bitterly resented German interference in Turkey's affairs were now consolidated and extended. The Turkish Empire was gone and nothing could bring it back; but Turkey herself could and must be saved—by Nationalism. To France, to Italy and, most important of all, to Britain, a firm front must be shown. They were there to overrun Turkey, to wipe her off the map, and would do it if the losers endured their demands with humility.

A few days after the signing of the armistice at Mudros, Mustapha Kemal made his first Nationalist move, and demonstrated what he meant when he said that these foreigners who desired to overrun the country must be checked at all costs. The British wished to occupy Alexandretta, to use it as a supply base for the revictualling of their troops at Aleppo. Mustapha Kemal would have none of it. Nothing would be gained by weakness, he wired to Constantinople. The British merely desired to get a foothold in Turkey. It was the thin end of the wedge. He had to give way eventually, but the experience hardened his resolve concerning resistance. To Constantinople he hastened, determined to overthrow the new ministry of Tewfiq Pasha on a vote of confidence. The politicians, not for the first time, played him false, assuring him of their support and then voting for Tewfiq.

Out of an interview with the crafty old Sultan—a complete rebuff in itself—inspiration came. Patently he would continue to be cold-shouldered by all Parties in Constantinople; they feared him too much to give him power of any sort. Hence Constantinople was no place for him, no place for a Nationalist who hoped to seize the machinery of State. The British, too, were over-powerful there, and would be only too ready to side with the Sultan to crush him if he inspired a revolt.

Anatolia (Asia Minor) he decided, was the most promising theatre for him, and by a piece of great good fortune he was able to go there as Inspector-General, an official appointment for which he was selected by the Sultan. National feeling was strong in Anatolia, owing to the menaces of the

Armenians and the Greeks. In March, 1919, an Anatolian Defence Rights Association had been formed. Mustapha Kemal hailed this development with joy ; and he must have smiled with sardonic amusement when the Sultan and the Grand Vizier, worried as usual by the threat of his presence at the seat of Government, nominated him as Inspector-General to stamp out the Anatolian Movement. On May 19, 1919, accompanied by his old friend Arif, a cavalry officer, and Colonel Refet Bey, who had been appointed Governor of Samsun, he landed at that Black Sea port. Four days previously there had occurred an event which brought the passions of the Anatolian peasantry to fever heat ; Greek troops were landed at Smyrna, the citadel of Turkey in Asia, with the sanction of Britain, France and America. On this threat of a Greek invasion of Turkey the surrendering of arms in Anatolia, as specified in the armistice, began to cease. If the hated Greeks were to be allowed to overrun the country, the arms would be urgently needed.

6

The Congress from which sprang the Turkish republic is set up. The National Pact offers a challenge to the Allies, who by their response consolidate Mustapha Kemal's position.

We have seen Mustapha Kemal in the important formative phases of his career, his character hardening, his resolution growing. As a soldier he has made a reputation and is now everywhere regarded as the best general in Turkey. But the policy of the lone hand has led him nowhere: Now he begins afresh in the wilds of Eastern Anatolia, away from the decadence and intrigues and conservatism of Constantinople. And in his new surroundings the same policy brings success in a comparatively short time.

Personal jealousies had played a major part in Mustapha Kemal's frustrated political career. In Anatolia, too, they were still present, but he conquered his enemies. The troops there, by arrangement with generals sympathetic to the cause—Kiazim Kara Bekir, Ali Fouad Pasha, and Rauf Bey—passed under his control. But the generals had their own ambitions and were not willing to see Mustapha Kemal as their master. With them he walked warily. With the people and notabilities of Erzerum on the other hand, he was demagogic, savage, unrestrained, lashing them into patriotic frenzy. They were puzzled at first that this general sent to them by the Sultan should preach a doctrine which urged them to act on their own responsibility independently of Constantinople. Soon Kemal's oratory made them forget their doubts. No longer, he thundered, was it of use to look to Constantinople for direction. The Sultan, alas, was now in the hands of foreign advisers, and the country was breaking up. The Greeks had already carried fire and sword to Smyrna. It was necessary for every patriotic Turk to be ready to rise against them, the natural object (with Armenians) of every Turk's hatred. A congress must be called in this moment of crisis—a congress representing all Turkey.

It was not so easy with the generals, for as the days passed their suspicions of Mustapha Kemal's personal ambitions rapidly grew. But he had his way with them. They met him at Amassia and signed a Protocol calling for the co-ordination of all the defence groups in the country.

Kiazim Kara Bekir, the staunch soldier-hero of Eastern Anatolia, was the most difficult to win over, but Kemal succeeded when he argued that the will of the people was paramount even though the general had sworn loyalty to the Sultan. After a meeting at Erzerum a congress with deputies from many parts of Turkey met at Sivas in September, 1919, and Mustapha Kemal was chosen as President. When jealousy showed its head once more, he came out into the open and declared : " Gentlemen, history shows clearly that in great enterprises and for the attaining of success, the leadership of an energetic and capable chief is absolutely essential. In moments of crisis the goal cannot be reached by discussion."

This Congress marked a new epoch in Turkey's history. From it sprang the Turkish republic. Yet of all those present only one man, Kemal, apparently realised the path that must be trod to reach the end. The truth of this was made evident when the newly-formed body forced the Sultan to hold another parliamentary election. They had been angered by an order coming from the Grand Vizier that Kurdish tribesmen should be sent to arrest the delegates and break up the Sivas Congress, and despatched an ultimatum to the Sultan : the Grand Vizier must go and elections for Parliament must be held forthwith. The Sultan reluctantly gave way and at the elections the Congress candidates secured a big majority. Then the question immediately arose : where was Parliament to be held—in Constantinople, or in Angora, which was now the official headquarters of the Kemalists ?

The deputies met at Angora previous to the opening of Parliament and agreed on the terms of the famous National Pact. But against the advice of their President, they rejected Angora and decided on the constitutional course—Parliament at Constantinople. Mustapha Kemal warned them against this course, but could do nothing to restrain them. They did not realise, he told them, that by their action they were putting their heads into the lion's mouth—for Britain, not the Sultan, was the real danger at Constantinople.

Events justified him, but the National Pact saved the cause. This document, consisting of six brief articles only, laid down the conditions on which the Nationalists would agree to peace. The tone of the Pact astonished the Allies, for the defeated had assumed a tone more fitting to the victorious. It laid down a " fundamental condition "— the complete independence and liberty of Turkey. Its challenge was received in silence. The rank and file of Turks were not slow to harry the Army of Occupation and break the terms of the armistice.

The silence was maintained until at last the Allies had to act. Forty leading members of Parliament were arrested and deported to Malta.

Two hundred miles away, in the wilds of Anatolia, Mustapha Kemal, who had been proclaimed an outlaw by the Sultan, must have laughed. These foreigners believed that Constantinople was still the centre of things ! If it had been true their action made it true no longer, because the deputies who had escaped arrest immediately fled to Angora, the place where they were safe from reprisals. There the Grand National Assembly was set up on April 23, 1920, Mustapha Kemal being elected President both of the Assembly and of the Government. Once more his luck had held. As head of a new Turkish Government over all territories not under foreign occupation he could get to work unfettered. The Allies had had their chance and missed it. If they had not procrastinated Turkey might have been wiped off the map despite the resistance of Mustapha Kemal. It was too late now ; a miracle worker had appeared to save Turkey and nothing was to hold him back.

7

The Turks chase the Greeks into the sea and the way is made clear for the Turkish triumph of the Treaty of Lausanne. Mustapha Kemal abolishes the Sultanate and the Caliphate.

On July 24, 1923, the Treaty of Lausanne, which officially ended the war between the Allies and Turkey, was signed. It was of supreme importance, from the Kemalists' point of view, for several reasons. In the first place it gave Turkey practically everything she had claimed three years before in the National Pact ; in the second place it was the only treaty of the Great War which was not imposed by the winners on the losers. Mustapha Kemal had defied the great Powers, and in the face of overwhelming odds had scored a tremendous military and political success. The Treaty concluded the military stage in the development of the Kemalist régime, and, in the normal course of dynastic evolution, the law-giver succeeded the warrior, with the difference that Mustapha Kemal combined both roles in one person.

This military period between April, 1920, and the signing of the Lausanne Treaty in 1923 saw momentous happenings in Turkey. The Lausanne Treaty replaced the Treaty of Sèvres, which was concluded in August, 1920, between the Allies and the Sultan's Government.

This last agreement gave Smyrna to the Greeks provisionally, where, as has already been mentioned, Greek troops had been landed in May, 1919, under the protection of the Allied Fleets. The fact that the Greeks had inaugurated their occupation with a massacre committed in full view of the Allied Fleets also gave a tremendous impetus to Turkish Nationalism.

The first recognition of the new Angora Government came from Russia. Shortly afterwards the Allies recognised

Angora at a conference in London held to amend the Treaty of Sèvres. The only important result of this meeting was a difference of opinion between the Allies on the question of Turkey, and in consequence in May, 1921, the neutrality of the Allied Governments was signified. This action left a clear field for the inevitable war between Turkey and Greece. During the summer of 1921 fighting in Anatolia resulted in victories for the Greeks, who advanced and threatened Angora itself. The Assembly, alarmed for the safety of the town that was later to become the capital of Turkey, turned to Mustapha Kemal to save the situation. In this crisis jealousies were forgotten and they invested him with the powers of dictator for a period of three months and waited anxiously to see how he would tackle an army that outnumbered their own by four to one. Within three weeks the Greeks were beaten back at the battle of Sakaria, and Kemal and his able generals Ismet Pasha (now Prime Minister of Turkey) and Fevzi Pasha were acclaimed as national heroes.

How the ill-equipped Turks managed to stem the tide is one of the mysteries of history. Soldiers were sent on to the field without rifles—they had to take them from the grasp of their dead comrades. Women worked in the lines of communication. The Nationalist Air Force boasted one aeroplane. On his return to a jubilant Assembly, Mustapha Kemal was made marshal and given the title of Ghazi—the victorious. It was a year before operations in the war were resumed.

After Russia, France was the next country to make peace with Mustapha Kemal. While Britain was still backing the wrong horse—the Sultan's Constantinople Government—France sent M. Franklin-Bouillon to negotiate a " separate peace." But one great problem occupied Turkish attention, beside which everything was of secondary interest. The Greeks must be driven from Anatolia. Peace by negotiation not unexpectedly failed, and on August 26 an army reorganised by the Ghazi went into battle inspired by his order of the day, which began : " Soldiers, your goal is the Mediterranean ! "

It was a brief war conducted throughout with Oriental savagery, in which natural enemies rioted in blood and atrocities. From the first day the issue was never in doubt.

The Turks swept down on the Greek army and smashed it, and within three weeks the remnant was driven into the sea. The fleeing Greeks put the towns in their path to fire and sword, with the result that nearly a million persons were homeless after the hurricane had passed. By September 13 the Turks had reached Smyrna ; as though to purge it of Greek sympathies for ever, the rich city was set alight and destroyed.

The Turkish " rush for the sea " created an international crisis, as they ended facing the Allied armies on the Asiatic shores of the Straits. In Thrace the Greek army was re-forming itself, and Mustapha Kemal wished to get at it while it was yet still trembling under his assault. But between the combatants stood the British Army of Occupation at Chanak, the immovable object. Anxiously the European nations waited to see if Mustapha Kemal was the irresistible force.

Again M. Franklin-Bouillon appeared to negotiate. On behalf of the Allies he promised the evacuation of the Greek army from Thrace and a restoration of Turkey's territory. The way to Lausanne was paved. Mustapha Kemal and his ragged army had triumphed.

Then came the law-giving phase of the Ghazi.

First the Sultan himself was tackled. The House of Osman had ruled for seven centuries. Mustapha Kemal brought its sovereignty to an end in a fashion hardly fitting to its long history. The Sultanate must go, he told the Grand National Assembly on November 1, 1922. It must go, lock, stock and barrel, in the interests of a homogeneous Turkey. The Assembly abolished it, and Mohammed VI, the last of the Sultans, wrote to Great Britain imploring protection ; on November 17 he took refuge in H.M.S. *Malaya* and escaped to Malta.

A new Caliph was elected, who gave up his claims to the Sultanate. Mustapha Kemal was determined to separate religion completely from the State. On October 29, 1923, Turkey became a Republic, with Mustapha Kemal for its first President, and with his chief lieutenant, Ismet Pasha, as Prime Minister. Again the thunder of a salute of 101 guns announced the rebirth of Turkey. Thereafter the Ghazi led the attack on Islam as the State religion. On March 3, 1924, the Caliphate was abolished.

In November of that year Kiazim Kara Bekir Pasha and
Rauf Bey, who had been watching Mustapha Kemal
suspiciously, fearing a personal dictatorship, formed the
Republican Progressive Party in opposition to the Kemalist
People's Party. It was a risky move to challenge the Ghazi's
supremacy. Ismet Pasha's ministry had fallen and Fethi
Bey formed a new Cabinet. It was then that Turkey was
thrown into a ferment by a Kurdish insurrection, caused by
the chieftains' antagonism to the centralising policy of
Angora, which threatened the wild freedom they had long
enjoyed. Mustapha Kemal struck quickly, first at the Kurds,
and next at the opposition, whose programme, he falsely
declared, had encouraged the rising. Fethi Bey resigned,
Ismet Pasha came back, and an ominous " law of maintenance and order " was passed. It cleared the way for the
assumption of dictatorial powers by the Ghazi and for a
reign of terror in Turkey.

The constitution of the Republic was admittedly more
democratic than that of England. A serious omission, however, was a clause placing the President above party,
and of this the Ghazi, with his People's Party at his back,
took full advantage. Once out in the open as a Dictator, he
revived the Tribunals of Independence, which had appeared
first when he was crushing the anti-Nationalists. With these
Tribunals, which meted out justice in the manner of Judge
Jeffreys, of infamous memory, Turkey reverted to feudal
conditions in a night. They consisted of three deputies of
the People's Party, two of whom took the part of judges,
while the third acted as prosecutor (the accused had to
defend himself as best he could and was not allowed counsel).
The Tribunals were sent first to settle accounts with the
Kurds. In one town alone forty-six men were hanged in a
square before the horrified eyes of the inhabitants.

When Kurdistan lay bruised and bleeding the Dictator
turned his attention to his political opponents. They, too,
were to be annihilated. On the flimsy pretext that a plot
against his life was germinating, he ordered the police to
secure evidence against the Opposition leaders and any of
Enver's friends who still remained in Turkey. Hitler's purge
of his party was severe, but the Ghazi's purge was more
severe still. Wholesale hangings of influential and insig-
nificant members of the Opposition, including his old

friend, Arif, took place simultaneously at Smyrna and
Angora, while the nation waited anxiously, half-fearing,
half-admiring the man without compassion into whose
hands its destiny had been committed.

<h1 style="text-align:center">8</h1>

*The introduction of hats into Turkey causes a revolt.   Sartorial freedom
is imposed on the Turks, and is followed by many other reforms.
What will happen when the " Father of the Turks " dies ?*

Having thus cleared all rivals and dissentients from his
path, Mustapha Kemal again turned his attention to the
westernisation of Turkey. A new system of education was
introduced, following the abolition of religious schools, in
which Islam had no part. On February 17, 1926, a new civil
code, based on Swiss, German and Italian models, was
adopted by the Assembly. Quickly the machinery of the
State was completely refashioned in the light of ultra-
Nationalism, to the bewilderment of the slow-thinking
peoples, particularly the trading communities, which were
now to be run by the Turks themselves instead of by Greeks
and Armenians. The army, the navy and the air force were
strengthened, for Mustapha Kemal was not likely to forget
that his country owed its very existence to its armed forces.
State construction of railways was carried out on a large
scale.

There are those, however, who hold that the Ghazi's
boldest reform concerned the dress of his people, in particular the abolition of the fez.

The fez, curiously enough, had been introduced (to replace
the turban) a century before as a reforming measure by a
Sultan who saw in it a Turkish equivalent of Europe's top
hat. The religious significance of the fez made it impossible
for any Turk to discard this head-covering, and although
the astrakhan kalpak had been introduced by the Young
Turks as a symbol of their emancipation, there was
no serious outcry against it because it was not a *hat* with a
brim such as infidels wore. Mustapha Kemal perceived that
he must change the outward appearance of his subjects

before attempting to change their ways of thought ; that he must first make them sartorially free. He began by issuing *képis* to the Republican Guard, and as no trouble was forthcoming, extended the peaked cap to the rest of the army. Then in September, 1925, dressed in a lounge suit and a panama hat, he made a speech in a little Black Sea town which had important consequences for Turkey. " We will wear," he said, " boots and shoes, trousers, shirts, waistcoats, collars, ties. We will add brims to the coverings we place upon our heads—or to speak more plainly, we will wear hats. We will dress in morning coats and lounge suits, in smoking jackets and tail-coats. And if there are persons who hesitate and draw back, I will tell them that they are fools and ignoramuses."

Turkey became " fashion conscious " overnight when the Assembly made the fez illegal and the wearing of it a criminal offence, and a collection of hats appeared in the streets of the large towns such as history has never seen before —battered boaters, antiquated bowlers, pieces of cloth with home-made cardboard brims tacked on, anything that appeared to resemble the head coverings of the civilised peoples of the world. In the country districts, however, a murmur of revolt went up against the sacrilegious law, because no true Moslem could pray properly with a head-covering with a brim. Once more the Tribunals of Independence were sent out, and before resistance finally collapsed many Turks had been hanged and imprisoned.

Mustapha Kemal followed up dress reform with the emancipation of women. Polygamy was legally prohibited ; the laws regarding marriage and divorce were altered to bring them into line with European practice ; the veil went the way of the fez. Before this, in January, 1923, the Ghazi had married Latifé Hanem, the " advanced " daughter of a Smyrna merchant. She had been to school in London and Paris, and in dress and manners and general demeanour could have been taken for a woman of the West. Good-looking and intelligent, she appeared to Mustapha Kemal as the embodiment of emancipated Turkish womanhood. After a stormy courtship they were married in a fashion new to Turkey, at the bride's house in the presence of a few friends. The faithful who prophesied that no good could

come of such an unsanctified wedding triumphantly proclaimed their powers of divination two and a half years later.
For in August, 1925, the Ghazi divorced his wife, and
although no official reason was advanced, it has been suggested variously that he found her interest in his work too
intense and individual for conjugal harmony, and that she
on her side was not prepared to overlook the marital lapses
of a Western reformer who in his private life had para-
doxically manifested truly Oriental ideas regarding the
purpose of women in the scheme of things.

Among the many reforms introduced by Mustapha Kemal
one or two others must be mentioned. When he ordered
that Latin characters must take the place of Arabic in
Turkish script he sent a whole nation back to its school lessons.
But this vast experiment is succeeding. Before the War
95 per cent of the population could neither read nor write.
Now every Turk is compelled by law to write the new script.
In the closing weeks of 1934 more important changes were
made. By decree every Turk was required to find a surname.
The Assembly made the first move by selecting the President's own name, which was Kemal Ataturk. Ataturk
means " Father of the Turks."

In addition the Constitution was amended to allow Turkish
women to have the parliamentary vote. All women who
have attained the age of twenty-three can vote, and those
over thirty may stand for Parliament. Seventeen now have
seats in the Grand National Assembly. Lastly, the religious
representatives of the Moslem, Orthodox, Catholic, Jewish,
Armenian and Protestant faith were forbidden to wear their
clerical attire in public.

The Ghazi has shut out the westernisation in a democratic sense of the machinery of government ; one party
alone, the Party of the Dictator, is permitted to exist in
Turkey. To a democratic critic the Ghazi might explain
that he has experimented with constitutional parliamentary
government, and it has failed. Turkey, he could answer,
is not ready.

The experiment was made in 1930-31, and it is hard to
decide whether cynicism or sincerity inspired it. In either
case it sheds an interesting light on mass psychology, and
demonstrates that no sooner does a dictator step down from
his pinnacle than he loses power and prestige.

A short-lived Republican Liberal Party came into existence in Turkey in 1930 at the behest of the Ghazi. Fethi Bey was selected as its leader and ten or twelve prominent deputies were ordered by Mustapha Kemal to form the nucleus of an Opposition. They were to attack the Prime Minister in the Assembly, hold meetings all over the country, and in every way conduct themselves as the official and recognised Opposition party. The censorship of the Press and the ban on free speech were lifted, and Mustapha Kemal made it known that anyone who wished could become a Republican Liberal without earning his displeasure. The ironical result was that Turkey rang with real and imaginary grievances ; a nation unaccustomed to political freedom stirred uneasily. Something must be wrong with the régime for this to happen. The Ghazi was their idol, but might he not after all have feet of clay ? So with loss of faith an atmosphere of disquiet grew, until a grave religious revolt at Menemen, in Asia Minor, led by a dervish, caused Mustapha Kemal to drop the experiment and resume the rule of the iron hand. " Long live our chains ! " was the loyal cry of the mob in the great days of the Spanish monarchy. Bound in their chains once again the Turks sighed with relief.

The way of the reformer is hard, and, in Oriental countries, dangerous. Physical and moral courage in the highest degree are needed by the man who would introduce new ideas into Eastern countries ; for him there may be waiting the dagger of the religious fanatic or the fury of a mob demanding his ruin and banishment. The Ghazi has braved both dangers and has emerged as the demi-god of Turkey. Not so fortunate was Amanulla of Afghanistan, who lost his throne because he tried to westernise a backward country.

To the question which is always asked when one man holds a country in his grip—what will happen when the " Father of the Turks " and perpetual President of the Turkish Republic dies ?—the answer is clear. Never can the country revert to her former backwardness. While Kemal Ataturk has been refashioning Turkey to his heart's desire a new and emancipated generation has grown up ; a generation which may have heard of the tragedy of Turkey's past and the humiliations of the fez, the veil, and all that they stood for, but knows them not.

JOSEPH PILSUDSKI

1

The Polish paradox never flung democracy by the board entirely, but throughout his dictatorship continued to wear a few democratic shreds and tatters. The Constitution adopted by Poland in 1921 was for long his bugbear.

DEATH removed Marshal Joseph Pilsudski, the Polish paradox, from the ranks of the dictators on May 12, 1935. He was born a Lithuanian, and if he had been true to a tradition of that country he would have hated Poland implacably ; on the contrary, he worked from his earliest youth for Polish nationalism. He started (like Mussolini) as a Socialist, despite his aristocratic connections ; he died an autocrat. In the World War he fought against the Allies ; yet he was arrested by the Germans and imprisoned. A civilian by upbringing, he was renowned for his military exploits, and it was he who saved large areas of Europe from being overrun by the Bolsheviks when he overthrew them at the Battle of the Vistula, in 1920.

Every dictator, of course, must be of a masterful disposition. Pilsudski's masterfulness was always overwhelmingly downright, as though he never allowed himself to forget that any degree of subtlety would bè lost on the peasants and the army, on whom he relied for support. Yet this is not to say that his lifelong devotion to the cause of Polish nationalism though ardent was indiscriminating. From early days, when he plotted against Russian oppression, down to his death he worked with tremendous skill and courage for Poland's welfare. His enemies said that the only consistent thing about him was a lust for power that was never satisfied : which is but a half-truth. Pilsudski, after a lifetime spent in setting Poland free, regarded

" Marshal Joseph Pilsudski knew what he wanted throughout his
life—and got it."

power as his natural right, to be employed in the way that was best suited to Poland's needs. As the re-creator of Poland, he considered that he alone was the arbiter of the country's destiny ; that anyone could *honestly* hold opinions contrary to his own he could not believe. If they did they were not merely knaves or fools, but dark forces sent unaccountably by Providence to be battled with—and scourged. Those scourgings of the politically unclean in the elections of recent years were not as violent as those seen in Germany and Turkey, but they lost Pilsudski a great deal of sympathy inside and outside Poland. There was persecution of opponents (particularly in the Ukraine), arrests on trumped-up charges, and the shaving of heads, which was the Polish counterpart of the Fascist castor-oil. Notorious, too, but harmless, was the Marshal's invective. No ruler of the country has ever used stronger language in public. " If I accuse my opponents," he said, " of terminological inexactitudes my friends do not know what I am saying. If I call them —— liars, my peasants understand and remember." In this connection, England seems to have taught him a lesson. In 1921 Mr. Lloyd George criticised Poland in outspoken terms. Annoyed, Pilsudski hastened to protest to the British Minister in Warsaw, who sought to justify the words used by Mr. Lloyd George by remarking that the weakness of Poland's position in international affairs had to be emphasised, and if Mr. Lloyd George had used milder terms he might have been misunderstood. After that the Marshal made a habit of using unmistakable words in order that he, too, might not be misunderstood. His most notorious outburst occurred in 1928 in an article, written throughout in barrack-room style, which attacked Deputies who had opposed him. His verbal whips and scorpions were such that they could not be reproduced in the English Press.

Yet, despite everything, Pilsudski never proclaimed an open dictatorship. While using dictatorial power he did not shed democracy entirely. In 1928 he tried to obtain a parliamentary majority, but when he failed he did not hesitate to browbeat his opponents into his own way of thinking, despite his lack of parliamentary authority. Two years later he again tried his luck at the polls, and by bribery, the arrest of opponents, and the use of the iron

hand in the Ukraine, he emerged with 248 seats out of 444
in the Seym, as the Lower House of the Legislature is called.
   Why did Pilsudski continue to wear the rags of democracy
when the easier course would have been naked dictatorship ?
The reason that suggests itself becomes very interesting when
Pilsudski is compared with Mustapha Kemal of Turkey.
Pilsudski was the oldest of the dictators ; in 1930 he was 63,
and Mustapha Kemal was 52.   One cannot doubt that
the younger man, had he been in the Marshal's place,
would have thrown democracy overboard completely.
The fact that past generations of Poles had given their
lives in order that their country might have a Constitution
would not have weighed with the Ghazi, whose realist mind
has not a tincture of reverence for the past.   Had he been a
younger man it is conceivable that Pilsudski could have
brought himself to the point where, shutting his eyes to the
ideal he had once considered all-important, the legacy of
the heroes of his race, he would have walked out into the open
as a dictator.   But he was 63, and at that age it is not easy
even for the great to snap the links that bind a man to the
traditional past.
   This may or may not have been the reason, but the fact
remains that he did not abandon Poland's 1921 Constitution ; he contented himself with reviling it on every
possible occasion, and immediately he obtained his majority
in 1930 set about reforming it.
   It was the Constitution that caused Pilsudski to retire
from public life from 1923 to 1926, for that Constitution
was framed with the especial intention of limiting the power
of the President of Poland, a country which had been
replaced on the map of Europe after the World War as a
republic, with nearly thirty million inhabitants.
   He retired, and from a distance looked with growing
anxiety at political developments.   Poland had adopted
proportional representation for the election of the Seym.
The creation of numerous parties was the result, and the
bloc system became the basis of the formation of ministries.
Personal animosities and the rivalries of the *blocs* led to
political crises, and the frequent fall and rise of ministries,
with the bewildering of the country as a consequence.   In
the first ten years of the existence of the Polish Republic,
no fewer than twenty-two ministries were formed.

It was the spectacle of the futility and pettiness of the politicians that brought Pilsudski charging back to politics, after an absence of three years, with troops at his back. There was a show of resistance and civil war, before he installed himself in 1926 as Poland's virtual dictator.

2

If dictators are made in childhood, the men who determined Pilsudski's career were the Russian schoolmasters of Vilna. He goes to Siberia for five years, and re-enters ordinary life full of zeal to confound the Russian taskmasters.

Every schoolboy knows, as Macaulay would have said, the term, Partitions of Poland. But only the Poles know the real meaning and tragedy of those three words. Prior to 1772 Poland was a country of over 280,000 square miles with centuries of history behind it. But in that year the first of the partitions was made by Russia, to be followed by further depredations in 1793 and 1795 by Prussia and Austria (the latter partition was rearranged in 1815). The final blow to Poland came in 1868, when the 50,000 square miles of the country that remained, with their twelve million inhabitants, were incorporated in the Russian Empire. The Russification of Poland began with the abolishing of self-government and the prohibition of the Polish language for public purposes.

Pilsudski was born in 1867, the son of a House sprung from princes of Lithuania, but now fiercely Polish in sympathy, and he took in with his mother's milk a hatred of everything Russian.

Where other children were entertained by fairy stories, the child Joseph Pilsudski was inspired by stories of Polish heroes who had given their lives for Polish freedom. It was dangerous in his childhood home at Vilna to be in possession of Polish books, for Russification was ruthlessly enforced. The Tsarists strove in vain to wipe out Polish independence by suppressing Polish customs, language and literature, but the Poles continued to derive inspiration from their national history.

Of all patriots, Pilsudski's mother was the most irreconcilable. She brought up her ten children in an atmosphere of hate against the oppressor. The nightmares of the young Pilsudski centred upon the Russian schoolmasters at his gymnasium at Vilna, whose aim was to crush the independence and personal dignity of the Polish youths. This gymnasium, with the ever-present possibility of unjust punishment, became a place of dread for him. Writing in after years of his school experiences he said : " How deep the impression this system made on my mind may be judged by this fact ; although I have since passed through gaols and Siberia, and have had to do with a number of Russian officials, it is still the Vilna schoolmasters who play some part in every bad dream."

Dictators are made in childhood, the psychologists suggest, and some of them believe that Europe would be a happier place to-day if the pastors and masters of the dictators of the world had possessed the knowledge that nothing does so much lasting harm to youth as unjust punishment. Pilsudski certainly never forgot the tyrants of his unhappy schooldays ; neither did Mustapha Kemal, whose bastinadoing at the hands of a cleric may well have been responsible for his later assaults on religion.

At the age of eighteen Pilsudski began to consider how he could best spread his gospel of political hate. Action against the Russians must be taken, he decided, and that action must be directed by one man, not by a body or a mass. The literature of the French Revolution had been assimilated by the adolescent boy, and that was the lesson he had gained from it. If a revolution was to mean more than a gesture, more than blood and barricades, it must be directed by one man. Already he saw himself as the leader.

At the University of Cracow, where he became a medical student, he was brought into contact with Poles of his own generation, and he found that those who were politically minded accepted Marxism almost to a man. Pilsudski, too, became a Marxist, although he did not like the creed or understand it. But any stick was good enough to beat Russia with, and as a Socialist (though hardly an Internationalist) he began eagerly to form a revolutionary society. In 1887, however, his activities were brought to a sudden halt. He was held to have been involved in an attempt to assassinate the Tsar Alexander III. Pilsudski, though not a direct participant in the conspiracy—his name was found in the note-book of an arrested man—was charged with complicity, and sentenced to five years' exile in Siberia. For his part in this same plot the brother of Lenin was hanged.

Pilsudski's Siberian experience began violently, and he was lucky to escape with his life. With twenty other exiles he reached the prison of Irkutsk after a three months' journey. At Irkutsk, the entire party, led by Pilsudski, rose in revolt, and troops were called out to quell them. Pilsudski was the first to be knocked out by two blows from the butt-end of a rifle. He was dragged into a court-yard and on regaining consciousness made a dash for the prison gate, where were waiting a cordon of soldiers. His legs gave way and he fell into the arms of a soldier, blood gushing from his mouth.

Such was his introduction to life in exile, and it must be admitted that on this occasion he went to meet trouble considerably more than half-way. His five years' banishment was an enervating, but not a nerve-wracking experience. The once popular idea—does it exist to-day?—that Siberia was synonymous with Gehenna was not borne out by the experience of Pilsudski or Lenin, who followed the Pole to exile in 1897. Pilsudski underwent no change of heart in exile. He returned to ordinary life in the autumn of 1892 eager to work for Polish independence and the overthrow of the Tsarist régime.

3

Pilsudski is condemned to prison for ten years, but gains his freedom by a ruse. From within Austrian territory he engages in guerrilla warfare with Russia. Slowly he builds up a tiny private army and when war is declared throws in his lot with Austria.

When Pilsudski returned to Vilna he found that the Polish Socialist Parties were co-operating on a programme of national independence somewhat similar to his own plans. Very soon he was taking a leading part in the formation and organisation of a secret National Socialist Party within Poland.

It was decided at a congress at Vilna in the summer of 1893 to publish a party organ, the *Robotnik* (The Workman), which, to avoid censorship, would have to be printed and circulated in subterranean fashion. Pilsudski was made editor, and threw himself into the work with enormous enthusiasm, not only editing the paper, but taking an active part in the distribution of that and other *bibula* (the slang word for uncensored and prohibited literature). If Pilsudski could have been persuaded to talk about his career, it is to this chapter in his life that he would doubtless have turned first. It was the production of the *Robotnik* that caused him to become the idol of the masses, for, despite a close watch by the police, he kept the whereabouts of his printing press a secret for six years. Legends grew about it, and the police were never certain if it really operated within Russian Poland or whether copies of the *Robotnik* were being smuggled into the country.

One of Pilsudski's most courageous helpers was his first wife Maria, particularly in the distribution of the banned journal. " Boyish " figures were not fashionable then, which was as well for the conspirators ; for Maria Pilsudski sometimes secreted as many as seventy-five copies of the journal on her person.

At length, in February, 1900, when Pilsudski was living at Lodz, the great textile centre, the police discovered the printing press hidden away in a cupboard in Pilsudski's flat. He was condemned to ten years' imprisonment.

After a term in Lodz prison he was sent to the Citadel at Warsaw, which he entered with some elation because it was an institution closely associated with the Polish martyrs of freedom. His life there was not entirely unhappy, but his supporters did not intend that he should languish for a decade in a Russian prison, and plots were hatched for his escape. He was confined to the notorious tenth pavilion, reserved exclusively for political prisoners, from which escape was a physical impossibility. First it was necessary to secure his transfer to a more accessible place. As an incurable disease would cause this to happen, Pilsudski was instructed by matchbox messages to feign madness and persecution mania. In accordance with instructions, the prisoner registered distress and panic at the sight of the gaolers, and ceased to eat food, which, he explained, his enemies might have poisoned. After a time it was contrived that the director of a certain lunatic asylum should examine the prisoner. This doctor had been in Siberia with Pilsudski and they spent a delightful hour together talking of their old friendship. A report was submitted that the prisoner's mental state was due to the conditions in the tenth pavilion and that with better surroundings, which the citadel could not supply, he would return to complete sanity. So Pilsudski was transferred to St. Petersburg to the section of the Asylum of St. Nicholas the Miracle Worker reserved for political offenders. From here the Polish Socialists confidently counted on being able to arrange for his escape.

A medical student and Socialist of St. Petersburg University named Mazurkiewicz, agreed to sacrifice his own career in an effort to set Pilsudski free. On the pretext that he wished to specialise in mental disorders, he obtained the position of house surgeon at the asylum. One night when the head physician was out, Mazurkiewicz ordered an attendant to bring Pilsudski to his consulting-room for a prolonged examination. A disguise for the prisoner had been arranged, and he made a hurried change. Then the doctor and Pilsudski passed safely into the outer world and made for Kieff where the *Robotnik*, still fomenting the Polish movement for independence, was then being printed. Although he could only remain for one night the former editor took a hand once again in the setting-up of the type. He was reunited with his wife and the two were smuggled over the Austrian border.

When the Russo-Japanese war broke out in 1904, Pilsudski went to Tokio to ask the Japanese Government for assistance in forming a Polish Legion to fight against Russia, but he was unsuccessful. During the revolutionary troubles of Russia, when the war with Japan went wrong, he regarded himself as being at war with Russia and with a handful of exiles under his command engaged in guerrilla warfare.

From such small beginnings something great emerged. He became to the Russians what Lawrence of Arabia became to the Turks—the embodiment of cunning, an elusive, legendary brigand chief. Round him the Polish patriots gathered, to take part in impudent, pillaging raids into Russian territory. The most famous raid occurred in September, 1908, at Bezdany, and he led it in person. In this coup he held up a Russian mail train and came away with two million roubles. No wonder his ragged little army esteemed themselves the greatest heroes since John Sobieski as they hurried away into Austrian territory with their haul.

As Pilsudski's supporters grew his ideas expanded. He realised, however, that there was only one thing which could ensure Polish independence, pin-prick the Russians as he might. That thing was a war in Europe, with Russia on the losing side. By the spring of 1914, incidentally, he had made a speculative disposition of the nations for that war. In a lecture in Paris, he declared that the independence of Poland could only definitely be solved when Russia was beaten by Germany, and Germany was beaten by France.

Having the permission of the Austrian authorities, he drilled his tiny army and applied himself to the study of the military art with great thoroughness. The years passed ; the time for the greatest clash of nations the world has ever known drew near. Pilsudski's little force of some two thousand men was wretchedly equipped, its arms were those discarded by the Austrian army—still, it could cause Pilsudski's breast to expand with pride when he contemplated it : it was a Polish army, the first that his country, once a race of warriors, had had for many years.

On August 6, 1914, Austria declared war on Russia. Pilsudski was ready. He launched one hundred and seventy-two men across the Russian frontier immediately, and followed himself with another two thousand—a modern version of David against Goliath.

4

Events move fast for Poland during the World War. Pilsudski never allows himself to forget that he must not become involved in other nations' troubles. The " miracle of the Vistula " saves Europe from the Bolsheviks.

The world lost its head in 1914—but not Pilsudski. That must be emphasised. While the dance of death continued he kept his eye steadily on his object, never allowing his gaze to be diverted though nations reeled. That object was Polish independence. It would serve little purpose to reconstruct the chaos and confusion that surrounded Pilsudski in the World War. The important thing is that he knew what he wanted, and got it. Although he sided with the Central Powers he insisted from the first that he should not be sent to the Western front. He considered himself to be fighting for the Polish cause, and for that alone, on Polish soil. Following the great Austro-German attack against the Russians in May, 1915, Warsaw was taken by the Germans. In September, 1916, Pilsudski resigned his leadership of 18,000 Polish legionaries following Germany's suppression of Polish institutions in Warsaw. In November of that year the Austrian and German Emperors proclaimed the independence of Poland. A few days later an Austro-German proclamation called for recruits for a Polish army to fight under German leadership. Pilsudski had rejoiced at the first proclamation, if only because it raised the issue he was fighting for on to an international plane, but the demand for a Polish-German army aroused his wrath. Although he had resigned his command, he hastened to harangue the Polish Legionaries on the folly of becoming involved in another nation's troubles. "Russia is beaten now, and we must fight Germany," was his advice.

Germany's reply was to disband the Legions and to arrest Pilsudski on July 22, 1917. He was imprisoned in the fortress of Magdeburg. One satisfaction at least he could nurse during incarceration, which was that the Powers were not now blind to Poland's hopes. For President Wilson had listened to the pleadings of Paderewski, the Polish pianist, who was on a visit to America, and on January 22, 1917, he made use of these words in his Message to Congress : " I take it for granted that statesmen everywhere are agreed that there should be a united, independent and autonomous Poland."

The end of the War drew near. The Central Powers collapsed completely. On November 11, 1918, Pilsudski, who had been released from the fortress of Magdeburg, made a triumphal return to Warsaw and took over supreme power from the Council of Regency. Three days later he notified the Governments of the world that a Polish Republic was in being. He was in control as Chief of State until a constituent assembly could give Poland a constitution.

While Pilsudski was reorganising the national defences at

home, his Prime Minister, Paderewski, was rendering patriotic service at the Peace Conference in Paris. Music had won recognition for Polish independence which the force of arms and the processes of diplomacy could not have gained.

The thirteenth of President Wilson's fourteen Points was that " an Independent Polish State should be erected which should include the territories inhabited by an indisputable Polish population, which should be assured free and secure access to the sea, and whose political and economic independence and territorial integrity should be guaranteed by international covenant."

Wilson meant well, but at the Peace Conference the phrasing of this Point caused interminable argument, with the words " indisputable Polish population " as the chief source of disagreement. Poland had her own ideas on what should become her territory—in a word, as much as possible. Her enemies and neighbours naturally resisted her demands. In the end the Peace Treaty provided that Danzig should become a Free City and that there should be a plebiscite in Upper Silesia. Poland secured access to the sea through the Polish Corridor, soon to be the cause of bitter friction between her and Germany.

With the Allied Powers, Pilsudski was suspect. In those days Europe was witnessing the emergence of Bolshevism, following the Russian revolution and the killing of the Tsar. The Allies were fearful of the new Communist enemy, fearful that other countries in Europe might go Bolshevik. Pilsudski had been a Socialist ; therefore he was identified with Bolshevism.

However, he soon demonstrated that the suspicion was misplaced, when, after a quarrel with Russia over frontier limits, he launched an army against the Bolsheviks.

All went well until the Bolsheviks, having crushed most of the " White " armies fighting against them, were able to give undivided attention to the Poles. They attacked, and surprisingly Pilsudski was forced to retreat three hundred miles in a month. Poland's position grew desperate, for now it looked as if she must be engulfed in the new Russia. The enemy swept on, with the wish not merely to conquer, but to spread their gospel of Communism. " The destinies of the world revolution," proclaimed their General, " will be

settled in the West. The way towards world-wide conflagration passes over the corpse of Poland." The Russians
pressed back the Poles towards Warsaw. Poland sought the
help of the Powers. The Bolsheviks made representations
which were backed up in England and France by Socialists
who threatened direct action in support of the " Hands-
Off-Russia " movement.

In August, 1920, the Bolsheviks began the encirclement of
Warsaw. Their patrols advanced to Praga, a Warsaw
suburb on the eastern bank of the Vistula. There was
fighting not far from the gates, and then, when hope was all
but abandoned, there was a dramatic change in Polish
fortunes : the "miracle of the Vistula " occurred. Pilsudski
waited on the enemy's flanks and then struck north, cutting
off the invaders from their base. By August 18, he had scored
an overwhelming success and won what Lord D'Abernon
has called the " eighteenth decisive battle of the world,"
since it stemmed the advance of Bolshevism into Europe.
Warsaw was saved and the Bolsheviks were routed, 60,000
being taken as prisoners. Their fourth army had to pass into
Prussia, where it was disarmed.

The Battle of Vistula was a startling success for Pilsudski,
and although his critics have said that the French General
Weygand was the real brain behind the victory, there is no
doubt that Pilsudski fully deserves the title of saviour of
Poland. Soon the Bolsheviks were rolled back well beyond
the frontier line drawn by the Allies, and the Riga Treaty
of March, 1921, helped to compensate the Poles for the
revision their claims to territory had undergone at Versailles.

On the close of the war with Russia the party " dog fight "
in Poland was resumed, with the Constitution as the bone of
contention. The victorious and overbearing Marshal found
himself confronted with the obstinate politicians, who
suspected and feared him. Before the new Constitution came
into force, Pilsudski was Chief of State under the authority
of the " Little " Constitution, and his struggle with his
enemies of the Right so embittered him that when the
Constitution was passed he refused to stand for the Presidency. Because they feared that he would abuse his
position, his opponents had imposed numerous and
effective restrictions on the power and prerogatives of the
President.

Poland's first President, Narutowiez, held office for two days and was assassinated. Wojciechowski was elected to succeed him, and with him Pilsudski soon had differences of opinion. The Marshal gloomily watched the unpleasing spectacle of Polish politics and the strife of many parties bickering and delaying while the work necessary for the creation of a new Poland remained undone. In June, 1923, after resigning as Chief of Staff and President of the Supreme War Council, he withdrew entirely, refusing to be associated with affairs which were going wrong, but in which he was powerless to intervene. The Marshal was solemnly voted an expression of the Seym's appreciation of his meritorious service to the nation.

In retirement Pilsudski lived the life of a comparatively poor man, refusing to spend the pension the State had granted him, and supporting himself by his pen. But he did not cease to watch Poland's political affairs closely.

Crisis followed crisis and ministry succeeded ministry. The national position became grave ; the country's finances were in a critical condition and a feeling of unrest was abroad. Yet another cabinet fell, and Witos, for the third time, became head of the ministry. General Maczewski was placed in charge of the War Office, and as this Maczewski was Pilsudski's old enemy the Marshal's friends in the army feared that they would lose their places. There were even fears for Pilsudski's personal safety, and it was reported that he had been shot at. From several regiments came a summons to Pilsudski to quit retirement, and at length he was persuaded to answer the call. At the head of three regiments he marched on Warsaw. Troops were sent out against him, but he seized Praga. There was a meeting between the President and the Marshal, who demanded that the Witos Ministry should be dismissed. The President refused. The Marshal was determined to impose his will, and civil war was the result. Fighting was short, but sharp, about six hundred persons being killed in the three days' fighting, which ended with Pilsudski's entry into Warsaw on May 14, 1926.

5

Pilsudski tries his luck at the polls, and in 1930 *succeeds in getting an absolute majority.   The vision of him that remains is that of a great patriot.*

Once again Pilsudski surprised his supporters by refusing to take office as President.   Instead, he secured the election of a friend as President and himself became Minister of War.   Then began Pilsudski's reign as veiled dictator.   His ministry was out-voted in the Seym, but the man who controlled the army and the police controlled Poland.   When the Ministry was twice defeated Pilsudski himself took office as Premier.   For two years Pilsudski ruled the State in the face of hostile parliamentary majorities, treating Parliament with contempt.   He denounced the politicians as renegades and worse, as men who were endangering Poland's existence.   To mark his disgust at the inefficiency of the Chamber, he resigned the premiership and returned to the War Office, and from this, his favourite post, he continued to guide the affairs of the republic through a cabinet of colonels.

The Government Party which he organised obtained a quarter of the seats at the polls in 1928.   Two years later, by methods which estranged democratic opinion abroad, he gained an absolute majority in both houses.   About his methods there is this to be said :   Poland during the transitional years had been in a state of political deadlock, and if the uneducated electorate had confirmed the position, Pilsudski might have found that his only course was to sweep away every trace of democratic government.   Instead he applied pressure and emerged as the chosen of the people.   Immediately he had obtained his majority he announced that his main task would be to reform the Constitution[1] and in these racy words summarised a state of affairs that had angered him for years :   " Since the May revolution I have tried to induce our Ministers not to worry about little formalities.   The time of a legislator and a Government should not be spent on intricate technicalities and legal quibbles.   Unfortunately I always have in my way a lawyer who tears

[1] The new Constitution came into force in April, 1935, a few weeks before Pilsudski's death.

his hair for all his bald-headedness. Believe me, when I was harping so often on the attempts of the former Deputies to be not only arch-President, but arch-chauffeur, arch-engineer, and arch-tram-conductor I had always before my eyes the tremendous misfortune of our country in having no proper divisions of sanctions between the President, the Government and Parliament. " The new Seym will have to accomplish a far-reaching limitation of its own competence in order that it may cease to have a finger in every pie and may give the Government a free hand to settle commonplace affairs. That is all."

The vision of Pilsudski that remains is of a man who chastened his country for what he considered to be his country's good. In short, a great patriot—the Cromwell of Poland.

IV

DICTATORSHIP IN RUINS

FRANKLIN DELANO ROOSEVELT

1

President Roosevelt, the unconstitutional despot, broke the Constitution on a magnificent scale until four poultry dealers went to law against the New Dealer.

IT is plain enough now that President Roosevelt *was* a dictator. Until the judgment of the Supreme Court on the validity of N.R.A. the matter had been in doubt.

According to his friends, Mr. Roosevelt was no dictator. According to his critics he was. They have uneasy consciences about dictatorships in the United States. They mistrust dictatorships with the mistrust which by repute is assigned in England to coalitions. Mr. Roosevelt was not lightly to be pronounced dictator. It was a matter on which opposing arguments had carefully to be weighed.

But since the judgment of May 27, 1935, all this has been changed. Doubts have been set aside. The Supreme Court made his position unequivocally clear. Mr. Roosevelt's claim to inclusion amongst the world's dictators was in effect proclaimed by the highest judicial authority in the forty-eight states. That he had been exercising despotic powers was plain before. After the judgment it was manifest that his despotism was unconstitutional. He had derived his authority from Congress, but Congress had granted powers not in its power to bestow.

Mr. Roosevelt, in fact, was an unconstitutional despot. His dictatorship offended against the Constitution more gravely, perhaps, than those of Hitler and Mussolini. And the judgment which proclaimed his dictatorship to the world left that dictatorship in ruins.

In the world of politics there is nothing more paradoxical than this conclusion to the first stage of Mr. Roosevelt's Presidency. His dictatorship, as we shall attempt to show in the sequel, was an attempt to restore American democracy. For three years he laboured on his New Deal which would restore the old prosperity to American industry and the vanished purity to American politics. The Supreme Court destroyed the labours of three years. It terminated the dictatorship, but it is to be doubted whether the judgment will be to the advantage of American democracy. It may—it may not.

The judgment brought a chapter to the end. The next chapter depends upon the strength and skill of the Presidential player. The New Dealer must deal again. If he can secure a legal and constitutional basis for continuing the designs of his first deal, if America can be led onwards towards the ideal he set before it, there will be confidence that all will be well. If the letter of the Constitution proves a permanent obstacle to advance, if there is a reversion to the conditions before the New Deal began, then the future will be full of doubt.

In the collapse of the New Deal the English observer will have found the latest cause for satisfaction with his own Constitution. The post-war dictatorships have been political expedients to which various countries have been driven as a means of finding a solution of the problems of these crisis years. In the United States of America, as in the Republic of France, the written Constitution has been an obstacle to the adoption of measures to meet the crisis.

In England there are no binding fetters of a written constitution. Our system is supple. We formed our National Government and we took the measures which we thought to be expedient. We stretched the doctrine of collective cabinet responsibility. There was no Constitution to forbid it.

In America they stretched the Constitution, and now it is seen that the Constitution cannot be stretched. Where our constitution is supple, theirs is rigid. Where we can make changes as circumstances require, they are fettered and can change only with difficulty. You may drive a coach and horses, so they say, through an English statute, but Mr. Roosevelt found that not all his energy would drive

" By means of the radio President Roosevelt keeps himself in closer touch
with the people than any American statesman before him."

a New Deal through the American Constitution. The
Supreme Court upset the coach, and now, in the President's
phrase, they are back to " horse and buggy days "—and he
spoke as a man who realised the limitations of the horse and
buggy in the age of the automobile.

The strict constitutionalist must rejoice at the vindication
of the law. As the world advances institutions must be
modified, but modification must be accomplished by constitutional means, for only in the Constitution is there an
assurance to be found for the preservation of rights and
liberties. With the growth of disrespect for the Constitution
the way of the dictator begins.

The vindication of the Constitution in America has
revealed its limitations, and the American Constitution
cannot easily be amended. Nevertheless, this amendment
must be secured if Mr. Roosevelt is to carry out the policy
of the New Deal. To this there are forty-eight obstacles—
the forty-eight States of the Federation, forty-eight " Little
Empires " which must be induced to sacrifice their independent sovereign right before the Federal Government can
legislate for the entire federation on points affecting national
social and economic problems

The constitution makers of 1787 decided in their wisdom
on a clause to prevent the creation of tariff barriers between
the various States. In the year 1935 this clause operated
as barrier to the Federal Government in fixing codes to
regulate hours and wages and to establish principles of fair
trading throughout the country.

Congress delegated to the President the power to promul-
gate rules for the conduct of business, but in so doing it
exceeded its own powers. " It is sufficient to say," pronounced the Chief Justice, Mr. C. E. Hughes, in his laconic
phrase, " that the Federal Constitution does not provide
for this."

No more staggering blow has ever befallen a Government
than that which was dealt to the New Dealer by the Supreme
Court. Mr. Roosevelt was at the very moment engaged
upon the task of providing for the extension of N.R.A. for
a further term. He could look back with a fair measure
of satisfaction upon the benefits which N.R.A. had produced;
he could look forward with a fair measure of confidence to
the extension of the benefits in the future. Then came the

devastating decision reached by the Court in the case of
the four brothers Schechter. The poultry dealers who had
violated the provisions of fair dealing under one of the
codes of N.R.A. smashed the New Dealer. Not since the
Capitol was saved from the Gauls by a gaggle of geese had
poultry played so prominent a part in history.

It says much for the steadiness of the American national
character that with so little disturbance it survived the
shock of the discovery that the President and Congress had
for three years been breaking the law of the land on so
magnificent a scale. It was a crisis from which worse than
chaos might immediately have resulted. The ordinances
which had regulated American industrial life, the paying
of workmen, their hours of labour, the production and selling
of goods were declared illegal, to have no binding effect
upon employers and employed, producers and salesmen
upon whom they had been imposed. It was not a mere
question of diseased poultry. It was the entire structure of
American industrial and economic life. The judgment
that re-established the Constitution destroyed N.R.A., and
all its subsidiary institutions, its boards, its administra-
tions, its authorities, its agencies, its codes, its control
over alcohol, over electricity, over agriculture, over labour
relations.

The President could do nothing to save his cherished
institutions from the legal wreckers. He and his advisers
and the country at large had to look upon the ruins in
amazement, with regret and disquietude.

It is already apparent that the Supreme Court judgment
has given a new orientation to American politics. There
must be a new alignment of political forces. The arena has
been cleared for a new fight. There will be new battle
cries. There will be need for new catch words for Senator
Huey Long and his " Share the Wealth movement," and
Father Coughlin[1] and his Union of Social Justice, if these
demagogues are not to suffer eclipse. The new issues will
transcend these, but they are for the future. In the past

---

[1] Senator Huey Long promised by his " Share the Wealth "
agitation to provide lavish old-age pensions, free university
education for all, and the abolition of unemployment by shortening the hours of work. Personal fortunes would be limited to

are the achievements of President Roosevelt's dictatorship, of which the survey that follows now becomes an obituary notice.

2

With the collapse of the American banking system the Roosevelt Revolution began. Under the President Reformer, get-rich-quick methods received a check.

To Franklin Delano Roosevelt belongs the credit for having attempted more to change the lives of millions of his fellow-countrymen than any statesman in history without violent change and bloodshed.

It was only a few months from the time when Mr. Roosevelt was a State governor—virtually unknown on the European side of the Atlantic—until he had flashed on to the international scene as a New Messiah. No one knew what he would achieve in his new eminence, but a new spirit of confidence swept across America.

Mr. Roosevelt's smashing victory in the Presidential campaign of 1932 was not so much a triumph for his own policies as a crushing defeat for Mr. Hoover and the " Old Gang." The country had inspected Mr. Roosevelt and liked the look of what it saw. He represented a new type of politician for America ; some were inclined to scoff at him as a mere idealist, but to the vast majority of voters the choice was a simple one—the Old Gang or something new.

Seldom in history was the stage more opportunely set for a reformer. Most Americans had lost so much that they felt they could not lose more even if the New Deal proved a failure. The Presidential campaign of 1932 was conducted

three million dollars, and personal incomes to one thousand dollars, and every deserving family would receive five thousand dollars. He claimed to have four million followers. Father Coughlin gained fame by his addresses over the radio on Sunday afternoons. He founded the Union of Social Justice to denounce private finance and the profit system and advocate a currency which would not change in purchasing power. He gained three million adherents, each registered under their district of residence.

with extreme skill. Mr. Roosevelt did not promise too much. He knew that every American in the country had contracted a stiff neck looking round the corner for prosperity at Mr. Hoover's behest. In frank, almost conversational talks, he addressed himself to the " Forgotten Man." Every citizen of the United States saw himself in the part ; the Roosevelt spell-binding technique had scored its first victory on the national scene.

Not even Herbert Hoover's most enthusiastic friend could describe his platform manner as picturesque. Both in appearance and outlook Mr. Roosevelt's opponent had the misfortune to be the personification of " Wall Street." At that stage it was not, as it became later, synonymous with abuse to suggest that any prominent American was a typical inhabitant of New York's principal business thoroughfare. But, as one would expect, the average mid-Western voter is not a great economist. He considered his own situation and drew his own rough and ready deductions. All that counted to him was that Herbert Hoover stood for the old order. In the last three years the mid-Westerner's farm had been heavily mortgaged, his son in the city had lost his job, he could not get a profitable price for his wheat and the bank where he kept his money was likely to close down at any moment. Such were the benefits, he reflected (not without injustice), which the old order had conferred upon him.

On the other platform stood Mr. Roosevelt. The voter did not know much about him, but he remembered Teddy Roosevelt with affection ; the name was as good a trade mark as an American politician could desire. The voter went to see the Democratic candidate at one of his meetings during the electoral campaign. Under a baking sun he saw a man, hatless but showing no signs of strain, talking quietly and confidently about the " more abundant life." He had heard that Mr. Roosevelt was a cripple : when he saw him he found that difficult to believe. It was true the future President did not walk about as he spoke. He stood leaning against a table with his full weight on his arms. But with his powerful frame, resonant voice and his mobile, expressive face, Mr. Roosevelt did not need to stamp about the platform. Always cheerful, he was the " Happy Warrior " incarnate.

In an age of "isms," how should we class the political philosophy for which this American presidential dictator has stood? Mr. Roosevelt himself, defining the nature of the New Deal, defended it from charges of Fascism and Communism. Americans have a passion for labels. Every new movement must be given a tag ; if no suitable word exists to describe it, then a new one must be coined, and preferably as long a word as possible. It was for this reason that one of the last ready-made remedies for the depression was christened "Technocracy." The word meant nothing in particular, but it was soon accepted and achieved such popularity that to-day no political writer in America ever uses the word "technical." In its place he calls mechanical and other matters "technological." It means no more than the older word, but the American reader, seeing it, attaches more significance to the technicalities in question. As soon as the New Deal began, writers sought to find a suitable high-sounding name by which to label it. The fact that within a few weeks it was attacked both as Fascism and as Communism was an indication how hard the Republican leaders were trying to find a catchword for it and how baffled they were by the unconventionality of Mr. Roosevelt's political outlook.

"It is not Fascism because its inspiration springs from the mass of the people themselves raٍher than from a class or a group or a marching army," wrote the President in the foreword to his book *On Our Way*. "Moreover it is being achieved without a change in fundamental republican method. We have kept the faith with, and in, our traditional political institutions. Some people have called it Communism ; it is not that either. It is not a driving regimentation founded upon the plans of a perpetuating directorate which subordinates the making of laws and processes of the courts to the orders of the executive. Neither does it manifest itself in the total elimination of any class or in the abolition of private party."

There was no ready-made peg on which the Roosevelt Revolution could easily be hung. Over and over again, when pressed to explain his plans, the President compared the work of his government with a game of American football. A plan of campaign is prepared before the match ; the play is frequently interrupted and the contestants " go into a huddle," in which they endeavour to determine their course of action for the next few minutes.

When Mr. Roosevelt first came into power, he briefly summarised the principal steps which he considered it essential to take without delay if America's social and economic life were to be rebuilt. His programme roughly divided itself into three parts. First was the necessity to eliminate by drastic measures special privilege in the social and economic structure by a numerically small but very powerful group of individuals who were dominating business, banking and the very government itself. Next on his programme was war on crime and graft, accompanied by a crusade " to build up moral values." Third, by some means or another it was the desire of the administration to seek a return of the swing of the national economic pendulum. For three generations it had been sweeping towards a constantly increasing concentration of wealth in fewer and fewer hands. What was sought was a swing back in the direction of a wider distribution of the wealth of the nation.

The New Deal was America's political reformation, the revival of her democracy. A century and a half ago Jefferson held it self-evident that " all men are created equal ; that they are endowed by their Creator with certain inalienable rights ; that among these are life, liberty and the pursuit of happiness." In the days when America still stood to the Old World as an Eldorado, when the frontier was ever expanding farther and farther westward and every settler had as good a chance as his fellow, the American Ideal was vigorous and practical in its application. But the building up of vast fortunes in the second half of the last century, the steady stream of immigrant Jews, Poles, Italians, Scandinavians and Germans, and the increasing conviction among Americans that there was no difference between value and price, all combined to make the honour paid to democracy largely a matter of lip-service. The outward and visible signs of a democracy remained, but they were formalities. Into the hands of the richest in the land there had gathered immense power over their poorer fellows. It is only in these latter days that Americans have been prepared to admit that the old tradition of " rugged individualism " does not necessarily dovetail with the " pursuit of happiness " by the majority. The Anti-Trust laws were a sign that even Congress had discovered there was a difference between liberty and licence. But it was not until Mr. Roosevelt entered the White House that an attempt was made to grapple with the ruthless character of the ethical code subscribed to by the industrialists, bankers and financiers who had been the real rulers of America for the previous generations.

It may be difficult for the English reader to appreciate either the esteem in which " Big Business" was held before 1929, or the peculiar conditions in which its magnates worked. It must never be forgotten that a large proportion of the citizens of the United States have had only one goal—to make the maximum of money in the minimum of time. This is the explanation of the Florida land boom and other phenomena of the " get-rich-quick " society which to the Englishman seem as incomprehensible as the South Sea Bubble. Gambling on the stock exchange (which in the United States is called " playing the market ") is as popular as betting on horses in England. The bellboy, the news-vendor at the corner of the street and the bootblack all speculated their savings throughout the boom years. Credit ran wild, high-pressure salesmen hawked doubtful securities from door to door, banks recommended issues without investigating them, wages soared and new sky-scrapers shot up with them ; there was a car to every six persons in the country.

The orgy of speculation had much to do with the origin of the depression and intensified the miseries brought in its wake, but it was by no means the root of the trouble. This is not the place for a treatise on international economics, but the problems which faced Mr. Roosevelt in March, 1933, and the necessity for the steps which he took cannot be appreciated without at least a reference to the dimensions of the crash. In England the decline in industrial production at the worst stage of the depression was less than 20 per cent. In America it had sunk 20 per cent by 1930 ; a year later it had sunk $33\frac{1}{3}$ per cent, and by June, 1932, production was less than 50 per cent of the 1929 level. Wholesale prices fell by one-third, pay-rolls by 60 per cent and factory employment by 40 per cent. America found itself with thirteen million persons—more than one-tenth of the population—out of work. It was said in 1932 that stocks had dropped so low that it would have been possible at current prices to purchase the control of the greater part of American industry for a sum little more than one-half the war debt owed by Great Britain.

The plight of agriculture was as serious as that of industry. A disastrous discrepancy regarding financial returns had grown up between the two branches of activity. In 1932 agriculture embraced 22 per cent of the population, but the farmers' total income was only 8 per cent of the national income. Between 1929 and 1932 farm prices declined 57 per cent; nearly half the farms in the country were heavily mortgaged. Prices for agricultural produce fell heavily, but the interest the farmer had to pay on the mortgages he had taken out in prosperous years remained unchanged.

Then came the Banking Holiday—the most dramatic moment of the whole depression. Besides the speculative mania to which reference has already been made there were other causes for this final collapse. There was the post-war inflation; American bank loans outstanding in 1919 totalled roughly £5,000,000,000, while in 1929 they approximated to more than £8,000,000,000, credit outstanding having been almost doubled in ten years. At one time there were thirty thousand banking units in America; State laws differed and many were appallingly lax. In consequence, banks failed persistently, over five thousand collapsing between 1921 and 1929, and public confidence in the banking system was slowly undermined. The rush of failures continued. In 1930 a total of 1345 banks closed their doors; in 1931 the number was 2298 and in 1932 it totalled 1456. Then the run on the banks began.

The financial situation in Europe was already most grave and gold began to filter rapidly from New York across the Atlantic. The Reconstruction Finance Corporation was set up by Mr. Hoover to lend Government money to weak institutions, but the run on the dollar continued. Foreign capital was withdrawn in increasing quantities as fear spread abroad that the United States would abandon the gold standard. In October, 1932, the public, which seemed to have been temporarily calmed by the activities of the Reconstruction Finance Corporation, took fright again; hoarding spread and the run on the banks assumed even more formidable proportions.

It has been suggested that the Senate blundered in ordering the Reconstruction Finance Corporation to publish the names of the institutions it had helped, together with the amounts borrowed. It may have been this step which destroyed public confidence, but whatever the cause, the run was resumed, and over a hundred more banks promptly failed. On October 31, 1931, a banking holiday was declared in Nevada ; Iowa, Louisiana, Michigan followed. By March 1, 1932, seven other States had proclaimed banking holidays, and on March 4, the day of Mr. Roosevelt's inaugural parade at Washington, the Governor of New York State followed suit. By next morning every State in the Union had done likewise. On the afternoon of Sunday, March 5, the Roosevelt Cabinet met for the first time.

Weeks previously the President-elect had unearthed a forgotten war-time emergency statute giving the Chief Executive authority in a crisis to close all banks. Mr. Roosevelt was convinced that although the closing was already a *fait accompli*, it was essential to give the bank holiday official endorsement if complete chaos were to be avoided when the normal time of opening was reached on Monday morning. Accordingly it was the first important action of the administration to declare a four days' national bank holiday. Every bank in the nation was shut. The American banking system had collapsed, but the Roosevelt Revolution had begun. The New Deal was called into being to save the old order.

3

The New Deal was an effort to do in four years what might normally have been done in forty. Co-operation in industry instead of unrestrained competition, and public works for the unemployed were bases of the Recovery Act.

The catchword of " the New Deal" served as a cloak for a mass of legislation which was generally assumed to be aimed at the creation of an American Utopia. The details of that legislation the average American did not pretend to understand, and many governmental experts were more in the dark than they would care to admit. Proof of this was forthcoming in December, 1934, when the Supreme Court criticised the laxity with which records of the new laws and regulations had been compiled and made available to the public, which was nevertheless expected to obey them.

A Committee of the American Bar Association estimated that in the first year of the National Recovery Administration alone ten thousand pages of orders issued by various departments became " law " by Presidential edict without adequate provision for notifying the public. The Committee estimated that between 4,500 and 5,000 methods of business conduct were prohibited by the codes and supplementary codes of N.R.A. in that period. It was found that of 6,910 executive orders issued in the nation's history, 1,013 were issued during the first half of President Roosevelt's term of office.

Nothing attested more vividly the position of the dictator in a hurry. Before he had time to settle down in the White House, Mr. Roosevelt had to take action to extricate the nation from the morass in which it was floundering. His job was to get the wheels of industry moving again, to start people buying and selling things once more, to put back to work some ten million men and women whose idleness meant that about thirty million adults and children were dependent upon relief, some of which came from the Government and some from private sources.

Mr. Roosevelt had to deal with the problem which was so urgent that it was bringing the nation to the verge of revolution ; he had to stop the financial panic which was closing banks all over the country and undermining the national credit, and to provide food for families faced by starvation. But he took a wider view of his responsibilities than that. He asked himself whether advantage could not be taken of the crisis with the weakening of conditions that it had caused to reorganise the whole social system on a saner basis.

The phrase " the New Deal," summing up in an ideal manner the hopes and convictions of Mr. Roosevelt and those near to him, seems to have been used without any realisation of its value in a speech which Mr. Hoover's opponent made on the eve of the Presidential campaign, when he accepted nomination at the Democratic Convention in Chicago. As he revised this acceptance speech while flying from Albany to Chicago, no advance copies were given to the newspapers, and correspondents hard pressed for time seized upon the reference to " New Deal " in dashing off their despatches.   In the same way the phrase " Brains Trust " was commonly used after it had appeared without any special hint of significance in the *New York Times*.   Its value was felt to be that it indicated how Mr. Roosevelt in preparing his plans consulted with experts on economic and allied subjects who had had no practical experience of politics.   This taking of academic advice was not a novelty in the United States, but it had never been resorted to before on such a national scale.

Mr. Roosevelt formed a circle of college professors including Raymond Moley, Professor of Public Law at Columbia University, Rexford G. Tugwell, Professor of Economics at the same University, and others such as Hugh S. Johnson, who although he was a retired brigadier-general, had been engaged for many years by Mr. Bernard M. Baruch, the financier, to collect and collate economic data.   This was his intellectual cabinet, his general staff of ideas.

By the time Mr. Roosevelt reached the White House he had a fairly clear idea of what he wanted to do, but it is doubtful if many of his fellow-countrymen realised how revolutionary his plans were.

Many of his proposals, as he admitted towards the end of 1934, in one of the broadcast speeches (by means of the radio he keeps himself in touch with the people more than any American statesman before him) were adopted long ago in supposedly old-fashioned England.   He referred to such proposals for social legislation as old-age pensions.   In fact it has been convincingly argued that the New Deal was only an attempt to accomplish in the United States in a short time what has been done in England gradually, that the New Deal was like a film being run through at top speed.   The New Deal became fairly simple when regarded as an effort to do in four years what could have been done in the previous forty.   What was amazing about it was the apparent change of heart of a whole nation, which was due to the fact that the leaders and philosophers who were formerly trusted were completely discredited in the collapse that followed the years of prosperity after 1929.   Few nations in history had undertaken more courageously the attempt represented by the New Deal to reorganise their corporate life on a new basis.

As Professor Beard put it in his book *The Open Door at Home*, the Recovery Programme "calls upon millions of individuals in industry and agriculture who have hitherto been pursuing their own interests at pleasure, to co-operate in adjusting production, setting prices and maintaining standards—thus making imperative a new economic education on a colossal scale, an education founded on conceptions of collective duties and responsibilities."

The National Industrial Recovery Act, now emasculated by the judgment of the Supreme Court, remains one of the world's most famous pieces of legislation. It was an attempt to substitute orderly co-operation for cut-throat competition in industry and to tackle the unemployment problem by means of a vast system of public works. It gave birth to the Blue Eagle, the sign which was adopted to indicate firms and shops participating in the National Recovery effort, and which received more attention than any other aspect of the New Deal.

In its early tempestuous days General Johnson, the Recovery Administrator, was a national hero engaged in a battle with recalcitrant manufacturers and capitalists to restrain production, largely by means of shorter working hours, and to increase consumption by raising wages. From August, 1933, onwards Johnson proclaimed : " If we don't get heavy industry moving we are sunk." One of Mr. Roosevelt's ways of getting things moving was what is called " priming the pump." The theory was that if the Government started spending money the normal flow of prosperity would be restored. One section of the National Industrial Recovery Bill authorised the President to spend £660,000,000 on public works of every description. That was only one item of the Bill that was later to be presented to the nation.

Estimates of the cost of the New Deal vary tremendously, and often according to the political convictions of the person who tries to make the staggering calculation. The sum of £2,700,000,000 had been appropriated to cover the period from the inauguration of the New Deal to the end of June, 1935, and more than half this vast sum had actually been spent by the end of 1934. At that date the Reconstruction Finance Corporation had advanced about a third of the money spent to railways, banks and industries, and most of it will probably be repaid. Of the balance of the sum spent a quarter was devoted to direct relief, which at the end of 1934 was costing £25,000,000 and more a month, and at least a half to various public works, while farmers received about £200,000,000 for producing less in 1934 than in 1933. Only about half of the emergency expenditure is ever likely to be repaid. At one period the recovery expenditure was at the rate of £6,700,000 a day.

Section 1 of the National Industrial Recovery Act declared a national emergency and provided machinery by means of which any representative trade or industrial association might draft a code of fair competition which would become effective on approval by the President, who was free to amplify and amend it. When he had approved it the code assumed the character of law, and fines could be imposed on persons who violated it. Every employer had to comply with working conditions approved or prescribed by the President, including maximum hours and minimum wages. All the provisions of the Act were to remain in force for two years. Such powers had never been conferred on a President of the United States, but the situation was desperate and as soon as the measure became law General Johnson set to work on the critical task of getting codes adopted by all the leading industries. The whole of American industry was closely if hastily examined and painfully overhauled.

Similar work was done in the agricultural sphere by another of the New Deal's alphabetical agencies, the A.A.A. (Agricultural Adjustment Administration), which by restraining production sought to adjust in accordance with demand and supplies of produce, from cotton to wheat, and from milk to pigs. Indeed, so many special agencies were created by the New Deal that a special Information Service Bureau had to be opened in Washington, and it published a " Digest of the Purposes " of as many as fifty of them. More than 23,000 new civil servants had to be engaged to run them. Amongst the most important besides those already named may be mentioned :

C.C.C.—Commodity Credit Corporation to deal in agricultural commodities and lend or borrow money on them.

E.C.W.—Emergency Conservation Work to provide employment by restoring depleted natural resources of the United States specialising in afforestation. The famous " C.C.C." (Civilian Conservation Corps) under this agency provided nearly 300,000 unmarried young men with healthy work in the forests, giving them an allowance of £6 a month.

F.C.A.—Farm Credit Administration, appointed to provide a complete and co-ordinated credit system for agriculture by making available to farmers loans of every description.

F.A.C.A.—Federal Alcohol Control Administration to deal with the innumerable problems arising out of the repeal of prohibition, which was one of the first acts of the Roosevelt administration.

F.E.A.P.W.—Federal Emergency Administration of Public Works to aim at reducing unemployment and restoring purchasing power through the construction of useful public works of every description and by means of low cost housing schemes.

F.E.R.A.—Federal Emergency Relief Administration to provide for co-operation between the Federal Government and the various States in relieving the hardship and suffering caused by unemployment.

F.H.A.—Federal Housing Administration to encourage improvement in housing standards and conditions.

N.E.C.—National Emergency Council. An important body to provide for the orderly presentation of business to the President, to co-ordinate the work of all the new federal agencies and to serve the President in an advisory capacity. The members included the principal members of the ordinary Cabinet and the heads of the New Deal agencies.

N.L.R.B.—National Labour Relations Board to investigate controversies arising out of the application of the National Industrial Recovery Act in the working of codes.

T.V.A.—Tennessee Valley Authority to supervise what was claimed as the biggest experiment in regional planning ever made outside Soviet Russia. The rivers of the Tennessee valley are being harnessed to provide electric power, a scheme of vital importance in the New Deal firmament, because President Roosevelt made clear his intention of imitating it in other parts of the country, thus striking a mortal blow at the supremacy of the public utilities companies and nationalising to a large extent the production of such primary things as electricity.

Such were the measures taken by the President under the authority unconstitutionally bestowed on him by Congress. It was a magnificent achievement in the re-ordering of a nation's affairs. A large part of the edifice he constructed has already collapsed under the blow of the Supreme Court. The fate of much of the rest was left precariously in doubt.

4

The cripple of the White House is a giant for work and has brought a novel note of informality to his duties. He succeeded in making his Press conferences a sounding-board for his policies.

The moral apathy into which the great mass of the American people had sunk by the end of the Hoover régime was practically a coma. They were convinced that political action could never again be a direct remedy for economic depression. Unemployment was increasing, banks were closed, farmers were starving, while crime, kidnapping and liquor lawlessness were making America a social shambles. And nothing, it seemed, could be done.

Mr. Roosevelt worked on the principal that the one essential thing was Action. It was not of primary importance what action he took ; mistaken action, he believed, was better than no action at all. Of all the qualities which combined to make him ideally fitted to lead the United States out of the depression, none was more valuable than his tremendous energy.

Circumstances had conspired in his favour. Three principal features assisted in his meteoric rise to fame. In the first place he is that rare feature in American politics, a gentleman. It is the people's knowledge that there is nothing of the " go-getter " about him, which was partly responsible for the fact that at the end of his second year in office he was still the most popular man in the United States. Even his brush with Colonel Lindbergh during the air mail contro-

versy—when it was by no means evident that the President
was in the right—did nothing to dim his popularity.

The second favourable factor was his upbringing. It
was one which, though comparatively rare in America,
would be considered usual enough in England for the only
son of a landed family. He was born at Hyde Park, New
York State, the estate of his father, James Roosevelt, on
January 30, 1882. On his father's side he came of a comparatively rich family, and the fact that he has always
been accustomed to a certain amount of inherited wealth
has given him a different outlook on financial matters from
that of most of his predecessors at the White House. His
fifth cousin, Theodore, joined President Grover Cleveland's
administration when Franklin Roosevelt was still a boy, and
became President at a time when Franklin was still young
enough for his ambition to be fired. During his boyhood
he spent much of his time in the country, learning to shoot
and fish and become an enthusiastic naturalist and yachts-
man. He went to school at Groton, which is still perhaps
the best known public school in America, and which bases
its methods on English models. Then he went to Harvard
where he edited the undergraduate magazine, *The Crimson*.
As soon as he had taken his degree he married his cousin,
Eleanor Roosevelt, and studied law at Columbia University,
being admitted to the bar of New York State in 1907.

When in the autumn of 1932 his mother was sitting at
Hyde Park listening to the wireless reports of the Presidential election, one of her guests asked her if she were not
excited at hearing how one district after another had given
her son a sweeping majority. Mrs. James Roosevelt made
an illuminating reply. Her thoughts, she said, had gone
back twenty-two years to 1910, when Mr. Roosevelt had
been running for the State senate. She recalled how she
had been on that day one of the only sympathisers he had
had among his own people. All the friends of his family
said it was shameful and absurd for such a fine young man
to mix himself up in so dirty a game as politics. They
hoped for his own sake that he would be defeated and that
the experience would teach him a lesson. When he won
his seat in the State senate, said Mrs. Roosevelt, they came
to commiserate with her.

If he had listened to his friends' advice Mr. Roosevelt

would not be in Washington to-day. But to him politics
have always represented the most fascinating career open
to a man. Experience at the White House has not made
him change his mind. Enthusiasm, energy and unbounded
zest have maintained him.

The third factor which cannot be overlooked in any
account of Roosevelt is his physique. In August, 1921,
when staying at his holiday estate on the Bay of Fundy, he
was attacked by infantile paralysis. For seven years he
was badly crippled, and he still has to wear metal braces
on his legs whenever he walks, generally leaning on the
arm of an attendant or White House official wherever he
goes. But his general health had always been so good that
after the first few years Mr. Roosevelt became no more of
an invalid than a man who has had a leg amputated. His
illness causes him no pain now, and apart from periodical
visits to the infantile paralysis clinic at Warm Springs,
Georgia (on the endowment of which he spent more than
half his private fortune) and occasional exercises he does
little about it. His nerves have certainly not been affected.

After Zangara had attempted to assassinate him at
Miami he was the least shaken of his party. The story is
told in Washington of how the friends who accompanied
him on his visit to Florida spent the night talking and
smoking, too agitated to go to bed. The following morning
they asked the secret service officer who had been outside
Mr. Roosevelt's door through the night whether the President-elect had been able to sleep. The detective admitted
to having experienced curiosity himself on the same point.
He had slipped into the room several times and Mr.
Roosevelt had been sound asleep every time.

Mr. Roosevelt is the only man who has survived an unsuccessful campaign for that most unenviable of positions, the
Vice-Presidency, and emerged with greater influence than
he had before. In 1920 James Cox (in 1933 he was one of
Mr. Roosevelt's delegates to the World Economic Conference) was the Democrat candidate for Presidency. Mr.
Roosevelt, as a gesture to the Wilsonian section of the
Party, was allowed to run for the Vice-Presidency. Everyone
knew Harding would win the election, and he did. For most
men the unsuccessful candidacy for the inferior post would
have been an inglorious end to a political career. But not

for Franklin Roosevelt. A year later paralysis seized him ; within eight years he was Governor of New York State, and within another five years was in Washington again, not as Vice-President, but as Chief Executive of the nation.

His illness gave him an opportunity to sit back and consider the state of the world—an opportunity which is vouchsafed to few busy men. It taught him to concentrate and deprived him of most of the recreations which might have interrupted his work. The labours at the White House which often prevent him leaving the building for days at a time are consequently less of a hardship to him than they would have been to any of his predecessors.

Throughout his career he has been fearless of criticism and has never hesitated to break with elements in the Democratic Party which he considered undesirable. In 1911, only a year after he entered State politics, he succeeded in blocking the appointment of a Tammany henchman to an important post. This move aligned him with the progressives, who were working to secure Woodrow Wilson the Presidential nomination in 1912 in opposition to a Tammany and Wall Street candidate. Wilson won, and Mr. Roosevelt was given the post of Assistant Secretary to the Navy, which he retained until the end of the Wilson administration in 1920. Roosevelt made an excellent job of his duties at the Navy Building, but he would be the last to deny that it was largely due to his family connections that he was first considered as candidate for the assistant secretaryship. The Wilson contingent was not renowned for social prestige, and Mr. Roosevelt was a distinguished addition to White House parties ; but it was not long before it became apparent that he was more than a cultured diner-out. His insistent advocacy of 110-feet submarine-chasers and a barrage against enemy submarines were both at first denounced as impractical, but both proved valuable when the United States entered the War.

The next stage of his career, as has been pointed out, would have been enough to remove most politicians from the arena. He was persuaded to run for the Vice-Presidency, the Republicans swept the country, and he was attacked by paralysis. For seven years he remained comparatively in the background. But in 1928 came in an unexpected shape his next opportunity. Al Smith was opposing Mr.

Hoover for the Presidency and wanted someone whom he could easily control to succeed him as Governor of New York State. Mr. Roosevelt, an invalid who had to spend weeks on end recuperating in Georgia, seemed to Smith the ideal choice. The Democrats were quarrelling over the nomination, and Al Smith's last-minute suggestion was received with acclamation. A long-distance telephone call was put through to Georgia and Mr. Roosevelt was persuaded at short notice to accept the nomination. But Al Smith had miscalculated. Mr. Roosevelt, as he had planned, was elected Governor, but Mr. Hoover conquered in the Presidential contest. Smith was left high and dry, and, to increase his chagrin, as soon as Mr. Roosevelt was installed at Albany (the seat of government of New York State) he dismissed the Smith myrmidons and set to work to create an active body of supporters of his own. From that time dates the animosity of Al Smith against Roosevelt.

Although his personal popularity in New York remains considerable, Smith is a disappointed man. He sits in his office high up in the Empire State Building, his own dizzy memorial to the departed boom. He built it himself, and so many floors remained untenanted during the early years of its existence that it is still generally known as the "Empty State." It is a safe prophecy that Al Smith will never be reconciled to Roosevelt.

At Albany Mr. Roosevelt gathered round him the corps of secretaries and assistants which became famous when it accompanied him four years later to Washington. It was at Albany also that Mr. and Mrs. Roosevelt began the cult of informality which they brought with them to the White House.

At 8.30 every morning the President is called by his negro valet. He has breakfast in bed, and consults five newspapers while he eats his eggs and buttered toast. Before he rises he generally has a few important appointments, and besides his secretaries one or two of the principal Cabinet or State officials frequently call on him. At ten o'clock he gets out of bed, and after he has dressed, in the oldest suit he thinks will pass muster, he is wheeled to his office. His dislike for formal clothes is typical of the new atmosphere in the White House.

Meetings of the Cabinet are infected by the spirit of

informality. The President addresses its members by their Christian names, and has a telephone in front of him on the table. He does not hesitate to interrupt the meetings by accepting important incoming calls—another innovation which at first troubled the official mind. In some such way, interviewing officials and important industrialists, he passes most of his business day. It may be that in the afternoon he has one of his bi-weekly Press conferences.

Mr. Roosevelt made a study of how to handle journalists when he was at Albany, and when he came to Washington he was in no doubt as to his ability to deal with them. When he announced that he proposed to talk personally to the Press at regular intervals he was assured by the wise-acres that it would prove impossible. Wilson gave up Press conferences ; Harding blundered in discussing international politics and never had another informal meeting with the Press ; Coolidge seldom talked to newspaper men, and when he did declined to allow himself to be directly quoted ; Hoover would answer no questions unless they were sub-mitted in writing beforehand, and then frequently ignored them, exasperating the Press more and more at every conference.

An average of 125 Pressmen attend each of Roosevelt's conferences, and the atmosphere, to the visitor from abroad, seems less like that of a political meeting than of a head-master's tea-party to his favourite pupils. The President has succeeded in making his Press conferences a sounding-board for his policies. He is well aware that newspapers exert more influence in the United States than anywhere else in the world, and no political correspondent could ask for a more sympathetic understanding of his requirements than he gets at the White House. When the President has no urgent news to impart he talks generally to the Press and provides what he calls " background "—information intended to assist appreciation of the fundamental objects of the Government.

Few things are more difficult than to discover where the work of Mr. Roosevelt leaves off and that of his advisers begins. Much has been written of the activities of the " Brains Trust." It is true that Mr. Roosevelt has a larger body of unofficial counsellors at his beck and call than any other President. But the influence of this constantly changing body of financial, political and social experts has been much exaggerated. Republicans and other opponents of Mr. Roosevelt try to describe it as some sinister cabala. In truth, many of the professors who flocked to Washington during the first year of the administration were invited very largely as a sop to public opinion which in America is inclined to place a greater value on self-styled experts than they command in Europe. But for some reason most commentators have failed to draw attention to the extremely important part that has been played in the Roosevelt Revolution by one of the President's advisers—one who has no claim to political prestige, but on whose judgment of persons and on whose talent for grasping public opinion he relies more and more —his wife.

When the Roosevelts first came to the White House, the President's wife was subjected to considerable criticism. Mrs. Roosevelt was so unlike any other White House chatelaine that for a week or so the " cliff-dwellers " (as the politically-minded old ladies of Washington are known by their juniors) were dumb with astonishment. Then they lifted up their voices in protest. Here was a President's wife who shattered convention ten times a day. She held Press conferences of her own with women journalists every week. She rushed all over the country-side at the wheel of her blue two-seater. No one knew when she would next take it into her head to leave the White House and disappear for a day, suddenly to appear unheralded in a mining town in a distressed district and insist on visiting the houses of the unemployed.

The politicians and their wives soon came to realise that the new President's wife was a very real social and political force. It is not surprising that Mr. Roosevelt relies on his wife's judgment so wholeheartedly. He married her when she was twenty and he was twenty-three ; in early days at Albany she never failed to adjust herself to the somewhat trying conditions of a life spent in State politics. When he was taken ill, it was Mrs. Roosevelt who insisted on his remaining in New York where a constant stream of people could call on him every day and ensure that he never faded completely into the political background.

5

" The More Abundant Life " for America.   *The President earns a
name as social reformer and as a crusader for higher moral
values.*

In his Message to Congress at the beginning of 1934,
President Roosevelt summed up the first nine months of
his assault on poverty and depression in the following
terms :

" This programme is an integrated programme,
national in scope.   Viewed in the large it is designed to
save from destruction and to keep for the future the
genuinely important values created by modern society.
. . . We would save useful mechanical invention, machine
production, industrial efficiency, modern means of communication, broad education.   We would save and
encourage the slowly growing impulse among consumers
to enter the industrial market-place equipped with
sufficient organisation to insist upon fair prices and
honest sales.   But the unnecessary expansion of industrial
plants, the waste of natural resources, the exploitation of
the consumers of natural monopolies, the accumulation
of stagnant surpluses, child labour, and the ruthless
exploitation of all labour, the encouragement of speculation with other people's money, these were consumed in
the fires that they themselves kindled :   we must make
sure that as we reconstruct our life there be no soil in
which such weeds can grow again."

At the end of two years he was in the position, unusual
amongst American Presidents, of being able to look forward
with some degree of confidence to a second four-year term
of office.   His experiment had naturally aroused bitter
criticism, although the extent to which he had been
supported, in view of the radical nature of his policies, was
really more surprising than the volume of resentment.
Then came the judgment outlawing the New Deal and the
situation was changed.   The structure was swept away,
perhaps to be renewed later.   There remained the record
of achievement to attest the vision of the social reformer.

As a social force Mr. Roosevelt has earned a reputation which all the judges of the Supreme Court cannot destroy. No one can deny that when, early in his administration, he spoke of the necessity of eliminating crime and " building up moral values " he was about to tackle what his countrymen would call a tough proposition. Since the War, America's average annual crime sheet has included 12,000 murders, 3,000 kidnappings, 50,000 robberies and 100,000 assaults. According to Government spokesmen 400,000 men and women were recently making their living by crime. The jealousy between state and federal authorities made Mr. Roosevelt's task of lessening crime even more difficult ; suggestions that fire-arms be licensed were howled down by local authorities as un-American and violating the liberty of the citizen.

Crime and politics were closely allied in practically every great city ; the public had a despairing way of deriving hearty amusement from the cleverness of crooks who " got away with it." Dillinger's picture was cheered in a Washington cinema during the height of the chase for America's Public Enemy Number One. Prohibition was largely responsible for the contempt in which all too many Americans still hold the law. But by repealing the Volstead Law, exerting all possible pressure to bring a better type of man into American politics and succeeding in considerably increasing the range of the Department of Justice at Washington, while at the same time improving its efficiency, Mr. Roosevelt has progressed appreciably towards his goal.

Special privilege has been eliminated throughout the business and political structure. Mr. Roosevelt has succeeded in giving the pendulum a violent jolt in the direction he sought—that of the more even distribution both of wealth and of influence throughout the nation. Whatever the future may hold, it is certain that Franklin D. Roosevelt will be remembered as one of America's major Presidents.

V

DICTATORSHIP OF THE PROLETARIAT

LENIN AND STALIN

1

The new dictatorship of the proletariat in Russia perpetuates the old despotism with Lenin and Stalin installed in the place of the Czar. The early lives of the revolutionaries.

RUSSIA since 1917 has lived under a dictatorship which has resembled almost more than it has differed from the Czarist autocracy which preceded it. It has been distinguished by a change of title to the official style of Dictatorship of the Proletariat. It has been distinguished by its theoretical basis of Marxian Communism as opposed to Imperial Capitalism. There has been a transformation of the economic scene, but nevertheless the continuation of the methods of political despotism is a link between the old Russia and the new.

Since 1917 Russia has lived under the dictatorship of Lenin, exercised in person until failing health took him from the scene, and then by deputy. Stalin is the name of Lenin's successor, but this personal succession has not been attended by any fundamental departure. For most practical purposes you can regard the rule of Lenin as having continued from 1917 until to-day.

Looking thus upon his career, one becomes impressed by the measure of Lenin's greatness. The dust and noise of acute political controversy obscured the Russian scene for long after his personal disappearance, but the achievements of Leninism are now beginning to emerge. The world can see the new Russian steam-roller, a mighty industrial machine created on the foundations which Lenin laid. It is the monument to the man who died at Gorky in 1924, but whose spirit has continued to animate the new Russia.

" Stalin, the Party man—it is plain enough to see the Party man in
Stalin—followed Lenin as Dictator."

Photographed in his office in Moscow.

Capitalist societies have been forced to reluctant admissions of the achievements of Leninism. Reluctant admissions, too, have been wrung from Socialists who foretold the dawn of the millennium with the rising of the Bolshevik sun. Bolshevism was to bring about the realisation of democratic institutions in their highest form, but now that the full sun of Bolshevism shines upon the Soviet, democrats see that the dawn of their millennium is not yet. Dictatorship of the Proletariat was the phrase that inspired democratic hopes. The democrat sees a dictatorship in Russia exercised not by, but over the proletariat by the new masters of Russia who rule in the name of Marx.

Lenin, no less than Hitler and Mussolini, trampled upon democratic institutions. It is one of the ironies of political history that the revolution in Russia for which men had been striving for a century should have resulted in the suppression of the Constituent Assembly upon which generations of seekers after liberty had focused their hopes.

The revolution of 1917 did not proceed according to the designs of any of the leaders of revolt. It was a revolution without design. It was not engineered by Lenin and the Bolsheviks, by the Mensheviks, the Social Revolutionaries, or the Bourgeois Liberals. Czardom simply faded away. It had survived many assaults. Its continued existence, despite the weight of opposition, was something of a political miracle. And yet its passing, when it came, was unexpected. On its fall its various adversaries sought to exploit the position to their own advantage, and of them all Lenin appeared to be least favourably placed. Various leaders of revolt gained places in the new régime. Lenin and his Bolsheviks were left outside. For a quarter of a century he had been a conspirator against Czardom. For six months in 1917 he conspired against the forces by which Czardom had been supplanted. Then came the revolution within the revolution, and Lenin and his Bolsheviks seized power.

.   .   .   .

The founder of Communist Russia was given no more than five years of life in which to lay the foundations of his new society. He died at the age of fifty-four, worn out by his exertions. The direction of affairs passed to Stalin, who adopted the creed of Leninism as Lenin had adopted the gospel of Marx. The work of rearing the Communist edifice proceeded as if the original architect were still alive. Only in the personnel of the master builders was change conspicuously apparent. As Stalin established his ascendancy, Trotsky's star declined.

Lenin, Trotsky and Stalin—these are the three great names in the establishment of Communism—the architect-in-chief; the man who beat off the foes which menaced the structure the architect was rearing, and the man who completed the edifice in the main to the architect's design; two dictators and the man who failed to be dictator. It is the measure of Lenin's greatness that he had no doubts about including in his team the ebullient and aggressive personality of Trotsky. It is a criticism of Stalin that he had to force Trotsky into exile. Lenin was a dictator whose intellectual supremacy over his fellows was such that by them his dictatorship was accepted unchallenged. Trotsky lacked that effortless superiority. He had push and drive and aggressiveness, but he lacked the political arts to recommend himself to the lesser men around him. Stalin succeeded to the inheritance, a dictator who contrived to make it appear that he did not dictate.

These three men were of the old guard of Bolshevism, underground conspirators, whose spirit of resolution to overthrow Czardom was intensified by detention in Siberia, and was fired anew by participation in the revolt of 1905.

The man known to history as Lenin was born to the family of Ul'yanov on April 22, 1870, and received the names Vladimir Ilyich. His home was at Simbirsk, on the Volga, in the midst of the vast plain of Central Russia. Mongol blood is believed to have flowed in his veins. His father was in the Russian Government service, rising to the rank of Director of Schools, and he became a small landowner. His wife, Maria Alexandrovna, inherited a small estate. Of their six children, Lenin's two brothers and three sisters, five became active revolutionaries at an early age. The eldest son, Alexander, was executed in 1887 for complicity in a plot to murder Alexander III, in which Pilsudski, of Poland, was supposed to have been implicated (see page 189). The loss of his brother was an inspiration to Vladimir Ilyich to dedicate himself to the cause of liberation of the people from the despotism of the Romanovs. He was seventeen at the time, and Karl Marx's *Das Kapital* gave him a a creed for revolt. At the age of twenty-five Lenin (he adopted as his revolutionary *nom de guerre* the name which his brother had used) was arrested after returning from a visit to the revolutionaries in Switzerland with a mass of illegal literature in his possession, plans for the production of a newspaper and a printing press. The result was that he was absent for four years from the political scene, serving a sentence of twelve months' solitary confinement, and three years' banishment in Siberia. His period of exile gave him the time to prepare his book, *The Development of Capitalism in Russia*, and it also enabled him to begin his married life with Nadeshda Konstantinovna Krupskaya, who proved the ideal wife for a revolutionary conspirator. She had got to know him when she was a teacher in a Sunday School, one of the means by which revolutionaries contrived to establish contact with the workers. She was arrested not long after Lenin, and whilst serving her sentence of exile was permitted to join him at the village of Shushenskoye, where their marriage took place.

Lenin was not permitted by the authorities to return to St. Petersburg, and he went abroad to join the circle of *émigrés* engaged from afar off in promoting the cause of revolution in Russia. He returned to take part in the rising of 1905.

Trotsky (Lev Davydovitch Bronstein), nine years the junior of Lenin, was the son of a Jewish farmer of the Province of Kherson. A year after he left school he was arrested for the part he played in organising a workers' union in South Russia. He was sent to Siberia, but escaped and he, too, joined the *émigrés* abroad. He, likewise, took part in the 1905 revolt. He was again sent to Siberia and again he escaped.

Stalin had an equally hazardous career as revolutionary. Joseph Visserionovich Dzhugashvili, in which name Stalin (the man of steel) began his life, was the son of a Georgian shoemaker. He was sent to a theological institution for training as a priest, but was converted to Marxism, and was expelled from the seminary. He joined the revolutionaries, allying himself with the Bolshevik supporters of Lenin. He gained a reputation for his cunning and daring in the execution of dangerous missions. Five times between 1902 and 1913 he was arrested, sentenced to exile, but

contrived to escape. It is difficult to understand how the
political police should never have recognised him as a previous
offender, for with his large figure and raven-black hair, he
is of striking appearance. Had such recognition taken place
the next sentence would have been not to banishment, but to
death. In 1913 he was sent to a place of exile within the
Arctic Circle, and it was the outbreak of revolution which
secured him his release.

2

*Bolshevism was born in London. A party split that makes history.
The Soviets, principal feature of the new Russia, originated
under the Czar, perhaps at his inspiration.*

London, city of finance, anathema to the Communist, may
yet be a Communist Mecca for those who wish to pay
tribute at the last resting-place of Karl Marx, their patron
saint, and at the place of birth of Bolshevism, which came
to be Communism.[1]

In the year 1903 there was a great gathering of Russians in
London at the second Congress in the history of the Social
Democratic Party, which had been formed in 1898. The
proceedings had opened in Brussels, but the Belgian authorities had intervened, and the delegates had to transport
themselves to London, where fuller licence was allowed to
agitators. The Russian Socialists were not to be disconcerted
by this break in the Congress. The Russian agitator was
accustomed to diving underground and continuing in
Geneva what had been begun at Munich. The transfer from
Brussels to London was accepted as a normal incident in the
round of agitation.

All the leaders of the new Russian Socialism had assembled
at Brussels, the men who still found it possible to live in
Moscow or St. Petersburg and indulge in precarious

[1] Karl Marx is buried in Highgate Cemetery. Lenin and
his wife lived in London under the name of Meyer at 30 Holford
Square, to the north of the Euston Road. The British Museum
Reading Room was a working place for both the founder and
prophet of Communism. Lenin also frequented Hyde Park,
where he made a serious study of the speeches of the open air
orators as a means of learning English.

propaganda, and the *émigrés* who had already placed themselves beyond the pale and must produce literature of revolt in the safety of Switzerland or England for circulation amongst the Russian masses.

There was the revered figure of Plekhanov, creator of the Liberation Party, Socialist philosopher with a European reputation, a man of words and theories. There was Vera Sassulitch, the woman revolutionary with a love of terrorism ; Paul Azelrod, who stood for development on the orderly lines of German Social Democracy. These were the seniors of the movement. Then there was Lenin, a younger man who was bringing a new energy and a new practicability to the ranks of the apostles of revolution. A few years before, Lenin had come to Plekhanov at Geneva as a disciple to a master. Konstantinovna Krupskaya, whom he had married in Siberian exile, was now editorial assistant and secretary to her husband in the production of the revolutionary paper, the *Iskra* (the " Spark "), the production of which had been one of the chief occupations of the *émigrés*. It was she who had control of the underground organisation necessary for the importation of this illegal journal into Russia.

Then there was the novice of the revolution, young Leon Trotsky, not long escaped from his Siberian prison. In two and a half years in prison and two years in Siberian exile he had learned the revolutionary ABC and now he was graduating among the *émigrés*.

There were over fifty delegates in all attending this, their Second Congress—fifty men assembled to discuss the means of overthrowing the Czar of all the Russias, the most despotic ruler in Europe. So hazardous was their position in their own country that they had to meet abroad to further their designs. Fifty men against an Empire. It might have been imagined that their weakness and the strength of their adversary would have imposed upon them the need for unanimity. Divergence of opinion is a luxury which only powerful political parties should permit themselves, but it is a characteristic of the agitator that he cannot work harmoniously even with his fellows. A life of agitation brings out a man's beliefs in hard uncompromising lines. Not even the necessities of the campaign could produce unanimity amongst the Russian Socialists in 1903. The Congress which was to have laid down a programme for joint action ended in disrupting forces it had been intended to unite.

The struggle resolved itself round the personality of Lenin, and his policy of uncompromising revolutionary tactics. There were " hard men " and " soft men " in the Congress. " Soft men " under Martov were in favour of action on parliamentary lines, to advance by making use of the aid of parties of the bourgeoisie. The " hards " led by Lenin were opposed to any association with contaminating bourgeois influences ; they stood not for gradual reform but for stark revolution.

The issue was brought to a head on a resolution regarding Party membership. Lenin and the revolutionaries sought the passing of a statute which would make the Party a disciplined centralised organisation, its membership limited to those, and those alone, who would accept the authority of the Executive. Lenin spoke scathingly of the Girondist who babbled about democratic claims and was frightened by the dictatorship of the proletariat ; the Jacobin was the real revolutionary Social Democrat. " Of such stuff Robespierres are made," declared Plekhanov approvingly in support of his disciple. On this resolution, however, Lenin was defeated and the Congress adopted Martov's formula, accepting alliance with the Liberals.

There followed a second resolution proposed by Lenin to the effect that in addition to the Central Committee of the Party in Russia, a second headquarters should be set up abroad ; that this second Executive should carry on publication of the *Iskra*, and be the supreme Party authority. On this point Lenin carried the day by the narrowest of majorities. The vote has passed into history by providing the title of Bolshevik by which the Communist is alternatively known. It was a simple origin for a name which has since sent tremors of alarm around the world. Bolshinstvo is the Russian word meaning majority ; Menshinstvo means minority. On the vital vote in the London Congress, twenty-five voted with the majority, the Bolsheviki, and twenty-three with the minority, Mensheviki, the latter including Leon Trotsky.

It was a division of affairs which persisted, for agitators do not find it easy to compromise. Lenin and the Bolsheviki were left temporarily in control of the organisation. The

Mensheviki declined to accept his authority and formed their own organisation and a campaign was started against Lenin, who was charged with dictatorial methods. Trotsky issued a pamphlet protesting against Lenin's leadership. There was much bitterness and the breaking of friendships. Men who had been associated in the production of the *Iskra* declined to write for it any longer—a strike of generals, in Plekhanov's phrase. Plekhanov had supported Lenin at the Congress, but the man of words and theories regretted the break with his old friends. And when he suggested a compromise to pave the way to their return, Lenin resigned from the editorial board.

The Party split of 1903 was a set-back for Lenin. He found himself almost isolated and deprived of the platform for the expression of his views. His health broke down. His prestige was affected. He did not come to hold the same position of pre-eminence until the fateful year of 1917.

.   .   .   .

There broke out in 1905 the risings which were a dress rehearsal for the final revolution. For a time it seemed that the Czarist régime was to fall, but though gravely threatened it survived. The rising ended in a butchery. It brought Trotsky to a new pinnacle of popularity, and then to Siberia for the second time, from which for a second time he escaped. Lenin, we are assured, gained nothing in personal fame, and he had to fly, an exile once more, sick at heart as never before.

Two lessons he took with him. The first was a practical demonstration of the methods of revolt, and of how to stamp out a rising. The second was of the value and importance of the Soviets—the new councils of the proletariat which had made their appearance.

The Soviet is the essential political organisation of the new Russia but it is not an invention of Lenin, though it was he who made the Soviets an alternative to parliamentary machinery. They originated as the spontaneous creation of the proletariat. The 1905 rising began with sporadic unco-ordinated strikes, and wherever a strike broke out a Workers' Soviet sprang into existence as a local council for the direction of affairs. The Soviet, indeed, is a cell which resembles the Fasci of Italy.

The Czar himself may have been the original inspiration for the creation of this feature of the Communist State. His Government had appointed a commission to inquire into the needs of the industrial workers and sought evidence from the workers themselves. Delegates from St. Petersburg factories had to be chosen and the choice was made by workers' councils. The Soviet of St. Petersburg workers came to have a pre-eminence above all others, with its nickname of the Proletarian Government, and during the 1905 revolt, Trotsky was the moving spirit of this Soviet.

.   .   .   .

3

How the revolution began in Lenin's absence. He returns from exile in a sealed train to begin a new conspiracy by which he disconcerts his followers.

The circumstances of the fall of Czardom in 1917 and the course the revolution took testify at once to the wideness of the range of opponents against the old régime and to their lack of co-ordination.

Successive Czars had declined to relax the completeness of their autocracy which they maintained through the bureaucrats and the police. They would permit no democratic participation in the task of ruling their vast dominions, with their inhabitants exceeding one hundred millions, a complex of many nations. The movement for the grant of a measure of self-government developed in various grades of Russian society—among the landowners, the Liberal bourgeoisie, the proletariat, the Social Democrats and the utter revolutionaries.

Immediately before the War the Czar stood, an isolated despot, amidst a people infected by discontent. Russia was in no condition to stand the long continued stress of a war, which strained even the more highly organised societies of the West. The Allies spoke of Russia's army as a steam-roller. It was a steam-roller only in respect of its ponderosity ; its essential machinery was lacking—equipment, munitions, organisation. Enormous casualties were the result. The *moral* of the fighting forces was in danger. The *moral* of the people was destroyed. Privation gave an added impetus to discontent. Food riots broke out among the population of the capital. Workers in some factories went on strike. The country blundered into revolution. There was no single overt act in March, 1917, to which it is possible to point and say : " Here the revolution began." There was no single body of people upon whom the responsibility can be placed. There was no co-ordinated revolt against Czardom. Rather did Czardom fall because there was no one to prop up its tottering fabric.

The food riots in St. Petersburg early in March were the heralds of the storm. " Give us bread " was the cry of the people in the streets. Revolutionary red flags and placards soon made their appearance. Factory workers were infected by the prevailing unrest. There was some looting of bread shops and Cossacks were called upon to assist the police.

On Sunday, March 11, the Military Governor of the City posted proclamations in the name of the Czar ordering the strikers back to work and calling upon the crowds to disperse. There was some firing on the mob, but the soldiers were reluctant to act as executioners. On Monday 25,000 troops mutinied. There was alarm in the Duma. It was proposed that the Grand Duke Michael should be appointed Dictator of St. Petersburg for the period of the crisis and a new Ministry formed. The Czar was appealed to by telephone to give his consent. He declined.

Events thereupon moved swiftly to their climax. The President of the Duma went to Prince Golitzin, President of the Council, and demanded the resignation of the Ministry. A report that the mob was marching on the Palace caused panic to the Ministers and their resignations were handed in. The country was left without a Government. Only the Duma remained, and this in defiance of the Czar, who had ordered its dissolution. The Duma demanded the Czar's abdication, and Nicholas faded from the scene. It was proposed that the Grand Duke Michael should succeed, but he declined the honour unless it were offered on the authority of a constituent assembly.

A Provisional Government was formed under Prince Lvov, a man whose only recommendation was his personal integrity. The Ministry was a coalition, ranging through various shades of Progressives to the Socialist Revolutionary

Kerensky, an eloquent lawyer and ambitious politician, who came ultimately to dominate affairs. The Provisional Ministry, several times reconstructed, remained in office until Lenin and the Bolsheviks carried out the second revolution.

.   .   .   .

In the month of April, 1917, an observer from the air, had he been minded to look away from the scene of armed conflict on every side, might have seen a train making its way across Germany. Had such an observer made a closer investigation he would have found that the principal occupants of the train were not allowed to make contact with the people of Germany. And the principal occupant of all was Lenin. The train was the historic sealed coach which was bearing him, after years of exile, back for the last time to his native land, back to the last hazards and the final triumph. Lenin and his associates (the thirty-two returning *émigrés* included nineteen Bolsheviks, one of them Zinoviev[1]) were at a pitch of expectation and apprehension. The Czar had been overthrown ; a Provisional Government reigned in his stead. What reception would await a leader of revolt—public acclaim or arrest and prison ?

The hours of the journey were the most anxious of Lenin's life. He had the full length of time occupied in travelling from Zurich to St. Petersburg, over railway systems disorganised by the War, to reflect upon the uncertainties of the destiny awaiting him. The day of the revolution, the day to which he had devoted his life's work, had arrived, but was it the revolution to which his years of striving had been devoted ? The announcement had come to him in exile in the form of a telegram with the brief information that the Czar had fallen ; that Ministers had been put in prison and that an executive of the Duma held the reins of power. There was a manifesto from St. Petersburg recalling in the name of the Provisional Government all exiles who had suffered for their country, but it appeared

[1] Zinoviev, whose real name is Apfelbaum, was so closely identified with Lenin's views that he was called Lenin's gramophone. The Zinoviev or Red Letter played a considerable part in the defeat of the British Socialist Party at the polls in 1924. The letter purported to give instruction to British Socialists to prepare for a revolution.

that there were exceptions to this welcome, and Lenin was among the exceptions. It was not easy for Lenin in a world at war to return to his own land. The Allied Governments had been informed by the Provisional Ministry at St. Petersburg that obstacles to Lenin's return could advantageously be employed. So Lenin looked to Germany. He toyed with the idea that he would pose as a deaf and dumb traveller as a means of getting back to his own country, but was warned against so hazardous an expedient. Approach was made to the German Government, but the negotiations for official sanction to Russian *émigrés* to pass were long drawn out, and it was not until Ludendorff had been persuaded that Lenin's return might work to the ultimate benefit of the German armies that consent was given. The condition was imposed that the Russians should remain in the carriages provided for them during the entire journey and have no relations with the outside world.

It was on April 8 that the sealed coach started on its way bearing a leader of revolt whose expectation was that he would be arrested when he stepped on to Russian soil. On the way he discussed with his friends the terms of the speech he would make in his own defence if he were to be put on trial by the Provisional Government. He reached Finland by train, and crossed by sledge to the Russian frontier, talked with soldiers while he waited, and took train again for the final stage. The faces of all the *émigrés* were grave as they neared their destination. " Shall we be arrested ? " The train came to rest at St. Petersburg Station, and cries rose from the crowd present round the platform. There came the singing of the Internationale and then cheers as Lenin stepped out on to the platform. He had come back to be acclaimed on behalf of the Soviets. " We hope," they told him, " that you will join as part of a united democracy in pursuit of the aims of the revolution." Welcome was expressed to him in the Czar's own waiting-room, and there, in a sanctuary of the old ruler, he proclaimed his faith in the new order. " I see a new soldiers', sailors', workers' vanguard of the army of the proletariat."

It was a triumphal return, and he was borne in honour to a royal palace, a man in threadbare clothes, to share apartments which had belonged to Mathilde Kzeczinska, a *prima ballerina*.

After years of exile and days of anxiety it must have been balm to his soul to have been received as the hero of the hour, but Lenin was not seduced by the pleasures of popularity to depart from his conception of the policy for the Bolsheviks. Mensheviks might make terms with the Government of the bourgeoisie and regard it as a transitional stage to the dictatorship of the proletariat, but Lenin was not prepared to compromise. He had declared at the Congress in 1903 for a revolution and to that policy he remained consistent. It cost him his popularity. Once again he was proscribed by authority. Once more he had to disappear underground, but it brought him to final victory in the days when the men of compromise met defeat.

.   .   .   .

The Bolsheviks in Russia at the time, even Kamenev, Chairman of the Central Committee, and Stalin, newly released from Siberia, entertained the idea of provisional support for the Provisional Government. Hostility to the Government which had succeeded the Czar's Government, and opposition to the War, which still went on, were not points of policy for politicians of St. Petersburg.

Bolsheviks quickly learned that their leader had other views. On the day following his arrival Lenin disconcerted his supporters by the address he delivered at a united meeting of all Social Democrats. His speech was a call to a new revolution. Power, he declared, must be transferred to the Soviets. Congratulations over the revolution were premature. The Government must be turned out for it was an oligarchy. The Government could not be overthrown at once ; the class-conscious minority of workers must win over the majority. Peace for the land and power for the Soviets were his appeals.

The speech was in a key for which the meeting had not been prepared. Lenin's arguments in the eyes of the others seemed scarcely attuned to the needs of the political position. The Social Democrats were indignant. The Bolsheviks were shamefaced. They strove to put forward excuses for their leader—he was but newly returned, he was tired after his long journey. When the speech was read in the papers supporters of the Provisional Government were elated. They had reckoned Lenin to be their greatest adversary, and now, they thought, he had destroyed himself by the extravagance of his views. Plekhanov broadly declared that his former disciple had gone mad. Muliukov rejoiced that his enemy would not recover from the reverse he had brought upon himself. The Government was even reproached by the Social Revolutionaries that it had raised obstacles to the return of an agitator who was capable of as little harm as Lenin.

Kerensky in those days seemed to stand for Russian Socialism. Bolshevism, belying its title, was a minority creed. Lenin was deserted. Only one person of note stood by him—Leon Trotsky, who had not been at his side since the split of 1903. Thenceforth Lenin and Trotsky worked together to rally the forces of Bolshevism to carry out the creed of Marx.

Lenin turned away from the political coteries and addressed himself to the people. For the first time in his life he could stand before the masses in his own capital and deliver in person the message which previously he had only been able to send surreptitiously from abroad. His slogan was : " Power to the Soviets, land to the peasants, peace to the peoples, bread to the hungry." It was just those ideas which expressed the wishes of the people.

Peace which would bring bread was the chief desire in Russia in 1917, but the Ministers in the Winter Palace were making their plans for a new offensive. Kerensky under pressure from the Allies whipped the Russian armies into a new offensive. Brussilov met with an initial success in the field, but when the Austro-German forces attacked, the Russian army retreated in a panic, retreated and began to melt away. Never has there been desertion on so large a scale as in Russia in 1917. The soldiers had a double spur —to put distance between themselves and the enemy and to get back home to participate in the redistribution of the land. Men who lagged in the race for home were spurred by the fear that another in advance would secure the land that he coveted.

The Government needed a scapegoat for their failure and Lenin was to hand. They accused him of being a pro-German, of having plotted with Ludendorff for Russia's defeat. Lenin's arrest was ordered on a charge of high treason. His friends would not permit him to stand his trial ;

it would, they urged, be suicide, for the Government were bent on his condemnation. Back Lenin went to the conspirator's life underground in the disguise of a soldier, peasant or factory worker.

While he led a fugitive existence his party grew in strength. Branches came to number over one hundred and members over 200,000. Lenin's policy was no longer discredited. His vision and foresight were now acclaimed. It was evident that whatever the Ministry and Kerensky might determine, the people were bent on peace. There was growing anger against the Government which had changed nothing, whose policy was still war. There remained only one party not contaminated by association with the Government—the party of Lenin and the Bolsheviks. But they were a minority among the people, not one in fifty of the population. But in the name of the proletariat the minority established dominion over the rest.

.   .   .   .

By the autumn of 1917 the Kerensky Government was bereft of the last shreds of prestige and authority. Kerensky was the shadow of a Minister. He had had his opportunity to mould the new Russia, but power had exposed his deficiencies. An eloquent lawyer, this Kerensky, of undoubted talents, some energy and no little courage ; but something more than these were needed to save Russia in 1917, some driving force and ruthlessness, some purpose withal. He was head of the Ministry now, a Provisional Government which had shed its members of the Right by successive defections. But of what use to be head of a Government if you could not govern ? In his person had been concentrated all the prayers of the revolution. That was in the summer, but now in October he had been left discredited by his quarrel with Kornilov. These two working together, the head of the Ministry and the head of the Army, might have saved Russia, but they placed their ambitions before Russia's needs. Each would have been dictator. Kerensky proclaimed himself as such, and generalissimo as well, dismissing Kornilov, but he was a dictator without the means to enforce his despotism.

From its inception under Prince Lvov the Provisional Government had suffered the fatal handicap of the existence of another and rival power in the land—the Soviets. Back in March the Petrograd Council of Workmen's and Soldiers' Deputies had issued their famous Order No. 1, arrogating to themselves the authority of a government and instructing the Russian forces to accept no orders other than those of the Council of Deputies. The effect on army discipline was devastating. Throughout the summer the influence of the Soviets increased and that of the Government declined. By the autumn Russia was in a state of anarchy. Workmen and peasants had thrown off restraints. Peasants seized the land, workers the factories. The Central Administration collapsed. The bourgeoisie and the intelligentsia sank into a state of lassitude, lacking the energy to organise even in their own defence.

In these months vigour and decisiveness in Russia was concentrated in the Bolsheviks. To them the fading of the forces of the old régime was an inspiration, and the followers of Lenin, unlike their opponents of the bourgeoisie, knew precisely what they wished to accomplish. To secure power they worked through the Soviets, where gradually they advanced to gain a predominant position. At the first All-Russian Congress of Soviets in June, the Bolsheviks were only a small minority, outnumbered by Social Revolutionaries and Mensheviks. By the autumn the Bolshevik representation had been greatly increased, largely through the propaganda in the army, for the Bolsheviks, as the advocates of peace at any price, could offer the most telling of inducements to war-wearied soldiery. The peasants who had seized land and the workers who had taken over factories looked upon the Bolsheviks as the best insurance against dispossession. The Moscow municipal elections in October attested the mounting influence of the Leninites, who returned 500 compared with 248 of other parties.

The final step in the Bolshevik assault was taken in October, when the Petrograd Soviet was induced by its Bolshevik members to appoint a War Revolutionary Committee. Comrade Trotsky was elected to its head. " A staff for seizing power " warned the Mensheviks, but the warning was unheeded. The Committee was contrived so that through its membership tentacles could be thrown out into every force which could be used in the attack on the final citadel of the State—the army, the fleet, the post office, the railways, the telegraphs. There were representatives, too, of factory committees, trades unions, labourers, peasants and of the Presidium itself, the Permanent Executive of the All-Russia Central Committee, the Parliament of Soviets. Under the drive of Comrade Trotsky the War Revolutionary Committee completed the arrangements for securing control of the arms, provisions and garrisons of the capital.

On the last day of October Lenin returned to Petrograd, herald, were it but known, of the second revolution. But there was still a price upon his head, and so, disguised by an ample mass of beard, he remained in the background while Trotsky executed the " categorical " orders of his leader for immediate revolt.

At the headquarters of the War Revolutionary Committee life was " at a boiling point " day and night. Even in the Winter Palace there was a moderate simmering. The would-be dictator by November 4 had been roused to a sense of his own danger. Members of his Government might assure the British Ambassador that they were " quite unmoved " by the reports of the imminence of a rising, and give assurances that the " Government had sufficient forces to deal with the situation." M. Kerensky felt less sure. Infantry and artillery were ordered to hold themselves in readiness and guns were placed to defend the Palace. What use these steps now when troops were no longer responsive to orders from would-be dictators ? Guns might be placed, but they would only be used against the Government they had been provided to protect. Not all the talents of Kerensky could avail now on November 7. Provisional Ministers have had seven months to provide something permanent for Russia and have failed. Now Russia is to be provided with another set of Ministers, much less pro-visional these, who will evolve a permanent order of another sort, not yet tried in the world before. But before that Provisional Ministers will have vanished in the maelstrom that swept away the order of Russian society that they knew.

On November 6 the cruiser *Aurora* was ordered up the Neva to a point where the guns could command the Winter Palace. In the fortress of St. Peter and St. Paul, too, guns were trained on the Government building. There was a final massing of troops and machine-guns at Bolshevik G.H.Q. At 2 o'clock on the following morning the Bolshevik advance was ordered. It was efficiently carried out.

By 7 o'clock that same morning the city was in the hands of the War Revolutionary Committee—the State Bank, stations, post and telegraph offices. The Ministers were surrounded in the Palace, all except Kerensky, who had posted off to obtain assistance from the army. For that it was now too late.

In the afternoon the attack on the Winter Palace was launched by two regiments, a thousand Red Guards, two armoured cars and two guns. It was a leisurely attack. At 6 o'clock the Ministers were called upon by telephone to surrender, but declined. At 7 o'clock the Bolsheviks won over the Cossack Guards from the defence of the Palace. At 9 o'clock some blank rounds were fired from the fortress and the cruiser. They failed to intimidate the Ministers, and the bombardment was begun in which there participated guns brought to assist in the defence, but surrendered to the Bolsheviks. Shortly before midnight the bombardment ceased. The Palace was swept by a barrage of machine-gun fire. Then the attackers poured in. There were hand-to-hand struggles from room to room, but the defenders, though valiant, were outnumbered. They were beaten back down to the cellars and were finally overpowered. In one room fifteen Ministers were discovered. They were placed under arrest. There were cries for Kerensky. The place was searched from attic to cellar and the searchers in their frustration threatened to shoot his Ministers on the spot, but the Ministers were spared and removed under heavy guard to a fortress.

The revolt was complete. Power was with the Soviets now. The greater revolution was to be fulfilled. Out of anarchy and chaos the new order of Marxism was to be brought into being.

4

*Lenin enters into his kingdom and his adversaries are thrown into the
dustbin of history. The destroyer turns creator and begins the
greatest economic experiment in history, having sabotaged
democracy.*

Towards midday on November 7, 1917, the stocky figure
of a man, shabbily dressed, wearing trousers which had
obviously been tailored for a person several inches taller,
might have been seen making his way through the streets
on the outskirts of St. Petersburg. On a public building a
notice was prominently displayed. The walker paused to
read it. It informed him that the Provisional Government
had been overthrown and that power had passed to the
Soviets. The walker continued his way, and in course of
time arrived some distance out of the city before the grim
building of the Smolny Institute, built by Catherine II for
young ladies of birth, but now the headquarters of the
leaders of the proletariat. The shabby figure disappeared
within. It was Lenin entering his kingdom. His life of
agitation was fulfilled. He passed through the threshold to
power.

Within, Trotsky was directing the completion of the
November Revolution. Lenin himself had had no immediate hand in the revolt. Like a generalissimo he had drawn
up the plans for the engagement, and then had stepped
aside for his Chief of Staff to carry them into effect. The
plans were based on the experience of the 1905 risings, and
the success which attended them is a tribute to their conception. A proclamation was issued even while the events
were in progress to inform the proletariat that a new régime
had begun. Citizens of Russia were informed that :

" The Provisional Government is deposed. The
authority of the State has passed into the hands of the
organ of the Petersburg Soviet of Workers' and Soldiers'
Deputies—the Military Revolutionary Committee, which
now stands at the head of the Petrograd proletariat and
garrison. The cause for which the people have struggled,
immediate conclusion of a democratic peace, abolition
of landlord property rights over the land, labour control

over production, creation of a Soviet Government—that cause is securely achieved. Long live the Revolution of Workmen, Soldiers and Peasants ! War-Revolutionary Committee of the Petersburg Soviet of Workers' and Soldiers' Deputies. October 25, 1917. Ten o'clock in the morning."[1]

Almost without bloodshed power passed to the new masters of Russia. The men in the Smolny Institute, conscious that they were starting an experiment the like of which had not been known in history, had not foreseen so simple a conquest.

In the evening in the main hall the All-Russian Congress of Soviets met. The rising had been specially timed so that delegates would assemble to be informed of the accomplished fact of the Provisional Government's over-throw. The fall of the Winter Palace and the capture of the Ministry was announced to the Congress at 2 o'clock on the following morning. There was a new confusion of Babel. Social Revolutionaries and Mensheviks raised bitter voices in complaint that they had been betrayed ; that members of the Government had been placed under arrest. They demanded the formation of a new coalition in which they should be included with the Bolsheviks. Trotsky made a reply to the men who not long before had sought his arrest and Lenin's : " What has taken place," he declared, " is an uprising, not a conspiracy. An uprising of the masses of the people needs no justification. We have been strengthening the revolutionary energy of the workers and soldiers. We have been forging, openly, the will of the masses for an uprising. Our uprising has won. And now we are being asked to give up our victory, to come to an agreement. With whom ? You are wretched, disunited individuals ; you are bankrupt ; your part is over. Go to the place where you belong from now on—the dustbin of history ! "

Into the dustbin of history passed the members of the Provisional Government.

In a room in the Smolny Institute Lenin and Trotsky snatched a few hours' sleep lying on the floor covered with

[1] By the old style Russian calendar it was still the month of October. The Gregorian calendar was not adopted in Russia until February, 1918.

a few blankets. Lenin began the first day of power with a rare admission that he had been moved by the stress of yesterday. " The climb from outlawry and vagabondage is too steep. One gets dizzy," he confessed.

Twelve hours later Lenin presented himself before the Congress of the Soviets to receive the formal mandate of authority. He was still dressed in his shabby clothes and the trousers tailored for a man several inches taller. The delegates received the undistinguished figure with thunderous applause. For once he appeared awkward in the face of an assembly, overcome by the realisation of the hopes to which he had devoted his life. He left the speaking to others. The delegates voted him President of the Council of People's Commissars[1] ; Trotsky was made Commissar for Foreign Affairs, and amongst the other Commissars was appointed Joseph Stalin in charge of Workers' and Peasants' Inspection. The voting being accomplished and the speeches made, Lenin at length rose to make his first speech as Dictator of all the Russias. He proclaimed anew his devotion to the task of building up the proletarian State. To the peasants he promised land ; to the workers control of production, and to one and all immediate peace.

.   .   .   .

Then began Lenin's greatest fight. He had been fighting throughout his life, but hitherto to destroy. Now he had to fight to preserve the new Government which he had called into being, and which had but a precarious hold upon existence. There were enemies on all hands and few courageous defenders. Many of Lenin's colleagues expected to survive only for a short while. He alone had unwavering confidence. There were adversaries around and doubters at his side but always to be gained was the support of the masses, the people who needed peace and bread.

Vera Sassulitch had once described Lenin as being a bull-dog with a death-grip. Trotsky described the same

[1] The Government was alternatively styled " Provisional Workers' and Peasants' Government " or " Soviet of the People's Commissars." " Commissar " was chosen by Lenin to escape from the odium attaching to Minister. The term was generally adopted throughout the ranks of Bolshevism so that any person who was a Soviet official came to bear the title of Commissar.

character in his illuminating phrase that Lenin's face showed " an expression of indomitability biding its time." It is only a man of indomitable tenacity of purpose who could have maintained himself against the odds that Lenin had to face. There was ca' canny throughout the Civil Service. From the heads of departments down to junior clerks there was a refusal to serve a Government of bandits. Lenin had a quick way with the non-co-operators. Telephone girls refused to work their instruments ; Lenin manned the service with ex-service men. Officials at the State Banks refused to open their safes ; Lenin ordered dynamite to be employed. At the Ministry of Foreign Affairs Trotsky found that all-important cases were locked and the keys missing ; two or three diplomats spent twenty-four hours in locked rooms and the keys were forthcoming. In the banks and railways and throughout the postal service employees declined to work. The bourgeois classes engaged in a conspiracy of passive resistance. Lenin turned to the masses for assistance. Manifestoes were issued informing the people of the obstacles which their commissars had to face. " While the situation calls for the most urgent and passive measures," a Government proclamation stated, " officials in the Government offices, banks, railways, postal and telegraph departments are on strike, stultifying all our efforts." Bourgeois obstacles were an inspiration to the proletariat.

On the second day of office Lenin had to face the counter-thrust of the dispossessed Kerensky who had fled to the army. He had assembled a force of troops and marched on St. Petersburg. Lenin attempted to organise resistance, but at the General Staff Headquarters he could find few officers to issue commands, and such commands as were given were received with mild curiosity by the soldiers. Had Lenin been dependent for his existence upon the troops, his régime would have fallen, but the Red Guards were mobilised. The counter-revolutionary forces were driven back, and Kerensky had to fly for his life.

There was the Commander-in-Chief of the Army, General Dukhonin, to be dealt with. He attempted to sabotage the negotiations for peace. The Chairman of the People's Commissars spoke by telephone to the recalcitrant general-issimo. Dukhonin was evasive. Lenin ordered his removal, and Krylenko,[1] who was still a cadet, was appointed to the head of the army. "Soldiers," wrote Lenin in a new manifesto, "if you want to go on with the war defend Dukhonin. You are not going to allow counter-revolutionary generals to tear away the cause of peace. You will surround them by guards to avoid lynchers who are unworthy of a revolutionary army. Soldiers, the days of peace are in your hands. If you want peace, protect the People's Commissars."

The soldiers showed their will to peace, but they gave no heed to the warning against lynching. Dukhonin was not long afterwards found dead, killed by bayonets.

Within the circle of his colleagues Lenin had other obstacles to overcome. Few of his associates were more than agitators, men of skill in argument, but untrained in affairs, and lacking the intellectual capacity which enabled Lenin to adjust himself to the responsibility of government. Out of the raw material of Bolshevism he had to fashion a new political machine which would take over the rule of 150,000,000 people, root up the old institutions and conduct society on new lines which had never been tested in the world before. Some of those at his side proved to be men of little faith. Rykov, Commissar of the Interior, and Miliutin (Agriculture) resigned from the Soviet of the People's Commissars. Zinoviev, Nogin and some others withdrew from the Central Committee of the Party. The Mensheviks and the Social Revolutionaries attempted to exploit the defections and to build up a new coalition. Again Lenin appealed to the masses, denouncing spiritless doubters who had allowed themselves to lose heart. Millions of copies of manifestoes declared the shame of the men who had deserted from the Red colours. After a few days the deserters came back begging for forgiveness.

· · · · · · ·

Early in the New Year Lenin had to face a problem on which depended the future constitution of the State. The Kerensky Ministry had made arrangements for the election of a Constituent Assembly and the nominations had taken

[1] Comrade Abram Krylenko had been a revolutionary since 1906. During the rule of the Provisional Government he was arrested for Bolshevik agitation in the army and was flogged.

place before the November Revolution, although the polls actually followed it. The Bolsheviks gained nine million votes, against twenty-two millions cast for the Social Revolutionaries. The Deputies who assembled in January were divided into one hundred and eighty supporters of Lenin and four hundred opponents. The anti-Bolsheviks came prepared with candles and sandwiches, fearing that the electric light in the Chamber might be cut off and the kitchens should be ordered to supply no meals.

There was something tragic about the meeting of this Assembly which had been the object of democratic hopes in Russia for a century. Before Lenin was born men had given a life of service, and life itself, in the cause of freedom, and to them the summoning of a Constituent Assembly had appeared as the ultimate objective. Now the Assembly met to find that there was a rival authority in the land— the Congress of Soviets. There was no room for both the democratic and the proletarian representative body.

Were Lenin to recognise the authority of the Constituent Assembly he would be forced to resign. He had no doubt as to the course to be pursued. To his followers he had announced that the Assembly must be broken up. Doubters impressed by the traditional importance of the Constituent Assembly were horrified, but Lenin was not going to surrender the hard won power in deference to parliamentary traditions. To recognise the authority of the Assembly was equivalent to quitting office and entering upon a new period of agitation. He had not gained power merely to surrender it. He had become Dictator in the name of the proletariat, to bring peace and bread. The safeguarding of his political existence was a political necessity.

A Latvian regiment composed of workers of unquestionable loyalty to the new régime was ordered to St. Petersburg for the day the Assembly was to meet. Marines in force were posted in the streets with orders to be ruthless in the suppression of disorder. While the Deputies assembled in the Taurida Palace, Lenin attended before the Central Committee of the Soviets. From the proletariat authority he obtained the formality of a mandate to suppress the rival democratic Assembly. It was a document which placed the responsibility for their suppression upon members of the

Assembly, who had broken bonds with the Soviet Republic, and were assisting the enemies of the Soviet in their struggle against the Government. The Central Committee accordingly resolved " that the Constituent Assembly shall be dissolved." Lenin returned to the Taurida Palace and gave instructions to the officer in command of the forces. The Commandant entered the Chamber and informed the President of the decree of dissolution. The Deputies were nonplussed. The officer reported that his men were tired, for it was four o'clock in the morning, and it would be a favour if the order could be obeyed without delay. So to oblige the officer and his tired men the sitting was abandoned and the Constituent Assembly faded out of existence.

Lenin was impenitent over the destruction of the symbol of bourgeois democracy. In a thesis on the Assembly he argued that Soviet democracy was superior to parliamentary democracy ; that Soviet democracy was the only form of government which would bring about a relatively painless transition to Socialism. He glorified the Soviet above the bourgeois model as giving the greater measure of democracy by placing the delegate in greater subjection to his electors.

There are few actions to which brilliant dialectic cannot impart the semblance of justification by appeal to the eternal verities (*vide* the works of George Bernard Shaw *passim*), but had Lenin been even more hard put to it to make the worse seem the better reason the Assembly would still have disappeared. His very existence required it.

The establishment of the Soviet form of constitution was finally ratified by the Congress of Soviets in 1918. The party Congress at Lenin's inspiration changed its name to Communist, the title originally adopted by Karl Marx. Communism was a word that Lenin preferred because it had a tradition behind it, recalling the Paris Commune. It also conveyed a declaration of complete independence from the bourgeois Social Democrats.

.   .   .   .

The life story of Lenin now merges into the wider history of Soviet Russia. It was a life of incessant toil. The greatest economic experiment in history had to be made by a Government which could only precariously maintain itself against its opponents within the State, and was soon to be assailed from without. Peace with Germany had to be negotiated, a task which Trotsky fulfilled at Brest Litovsk.[1] The Treaty which was finally signed on March 3, 1918, was agreed to reluctantly on both sides. Russia had to consent to surrender half a million square miles of territory, with sixty-six millions of inhabitants, and to pay a heavy indemnity. The Central Powers would not have been satisfied with these exactions had the situation on the Western Front permitted them to delay. This Russian Bolshevism was in their eyes a European peril. " If we had the power it would be right to refuse to negotiate altogether with these people, to march on St. Petersburg and restore order." But they had not the power. Germany needed every man to fight the French and British. It was the Allies who sent men, money and munitions to fight the European peril of Red Bolshevism.

5

Trotsky's achievements. Having made peace he wages war. The peripatetic generalissimo whose G.H.Q. was a train.

When in January, 1919, the Soviet announced cancellation of all foreign loans contracted by the Czarist régime, the Allied blockade was extended to Russia. Troops followed to reinforce the effects of blockade—British troops, American troops, French troops at Odessa, and Czechoslovak deserters. The Red Soviet was ringed by White attackers. There was Admiral Kolchak in Siberia, General Denikin in the South, General Wrangel in the Crimea, Yudenich in the North-west, Mannerheim in Finland, the Polish Haller, the Cossack Hetman. Armies of Russia which had been disbanded had to be re-formed.

[1] The negotiations at Brest Litovsk were used by the Bolsheviks as a means for world publicity and were adroitly prolonged by Trotsky. Von Kuhlmann and the German negotiators found to their surprise that although they were dealing with a beaten foe, the Russians so far from suing for peace adopted a truculent attitude—" behaved more like victors than vanquished." The Armistice negotiations opened on December 3, 1917, and the peace was not signed until March 3, 1918.

Trotsky, negotiator of the peace, had next to become leader in war. A halt was called to the suppression of army officers ; the revolution had need of generals. The presence of foreign invaders on Russian soil rallied young officers around the Red colours. The peasants, too, became supporters of the Soviet, though distrustful of Soviet policy, and herein was Lenin's vision justified beyond that of his followers.

There had been an outcry against him in that he had relaxed the rigid rule of Communism in the peasants' favour. In his first month of power he summoned an All Russian Peasant Congress at which he announced the land decree. This abolished all private ownership in land, without compensation, and transferred all private properties and estates of the Crown and the Church to district Soviets. The old owners of estates were dispossessed, but land did not pass to the Soviets. It was taken over by the peasants, and thereby Lenin gained millions of supporters for his régime.

He was challenged at an All Russian congress in which the Bolsheviks had only one-fifth of the seats. A delegate from the provinces, speaking from among the Social Revolutionaries of the Left, attacked the Government for failing to give representation to the peasants. " As long as the peasants are not represented," he declared, " we refuse to recognise you." Lenin had difficulty in obtaining a hearing to make his reply, but he persisted and at length made himself heard. " What is it you want ? " he asked. " You have your farms. Keep them. But if we no longer rule, everything will be taken away from you." He had to break off his speech to calm his own followers, who were outraged at this departure from the pure gospel of Communism. They threatened to leave the hall, but he commanded them to remain.

When his speech was finished the peasants had been convinced. Their holdings, newly won, were not to be taken away and held by the proletariat. " Lenin," they said, " is not against us after all." This private ownership of the land raised its subsequent problems for the People's Commissars, but it helped the Government to survive the menace of the invasions, for, where the Whites succeeded in gaining control, lands were restored to former holders. It was in the interest of the new peasant proprietors to support the Soviet Government. By relaxing the rigid rule of Communism Lenin

gained adherents of vital importance while he was struggling
for his existence.

.   .   .   .

The peasants helped, the soldiers helped, the Red Guards
helped, but it is to Trotsky to whom chief credit belongs for
saving Soviet Russia from invaders. Trotsky was the
organiser of the Red Armies. He refashioned the weapons
of the old order to fight the enemies of the new. He directed
the organisation of the men. He stimulated the provision
of munitions. His indefatigable energy was the inspiration
of the campaigns. For two and a half years he lived the
life of a peripatetic generalissimo, journeying from front to
front in the train which was his travelling G.H.Q. In his
autobiography[1] he tells the story of this train of the Pred-
revoyensoviet—the train of the Chairman of the Revolutionary Military Council, which, like Trotsky himself, was
awarded the decoration of the Red Flag for Service. In
the train travelled the secretariat, the printing press, telegraph station, radio station, electric power station, a garage,
a library and a bath. By its means the Chairman of the
Revolutionary Military Council was able to organise the
defence on the various fronts from the Baltic to the Pacific,
from the Ukraine to Siberia. It was an administrative,
political and fighting institution. The mere appearance of
Trotsky, his staff and his landing parties (as the armed
detachments were termed) had an immense psychological
effect, turning expected defeat of demoralised men into
victory.

In August, 1918, when Trotsky entrained for his first
engagement on the Volga, the territories of the Soviet had
been reduced to the size of the ancient principality of
Moscow. There were enemies on all sides and the road
to Moscow depended on the fate of Kazan. Kazan fell, but
Moscow was saved. The arrival of Trotsky and his train
worked like a tonic on officers and men. Disorganised
units were animated into fighting forces.

When Trotsky took the field he had as many dangers to
face from enemies on his own side as in the ranks of the
enemy. He says : " Treason had nests among the staff and

[1] *My Life :   The Rise and Fall of a Dictator.*

the commanding officers, in fact everywhere. The enemy knew where to strike and almost always did so with certainty. It was discouraging. Soon after my arrival I visited the frontline batteries. The disposition of the artillery was being explained to me by an experienced officer, a man with a face roughened by wind and with impenetrable eyes. He asked for permission to leave me for a moment, to give some orders over the field-telephone. A few minutes later two shells dropped, fork-wise, fifty steps away from where we were standing ; a third dropped quite close to us. I had barely time to lie down, and was covered with earth. The officer stood motionless some distance away, his face showing pale through his tan. Strangely enough, I suspected nothing at the moment ; I thought it was simply an accident. Two years later I suddenly remembered the whole affair and, as I recalled it in its smallest detail, it dawned on me that the officer was an enemy, and that through some intermediate point he had communicated with the enemy battery by telephone and had told them where to fire. He ran a double risk—of getting killed along with me by a White shell, or of being shot by the Reds. I have no idea what happened to him later." Even as his train drove away it was bombed by a plane and shelled by artillery, doubtless under the orders of the same artillery officer.

In the summer of 1919 Petrograd[1] was again menaced by the invaders under Yudenich, C.I.C. of the North-Western Army of the Whites. Lenin was induced (for this Trotsky puts the blame on Zinoviev) to agree to the evacuation of Petrograd as a means of shortening the front. Trotsky, however, urged that the city must be saved at all cost and persuaded Lenin to change his mind. A back to the wall order was issued " to defend Petrograd to the last ounce of blood, to refuse to yield a foot and to carry the struggle into the streets of the city." The 7th Soviet Army was in no condition to render effective opposition. Yudenitch advanced to within ten miles of Petrograd. Trotsky mobilised the male population of the city, the workers from

[1] St. Petersburg was renamed Petrograd by the Bolsheviks, and later Leningrad in memory of Lenin. In March, 1918, Lenin transferred the capital to Moscow, the ancient site of Government.

the factories to take their place beside the army, the marine battalions and the military students. There is the testimony of his adversary that he induced his forces to fight like lions. " They attacked the tanks with their bayonets, and although they were mown down in rows by the devastating fire of the steel monsters, they continued to defend their positions." On October 21 the enemy advance was checked. On the day following the Red Army took the offensive. By the 23rd a few outposts had been retaken. Encouraged by their successes the Reds rolled back the Whites to the Esthonian frontier.

In February, 1920, Admiral Kolchak was captured and shot. In the South General Denikin was defeated and fled, leaving his command to General Wrangel, who held out in the Crimea until November, when he, too, gave up the struggle, and Russia, after six years of war, was at peace. Trotsky's leadership had not merely enabled the invaders to be driven off, but permitted the war to be carried beyond the Russian frontiers in the manner of crusading invaders into Poland. This expedition (Trotsky claims that it was made against his advice) was entered upon with the object of overthrowing the new Polish Government and establishing a Soviet, but the Russian forces were defeated at the Battle of the Vistula.[1]

.   .   .   .

6

The murder of the Czar and his family in the House with a Special Purpose. An attempt to kill Lenin and the Terror that followed.

The revolution of a people on so vast a scale as the cataclysm in Russia takes its inevitable toll in human lives. The poor perish in their thousands, for they are easy victims, able to offer little resistance. Revolution of mass against class involves the lives of less humble folk as well—the rich, the eminent and the aristocrat. In Russia, as in England in 1649, and in France in 1793, the lives of the Royal ruler and members of his house were forfeit. The Romanovs perished at the hands of their Bolshevik gaolers. Perished —was it murder or execution? They were killed without the formality of a trial, and whether it be called execution

[1] See pages 194–195.

at the order of high authority, or whether murder by men who panicked at the near approach of counter-revolutionaries, depends upon the measure of responsibility to be placed on the Soviet leaders in Moscow.

Was Lenin responsible for the deaths of the Romanovs? Was he privy to the shootings at Ekaterinburg? Was he not merely privy to the shootings, but did he not give the order for their carrying out? The account of the killing of the Romanovs sedulously fostered by the Bolsheviks has been that the shootings were resolved upon by the local Soviet without reference to Moscow. Such mystery has hung over the fate of the Imperial family that it has not been possible definitely to apportion responsibility. But there has now been published an account of the circumstances by an officer formerly in command of the personal guard of the Dowager-Empress, who took part in the investigations at Ekaterinburg made at the order of Admiral Kolchak when Supreme Ruler, or Regent acknowledged by the Royalists. This officer, Captain Paul Bulygin, was appointed assistant to Sokolov, the Special Investigator, and on the strength of the investigations he pronounces that

Lenin knew of the preparations for the murder.
Lenin sanctioned the murder.
Lenin murdered the Imperial family.

They are charges plainly made and will be as plainly rejected by admirers of Lenin, who claim that he was opposed to the execution of the Czar on the double grounds of international policy and common humanity. It is a matter difficult to prove. Before submitting the testimony, the history of the Imperial family following the March revolution must briefly be traced. From Kerensky's record published in the same book[1] we gain a vivid picture of the last months on earth of members of the Russian Royal house.

Immediately on his abdication in March, 1917, Nicholas, Czar of All the Russias, became a cypher in Russian affairs, a person of such inconsiderable political significance that the Provisional Government did not deem it necessary to order

[1] *The Murder of the Romanovs*, by Captain Paul Bulygin, with an introduction by Sir Bernard Pares and foreword by Alexander Kerensky. (Hutchinson.)

his confinement, and he was even suffered to visit the army. He constituted no danger to the new régime as he was so completely deserted by all persons of consequence. Politicians and courtiers fell shamelessly away from the man who had been Emperor, and only a few faithful retainers dared to brave the odium of serving their fallen master. For his own safety, such was the intensity of popular hatred,. it was necessary he should be placed in confinement He, the Empress, his son the Czarevich, and four daughters› the Grand Duchesses Maria, Tatiana, Anastasia and Olga› were accordingly deprived of their liberty and confined in the Imperial Palace at Tsarskoe Selo, not far from St. Petersburg. Their detention was not expected to be prolonged beyond the few days necessary for the completion of arrangements for their removal to England, traditional refuge of dethroned royalty. On the day of the arrest the British Ambassador, Sir George Buchanan, informed the Provisional Government that asylum in England was available, but unhappily before the arrangements for the conveyance of the Imperial household could be arranged political developments in England caused a reconsideration of the offer of her hospitality. The Czar had to remain in Russia until a new refuge could be found. It became increasingly dangerous for him to be confined so close to St. Petersburg and the revolutionaries. Kerensky, therefore, made arrangements for the transfer of the prisoners by train and boat to far-away Tobolsk in Western Siberia, chosen as an out-and-out back-water, removed from centres of danger.

In Tobolsk the prisoners remained from August, 1917, to the following spring. With the downfall of Kerensky and the coming of the Bolsheviks to power their position was one of increasing peril, which was added to by the injudiciousness of the Royalists, who made futile plottings with the object of contriving a rescue. The plotters had never any real prospect of success, but even had the chances been otherwise favourable treachery would have rendered escape impossible. Soloviev, son-in-law of Rasputin, was sent to Tobolsk by the Czaritsa's favourite, Anna Vyrubova, to save and protect the family, but he turned traitor to the cause and betrayed all Royalists whose secrets he gained to the Bolsheviks.

In the spring of 1918 the prisoners were once again given a new place of confinement. They were removed to the town of Ekaterinburg, founded by Catherine the Great in a depression in the mighty chain of the Ural Mountains, where the ancient pass leads from Russia to Siberia. Ekaterinburg has acquired a new name since then—Sverdlovsk, which commemorates Jacob Sverdlov, first Chairman of the Bolshevik Central Executive Committee, who is alleged to have had a hand in the arrangements for the shootings. The transfer was the sequel to an attempt by the German Government to save Nicholas and his family. It was represented to the German Ambassador—he was in a position to bring considerable diplomatic pressure to bear upon the Soviet Government at that juncture in its affairs—that messengers sent to remove the Imperial prisoners from Tobolsk to Petrograd had been defied by the Ural Bolsheviks, who insisted on keeping Nicholas a prisoner. This explanation is claimed as an example of Lenin's trickery and duplicity—a device to retain the Imperial prisoners and to evade German displeasure by putting the blame elsewhere.

At Ekaterinburg, Nicholas and his family found a prison in Ipatiev House—the House with the Special Purpose, a two-storied building in which they were allotted five rooms on the upper floor. The conditions of confinement became more rigorous. The Emperor and his daughters had previously been in good spirits, but they became sad and worried. On July 14 Divine Service was held in the house. When the deacon sang the prayer " Rest in Peace with the Saints " one of the Grand Duchesses burst into sobs, and all had tears in their eyes. There was a foreboding of tragedy and the fulfilment was not long delayed. On the night of July, 16–17 the entire family with their personal attendants were shot. Here are the circumstances as reconstructed from the official investigations by Captain Bulygin :

At twelve o'clock, midnight, Yurovsky (Superintendent of the House) awakened the Imperial family. The prisoners rose, dressed, washed and came downstairs. They were taken outside into the courtyard and down through another door into the far end of the building, where they were led right down the basement corridor, past several doors, to the last room, which communicated only with a locked and sealed cellar. Yurovsky told the Czar that in view of the approach of the Czechs and the White Army bandit gangs they would have to be taken away from Ekaterinburg—such was the decision of the Ural Regional Soviet. In the meanwhile they would have to wait there, pending the arrival of the motor-cars to take them away.

The unsuspecting captives entered the trap and asked for chairs to sit down while they were waiting. Yurovsky ordered three chairs to be brought. The Empress took one, the Emperor sat down on another and supported the Czarevich, who sat on the third. Three of the Princesses stood behind the Czaritsa's chair and the fourth, the Grand Duchess Anastasia, stood a little to the right of the Czar. Dr. Botkin, Czar's physician, leaned on the back of the Prince's chair. To the left, near the wall, stood the valet Trupp and the chef Kharitonov. In the left-hand corner was the parlour-maid, Demidova, who held a pillow in her hand : she had brought two pillows with her into the room : one of them she placed on the Czaritsa's chair, for comfort, but the other was held tightly in her hands—inside it was a box containing the Imperial family's jewels.

They did not have to wait long before the murderers came in. Apart from Yurovsky, there was Paul Medvedev, Nikulin, two members of the Executive Committee— Voikov and Goloshchekin—and seven Hungarians. Yurovsky had already distributed the heavy revolvers. He stepped forward and addressed the Czar :

"Your relations have tried to save you ; they have failed, and we must now shoot you. . . ."

The Emperor rose from his chair—his arm still round the Czarevich—and had time to cry out : " What ? . . ."

Yurovsky fired point-blank at his head and the Emperor fell dead.

This was a signal for haphazard firing by the other assassins. The Empress had only time to raise her hand to make the sign of the cross before she, too, was killed outright with a single shot. Equally quick was the death of the Grand Duchesses Olga, Tatiana and Maria Nikolaevny, who stood together behind her Majesty's chair. The Czarevich was still quivering as he lay in the arms of his murdered father, when two more shots, aimed at his head by Yurovsky, put an end to his life. Botkin, Trupp and Kharitonov fell one after the other. Demidova was the last to fall ; she held up her pillow as a shield, and the box of jewellery which was inside stopped some of the bullets, protecting her heart and her stomach. She ran this way and that along the far wall, and screamed. They eventually murdered her with bayonets, borrowing rifles for this purpose from the guards who had led the captives across the courtyard.

When the smoke of the firing cleared a little and the murderers began to inspect the bodies they found that the Grand Duchess Anastasia was alive and unhurt. She had fallen in a dead faint when the firing began, and so escaped the bullets. When the assassins moved her body the Grand Duchess regained consciousness, saw herself surrounded by pools of blood and the bodies of her family, and screamed. She was killed. The bodies were then wrapped up in bed-sheets brought from upstairs and in long pieces of khaki cloth which had been prepared for this special purpose. They were carried out to the lorry (which had been standing in readiness outside all night), taken ten miles out of town into the woods, to the abandoned mine called " The Four Brothers," and there destroyed by fire. Such parts of the body as were particularly difficult to burn—the thigh bones, for instance—were dissolved in acids.

Thereafter Captain Bulygin sets out the evidence which convinced him of Lenin's complicity in the crime—that he " stood behind the murderers both before and after the act." It is for his readers to play the role of jurymen, and on the evidence he adduces to give a verdict. This evidence consists in the main of telegraph tapes of messages that passed between Ekaterinburg and Sverdlov, " Lenin's right-hand man."

In addition to the Emperor, his wife and children, other members of the Imperial family perished in that month of July—on the 13th the Grand Duke Michael and his English secretary, who had been imprisoned at Perm, and on the 17th the prisoners of Alapaycvsk, the Grand Dukes Sergius, Ivan Constantine and Igor, the Grand Duchess Elisabeth and Prince Vladimir Paley. With them, says Captain Bulygin, was Romez, secretary to the Grand Duke Sergius, and a nun, Barbara Yakovleva, who had come from the Moscow convent of SS. Martha and Mary to join the Grand Duchess Elisabeth, its founder. Both Yakovleva and Romez stood by the Royal captives until the end and shared their fate. Captain Bulygin writes :

On the night of July 17, that is to say about twenty-four hours after the Ekaterinburg tragedy, the captives were taken outside the town to an abandoned mine and thrown down the pit shaft—alive. The Grand Duke Sergius alone died before his body touched the bottom of the pit, because at the last moment he had gripped one of the murderers by the throat, and a bullet through his head saved him from the more terrible fate. The others were pushed over the edge alive and survived the fall.

The murderers then threw hand-grenades at the martyrs, but Romez alone was killed in this way, his body being terribly burnt in the explosion. The others survived only to die a more lingering death of starvation, exposure and injuries. The Grand Duchess Elisabeth had apparently used her handkerchief to bandage the Grand Duke Ivan's head, which was bruised in the fall, and a witness—a Muzhik who was hiding in the bushes near the mine—heard them sing " The Cherubim Hymn."

When the martyrs' bodies were found by the Whites, a post-mortem revealed the presence of earth in the mouth and stomach of the Grand Duke Constantine. Needless to say, it is possible for earth to find its way into a dead man's mouth, but only a living person could swallow it. It can be assumed, therefore, that the Grand Duke was alive for at least three days, because at least that period of starvation is required to make a man eat earth to appease the pangs of hunger.

. . . .

The Russian terror, prompted by fear of the enemies within the State, was raised to its highest pitch by the attempt made on Lenin's life in August, 1918, by Dora

Kaplan, a Social Revolutionary. The attempt was made at a meeting of workers. Dora Kaplan, a Jewess, advanced to present Lenin with a slip of paper, and she shot him as he accepted it. He fell, gravely wounded, and was carried to the Kremlin. For four weeks he was incapacitated. The country was roused into a new state of ferment by the anxieties of the Communist chiefs and the hopes of their opponents. An offensive was declared against sabotage and counter-revolution.

Lenin issued an order informing the people that the fatherland was in danger. The Soviet Government must protect itself. To this end " the bourgeoisie must be brought under control and mass terrorism instituted. The universal watchwords must be Death or Victory." The Cheka[1] (that is the Extraordinary Commission to combat Counter-Revolution, Speculation and Sabotage) was placed under the control of Felix Dzerzhinsky, whose picture is painted by Trotsky as that of a man of tremendous will, passion and high moral tension. His was the part in suppressing internal enemies of the State that Trotsky played in fighting enemies from without. The Cheka was more to be feared than the Red Guards. It worked in secret ; it had power to arrest, to try and to execute. No official statistics have been issued as to the number of its victims. In the stress of the times there was doubtless little concern to keep a record of their names. According to a French estimate they numbered :

Bishops	28
Priests	125
Professors and teachers	6,775
Police officers	10,000
Army officers	54,000
Soldiers	260,000
Constabulary	48,500
Landowners	12,950
Intelligentsia and middle classes	355,350
Peasants	815,000

[1] The first secret service of the Czars was the Opritchina ; the Okhrana succeeded it and lasted until 1917 ; the Cheka was established by the Bolsheviks in December, 1917, and was superseded in February, 1922, by the Ogpu—the Unified State Political Administration.

The French should have better reason than most for skill in estimating the victims of a revolution, but it is questionable whether they could enumerate the victims of their own guillotine with such appearance of accuracy. There is no question but these totals are exaggerated. General Graves, the United States Commander who supported Kolchak, takes another view of the terror. " There were horrible murders committed," he says, " but they were not all committed by the Bolsheviks. I am well on the side of safety when I say that the anti-Bolsheviks killed one hundred people in Eastern Siberia to every one killed by the Bolsheviks."

There is no questioning the ruthless efficiency of the Cheka. Dzerzhinsky justified his efforts by breaking the back of the counter-revolutionaries.

7

Communism in a hurry causes new difficulties for Lenin, who orders a retreat. N.E.P. is inaugurated and Lenin dies.

Under the stress of these years the foundations of the Communist State were laid. Only a man of the single-minded purpose of Lenin and with his infinite capacity for shutting the eyes to difficulties would have dared to try to launch a completely new order of society as head of a Government faced with such an intensity of opposition from without the State and within. Indomitable will-power carried him on over these obstacles, but others arose—famine and the opposition of the peasants—and these he could not march over or brush aside. The famine was largely the result of the peasant opposition, and this in great measure was the consequence of Communism in a hurry.

The transfer of industry from private to national owner-ship was carried out at a pace which would have led to complications in a society where greater efficiency of organisation was possible than in Russia during the height of a revolution. The proletariat in their zeal outreached Lenin in his discretion.

Everywhere men wished to be rid of their masters. The suppression of the bourgeoisie led to an inevitable shortage of organising and executive ability, which factory Soviets could not replace by mere enthusiasm. A partial break-down in the industrial machine was the result. The transport system was threatened at one stage with total collapse. Peasants who had seized the land were not disposed to join in the new Communism. They declined to surrender their surplus products to the authorities for sharing out amongst the proletariat. A food army was despatched throughout the country-side to commandeer the requisitions which were not voluntarily forthcoming. The peasants resorted to the opposition tactics of country people the world over—passive resistance. Drought accent-uated the difficulties which the peasants created. The grain harvest in 1921 was 60 per cent below standard, and Russia was ravaged by famine, the worst in the history of the country. Over a quarter of the population were reduced to privation, and it is estimated that no fewer than five millions died from want of food. Millions more would have perished but for the humanitarian efforts of inter-national relief organisations directed from capitalist countries in which America played an exemplary part.

Lenin was faced with a general peasant rebellion. There was open revolt in the district of Tambov. Disaffection spread. In Kronstadt the Baltic seamen mutinied. Dis-content grew. There were cries of " The Soviet without the Communists." The newly won stability of the Govern-ment was threatened. Lenin decided to make a strategic retreat, to temper the wind of Communism to the Soviet lamb, to permit a reversion to hated methods of capitalism, restricted, but capitalism nevertheless. The new policy was authorised in March, 1931, at the 10th Party Congress which adopted the N.E.P.—New Economic Policy. In place of the compulsory surrender of all surplus corn, a graduated tithe was imposed upon the agricultural com-munity ; the farmer remained free to sell the rest of his harvest. Other concessions permitted a restricted return to private trading, private industrial enterprise and private ownership of houses.

The pure gospel of Marx was thus rewritten in accord-ance with the dictates of political and economic expediency. The Party, declared Lenin, had to change its tactics from assault on capitalism to siege. The peasant must be allowed the opportunity of a certain freedom of

exchange as an inducement to the development of product-
ivity—" Freedom to buy and sell means freedom to trade.
Freedom to trade means the return to capitalism." It was
a frank admission. The strategic retreat was the last major
operation of Lenin's leadership. It saved his régime and
it enabled the foundations to be safely laid for the great
advances of the two successive Five-Year Plans. But these
advances the leader was not to see. He had borne the
burden and heat of the struggle, but he was not permitted
to witness the glory of the second Soviet dawn.

In 1922 his health began to fail. He was fifty-two, and
for thirty-two years he had laboured in the cause of the
proletariat without regard to his own needs. He had
brushed aside the rules of health as brusquely as the laws
of the bourgeois State, but the laws of nature cannot be held
perpetually at defiance. His constitution broke down under
the strain of overwork. He suffered a stroke and lost the
use of his right arm and leg. He had to rest and then,
partially restored to health, he returned to his desk. He
was able to attend the celebration of the fifth anniversary
of his rule. With his friends around him he spoke briefly
of the measure of achievement. It was better, he agreed,
than the old régime, but he did not pause to dwell on past
achievements. He pointed inexorably to the future. " We
have not yet got far. Our task is to make the needed
developments. Let me close with the expression of my
conviction that we shall achieve the solution of our
problems."

Before spring had brought the leaves to the trees he was
ill again, and he was borne to a villa at Gorky at the
edge of the forest near Moscow to pass little by little from
the activity of life. He lingered through summer and
autumn into the winter. The snows came down upon the
trees in the forests. The silence and sleep of winter fell
upon Gorky, and in the tranquillity the soul of Lenin fled
from the world of struggle and strife into the proletariat of
eternity. His mortal remains were laid to rest in a tomb in
the Red Square of Moscow—a shrine which is now the most
sacred object of veneration in Russia, to which hundreds
and thousands of worshippers make a pilgrimage to pay
reverence.

8

Trotsky versus Stalin, which shows that the greater man does not always win in politics. A tale of intrigue and exile.

Lenin left Communist Russia as his legacy, but he did not name the legatee. Who was to succeed?[1] In the ranks of Communism there was only one figure comparable in stature with Lenin's own. Leon Trotsky was the only man of outstanding capacity in the ranks of the lieutenants. The rest were able manipulators of the Party machine. Some of these able men resolved that the mantle of Lenin should not descend upon Trotsky. They were actuated, perhaps, by personal malice, perhaps by principle—it is difficult to determine. Whatever their motive they succeeded. Stalin, the Party man—it is plain enough to see the Party man in Stalin—became the new dictator.

Trotsky went into the wilderness to reflect bitterly on his fall, and to reflect upon the men who caused it. His autobiography, *The Rise and Fall of a Dictator*, is largely his reply to his opponents, and his attack upon them. Trotsky emerges as a fine figure of a man, dwarfing even Lenin. The others, Stalin, Zinoviev, Kamenev and the rest, flit in and out of the pages as lesser fry, diminutive also-rans. Trotsky is seen on the scale of Brobdingnag ; Stalin on that of Lilliput. This scale of values can scarcely be accepted, but it is not easy to correct, for while Trotsky's case is amply set before the world, we lack Stalin's apologia.

Even from his own pages, however, the cause of Trotsky's fall stands revealed. He makes much of questions of principle ; tries to prove in answer to detractors that he was always a Leninite. But principles are not at the root of Trotsky's fall ; it is a matter of personality. Trotsky has some of the qualities of the dictator, but not the finesse

[1] Trotsky in his book represents that Lenin intended shortly before his death to name Trotsky as his deputy and successor in office as chairman of the Soviet of Peoples' Commissars. He records, too, that Lenin left a " Will " in which Trotsky was described as being the ablest of the Bolsheviks, " his defect is his excess of self-confidence," and Stalin was depicted as " rude, disloyal and capable of abusing the power he derives from the apparatus ; he should be removed."

that makes a dictator acceptable to those around him.
Given tact and political sagacity, Trotsky might have
succeeded to the place of Lenin. Trotsky represents the
opponents who eventually evicted him as little men, but
nowhere does he show that he went out of his way to con-
ciliate them, and it is the little men in politics upon whom
the greater men must rely. Trotsky might have taken to
heart the advice of the French moralist : " *Entre nos ennemis
les plus a craindre sont souvent les plus petits.*" The tactful man
in politics follows La Fontaine and conciliates. Trotsky
rode rough shod over the smaller fry and these lesser
men banded against him.

You can see Trotsky's weakness revealed back in 1905
when he was serving his apprenticeship on the St. Petersburg
Soviet, of which the President was a young lawyer named
Khrustalyov. Trotsky had a contempt for this " accidental
figure " in the revolution, a man with no real political
leadership, and he quotes from the memories of a colleague.
" Khrustalyov was a man with an exaggerated vanity,
which was almost an illness with him. He came to hate
Trotsky because of the very necessity of referring to him
for advice and direction." It is dangerous to know better
than your fellows when your better knowledge serves
merely to make them conscious of their own inferiority.

Trotsky was successful in beating off the enemies of the
revolution. He rendered inestimable service to his country
and he raised up for himself a host of enemies. A man of
drive and action needs the gift of tact to a supreme degree
if he is to avoid the enmities of little men, but tact and
Trotsky have never been united. Even he realised that it
was no cause for wonder that his military work created so
many enemies for him. " I did not look to the side," he
says. " I elbowed away those who interfered with military
success, or in the haste of the work trod on the toes of the
unheeding and was too busy even to apologise."

Stalin and Zinoviev were two whose toes were hurt.
Trotsky need not look farther than that for the cause of his
overthrow. He need not speculate upon principles, if his
record in this respect is correct, nor need he try to demonstrate his consistent loyalty to Lenin. Clearly it was
personality and not principle that caused the fall. So up
to a point we can accept the picture Trotsky gives without

necessarily subscribing to the accuracy of every detail. During the last months of Lenin's semi-retirement we can see Stalin and Zinoviev and Kamenev drawing together and mustering their forces to ensure that the ruthless treader on toes shall not gain the position of permanent dictator. Stalin had been appointed General Secretary of the Communist Party, a position under Lenin, which was not suspected of having influence or importance. It was a position, however, which Stalin was able to exploit to advantage in securing the appointment of men of his own mind to important posts in the Party. Trotsky sneers at the man who worsted him in the political conflict, at his ignorance, his narrow political horizon, his moral coarseness. " His ignorance of foreign languages," says Trotsky, " compels him to follow the political life of foreign countries at second hand. His mind is stubbornly empirical and devoid of imagination. To the leading group of the Party (in wider circles he was not known at all) he always seemed a man destined to play second and third fiddle." It is a picture which does less than justice to the Dictator, diminishes indeed the stature of the vanquished that such a Lilliputian could have caused his overthrow. Trotsky, vigorous and aggressive, cannot appreciate the qualities of the other. Stalin has the political tact which Trotsky lacks and some of the subtler qualities necessary for the political conspirator. " The outstanding mediocrity of the Party " was Trotsky's sneer. Perhaps Stalin thought it was wise not to draw the limelight too much upon himself lest the enmity of other little men should be aroused. Trotsky pursued the flamboyant way of the dictator. Stalin contrived it so that the actions he took should seem to be the fulfilment of the wishes of the Party rather than of his own desires. The " outstanding mediocrity " showed himself to have the talents that make the greatest Party man.

Lenin died in January, 1924. Early in 1925 Stalin secured his rival's discomfiture. Trotsky was deposed from his position as Commissar for War. Many of his followers were removed from their offices. Trotsky was sent " for his health " into temporary exile and only a minor post was given to him on his return. It was a personal struggle, but fought on questions of principle. In the years immediately following Lenin's death, the vital question for

Communism was the extent to which concessions towards capitalism authorised by the late leader should be sanctioned. Stalin was in favour of caution and compromise. Trotsky declared for the uncompromising application of Communism. Trotsky was for developing revolutionary propaganda in the capitalist states of the world. Stalin, perhaps with a keener appreciation of realities abroad than might be expected from the man who had to " follow the political life of foreign countries at second-hand," could see no immediate prospect of results from propaganda crusades abroad, and was in favour of concentrating upon developments at home. Trotsky desired to end the concessions which Lenin had been forced to grant to the peasants ; he wished to suppress the Nep-men out of existence. Stalin advocated the path of conciliation and of advance step by step.

Stalin secured the endorsement of his views. Trotsky experienced the mortification of defeat. He has placed the blame on intrigue and the packing of Party congresses against him. Here again, perhaps, bitterness has distorted his judgment. Trotsky would have perpetuated the temper of the revolution, but societies are not tuned up perpetually to this rate of progress. After the crisis is past, they prefer gradualness to sudden change. Trotsky failed to adjust his personal outlook after the passing of the initial crisis and the emergence of the stability of the Soviet.

After Trotsky's discomfiture Zinoviev and Kamenev soon fell from grace, for Stalin threw off his allies once they had served his purpose. Trotsky rejoiced at their fall, for they had contributed to his own, and he sought to exploit the allies Stalin had cast off. Trotsky, Kamenev and Zinoviev conspired against the Man of Steel, and he gathered new supporters about him, headed by Rykov (successor of Lenin as Chairman of the People's Commissars) and Dzerzhinsky, head of the Ogpu, the successor of the Cheka. At length Stalin was able to place the trio in a position in which they could be charged with the crime of " illegal organisation of an opposition group." Their expulsion from the Communist Party was ordered, and in 1928 they were sent to exile. Trotsky even from exile continued to agitate against the new Dictator. He could not bend himself to compromise. Kamenev and

Zinoviev showed themselves to be men of another breed by recanting to secure their reinstatement in the Party, but they, too, despite their recantation continued to intrigue against the Dictator.

Towards the close of 1934 they were again involved in new charges of counter-revolutionary conspiracy. On December 1, Kirov, Stalin's right-hand man at Leningrad, was assassinated. It was the first step in a conspiracy aimed at Stalin's overthrow. The actual assassin, Nickolaev, was only a minor figure in the Soviet organisation, but he was shown to be a pawn in the latest intrigue staged by Zinoviev and Kamenev as a means for revenge on the man who had used them for his own ends and then thrown them aside. For a month there was a minor reign of terror as the Ogpu judges removed lesser suspects. Then finally Zinoviev and Kamenev were put on their trial. A confession was presented from Nickolaev to the effect that there were two groups of terrorists who had combined their activities against the Stalin régime. Both made the Dictator's murder their ultimate intention. According to the confession a foreign consul agreed for a bribe of 5000 roubles to forward a letter to Trotsky in his exile, inviting his participation in this new plot against Stalin.

Fourteen leaders of the Leningrad Soviet were shot for Kirov's murder. Zinoviev and Kamanev feared that they too might meet their fate before a firing-party. No Bolshevik of the old guard had thus far been sentenced to execution, but there had not previously been so grave a challenge to authority as the assassination of Kirov. Under the guidance of local leaders, factory councils throughout the country passed resolutions inviting the Court to proceed to the extreme penalty. The Court, however, was ordered to temper justice with mercy. Stalin was not prepared to order the execution of his former fellow-plotters. Zinoviev received a sentence of ten years' imprisonment, and Kamenev one of five.

9

The record of the Five Year Plan, first and second instalments. Russia is a country without workless.

Under the rule of Stalin the Communist régime was firmly established and regularised.

The most important development in the Soviet under Stalin's rule has been the industrial push to which the name of the Five-Year Plan, in first and second instalments, has been given. Piatiletka, the Five-Year Plan of national development for the period 1928 to 1933, superseded the Nep policy. It was drawn up by a State Planning Commission, or Gosplan, the aim being to provide for the direction of the entire national economy, industry, agriculture, transport and trade five years ahead. Russia, which lagged far behind other countries in development, was to be transformed into a highly industrialised State, and to be made entirely self-supporting. The Plan provided for a rate of industrial expansion which would have taxed the resources of a country already well organised. For a State lagging behind as greatly as Russia at the time of its inception, the Plan seemed to be the pointing out of an ultimate ideal rather than an expression of practical politics. But the steam-roller was set going cumbrously, with the spirits of its operators whipped up to a high pitch of endeavour. Such progress was made during the first two years that a further speeding up in execution was called for and the original period of five years was cut down by nine months, while the scope of the Plan was considerably enlarged.

All the paraphernalia of modern publicity was employed to stimulate the workers. Like troops in some industrial war, they were spurred on by their leaders. Shock brigades of the proletariat led the advance and the opening of new plants and new factories was the signal for celebrations of a victory on the battle-front.

There were difficulties—every commander has some reverses to admit. There was a shortage of skilled labour. The workers' control in the factories was not conducive to high efficiency. The development of transport did not keep pace with increased production and perishable goods rotted in thousands of tons before they could be removed. There was sabotage on the farms and passive resistance. The Kulaks (the richer peasantry who under the Nep concessions had by their enterprise risen above the common level of the peasantry and were employing farm hands on the old capitalist model) were opposed to the policy of collective farming, involving the loss of the ascendancy their enterprise had won. There was wholesale slaughter of live stock, Kulaks preferring to destroy their beasts rather than allow them to be appropriated to Communism. The Bolsheviks organised drives against the Kulaks, many of whom were killed in offering resistance and many sent to Siberia. The rigour of the first Five-Year Plan antagonised even members of the proletariat, and concessions both to them and the Kulaks had to be granted under the scheme for the second quinquennium.

Nevertheless, there is an impressive record of statistics attesting to the achievements of Piatiletka.[1] The volume of large-scale industrial output in 1932 was 220 per cent of the total for 1928, and 330 per cent of that of 1913. Electrification of the Soviet, one of the principal items in the Five-Year programme, did not come fully up to the Plan. Nevertheless the advance was striking. In 1928 the capacity of all electrical plant was 1,874,000,000 kilowatts ; by 1932 it had been increased to 4,567,000,000 kilowatts. Industry was de-centralised. It had been concentrated in four districts under the old régime. Under the Five-Year Plan the tentacles of industry were spread out over a wide basis. A beginning was made with the exploitation of rich resources of mineral wealth previously neglected—the iron ore of the Urals and Siberia, the non-ferrous metals in Central Asia. The output of coal in 1932 was 64,000,000 tons, compared with 35,000,000 in 1927, and 29,000,000 in 1913. The total of 64,000,000 tons did not, however, reach the estimate under the Plan of 75,000,000. In 1928 there were 69 blast furnaces

[1] The record of achievement is admirably set out in *The Second Five-Year Plan* by W. P. and Zelda K. Coates. (Methuen.) The figures of the first and estimate of the second quinquennium are exhaustive and official.

in the Soviet Union ; by 1933 there were 102. Twelve pig-casting machines were operating at the end of the period ; there had not been one at the beginning.

One of the Chief aims of the Plan had been progress with the machine construction industry. Russia had not the money to buy from abroad the machinery needed for the development of her industrial processes. Credit was difficult to obtain. It was a vital necessity that she should build the plant which she could not purchase. The Plan aimed at stimulating production sufficiently for the output of machinery at the end of the Plan to be three and a half times greater than at the beginning. This was achieved by the end of 1931, and in the year 1932–33 the estimate of output was exceeded by over 50 per cent. By that time Soviet farms were being supplied with machinery as up-to-date and of as good quality as that obtainable in America.

The development of large-scale farming was another vital feature of Piatiletka. The mechanisation of farming can only proceed successfully where the holdings are extensive. The peasant holdings were allotments, not farms. It is calculated that as much as 97 per cent of the cultivated land in Russia in 1928 was portioned out in individual plots and that the average area (Kulak holdings excepted) was well below ten acres. The rationalisation of farming was the most difficult task of the Five-Year Plan, owing, as has been ex-plained, to passive resistance of the peasants. Two methods were resorted to for the creation of larger agricultural units— the formation of Soviet State farms (Sovkhozy) and the formation of collective farms (Kolkhozy) by the pooling of resources of individual peasants. The official figures of the progress made reflect the ruthlessness shown in the application of Communist principles. In 1928, 417,000 farms had been collectivised with an area of some 3,000,000 acres. In 1932, well over 14,000,000 farms had been collectivised with an area under crop of over 200,000,000 acres. The number of State farms increased from 3000 with some 4,000,000 acres in 1928 to 10,000 with over 30,000,000 acres in 1932. It could be claimed that by the end of the quinquennium the Soviet Union had become a country of the largest scale farming in the world.

The administrators of Communist Russia could look round their country in 1932 and take pride in the transformation which had been wrought. An entire people had been set to work by the direction of the State in a manner no people have worked before, except in time of war. They could claim that there had been a striking advance in the conditions of life of the people. Wages were calculated to be 66 per cent above those of 1928.

There had been a notable reduction in sickness ; there had been a decline in the mortality rate. The people were better housed and better educated. Even in 1928 only half the population were literate ; by 1932 illiteracy had been reduced to 10 per cent. There was a total of 22,000,000 children at school, compared with 11,000,000 in 1928 and 8,000,000 in 1913. The advance in education is reflected in the increase in newspaper circulation. In Czarist Russia in 1913 all newspapers had a circulation of less than 3,000,000 per day. At the beginning of the Five-Year Plan circulation was still under 9,000,000, but at the close it had reached a figure of 36,000,000. The circulation management of the newspapers of capitalist states must cast envious eyes upon the opportunities which have existed for pushing sales in Soviet Russia.

The circumstance which above all others would have caused satisfaction to Bolshevik administrators in 1932 would have been the employment situation. From the world over they would have received reports of acute unemployment resulting from the world economic crisis. They would have noted with pitying superiority the issue by the International Labour Office of figures showing that twenty or thirty millions of persons in various countries of advanced industrialisation were unable to obtain the opportunity to labour for their own support. And they would have pointed to the contrast in Soviet Russia, where not merely was unemployment non-existent, but an acute shortage of labour was being experienced. They would have claimed that here was plainly shown the superiority of a system of national planning over the haphazard arrangements under capitalist society.

Before the first period of five years had closed the second Five-Year Plan had been drawn up to consolidate and exploit the gains of the first industrial offensive. Its aim was the final extinction of private ownership, the completion of national reconstruction and the final triumph of the dictatorship of the proletariat by the evolution of a classless society. An enormously increased industrial development was aimed at with the further exploitation of undeveloped resources, the establishment of new works and factories, and the tuning up of output to still higher levels. Plans were laid for merging the peasants, who form so large a proportion of Russia's millions, into the proletariat by the urbanising of the country-side and the industrialising of the farms.

The fulfilment of the second Piatiletka would mean that employment in the Soviet Union would have been increased by 25 per cent, and it might be wondered how this could be possible in a country in which unemployment had already been eliminated. Partly it would be brought about by the natural increase in the population and partly by bringing more women into the industrial sphere.

.   .   .   .

10

Women under the Soviet are on equality with men.   Marriage, divorce and children.

The position of women in Communist Russia contrasts with the theories of the new masters of Germany and Italy. Both Hitler and Mussolini have made it a cardinal point in their policies that the place of a woman is in the home ; that her duty is the rearing of new members of the State. The Soviet on the other hand have aimed to make women independent of the economic support of men and to place the sexes in a position of industrial equality.

There is no field in the social and political, cultural and economic life of Russia in which women are not working, and millions of them are in the front ranks in the struggle for economic reconstruction. The number and influence of women in administrative and governing bodies is growing, although strong opposition on the part of the men had to be overcome, especially in the country. At the 15th All-Russia Soviet Congress nearly one-quarter of the delegates were women. The Soviet Union is the only country in which equal pay for men and women is a national principle. It is estimated that already one-third of the whole labour force of the Soviet Union consists of women. An increasing number are employed on skilled labour, and in Moscow and Leningrad several factories have a woman at the head. Only a few are to be found in the ranks of the Red Army to-day, reminders of the "Daughters of the Revolution." During the civil war sixty-three women in the Soviet Union were decorated with the Order of the Red Banner, and the majority of these women soldiers, who were no longer young, died prematurely as a result of the hardships.

It is to Lenin that the Russian woman owes her emancipation. Although facing dangers within and without, he found time before the close of 1917 to issue a decree replacing the Czarist marriage law by the Soviet code which repudiates the conception of marriage based on inequality and indissolubility, with the "headship of the family" vested in the husband. Ten years later, on January 1, 1927, the complete marriage code came finally into force, establishing the Soviet on the hearth. This code aims at safeguarding the independence of both spouses, and directing marriage "along the path of comradeship." It is also laid down that property acquired before marriage does not become common, but all property acquired by their work during marriage is jointly held. The housewife's labour is counted as of equal value as the man's in his sphere.

As marriage is simplified, so is divorce. No country in the world grants dissolution on simpler terms—at the request of either member of the union. There are no longer divorce suits. The person desiring the dissolution is not required to give any explanation, for divorce, like marriage, is considered to be entirely a private affair.

As regards the children, if agreement is reached between the parties it is recorded on the register of divorces, and in case of disputes judgment is given solely in the interests of the children. In practice the custom is to leave them with the mother till the age of eight ; sometimes a child is placed in a home, both parents contributing to its support, according to their means.

The Soviet has solved the question of the illegitimate

child by abolishing illegitimacy. Birth and blood relationship have been made the sole basis of legal relationship and nowise legal marriage. Children born out of marriage are placed on an absolute equality with those born within the ties of wedlock. Equally the problem of the unwanted child has been reduced, for in no city in the world are there such facilities to prevent unwanted births. Attached to the Moscow Institute for the Protection of Mothers and Infants is the only establishment of its kind in existence—the Laboratory for Preventions. Under the direction of twenty doctors it conducts scientific research into all questions of preventive intercourse and measures to check conception. It engages in widely spread propaganda, which has reached the villages.

Furthermore, abortion is legalised in Russia. Every woman is at liberty to undergo such an operation on condition that it is performed on licence in a public hospital. A fee is charged, graded according to income, but in Moscow there is a free abortarium. It is laid down that abortion is not performed for a woman in her first pregnancy; that artificial abortion may not be performed on the same woman more than twice in one year. The thirteen abortaria which have been established in Moscow and the neighbourhood have proved unequal to meet the demands. The women remain after the operation for a period of from three to five days in order to recover, and then return to their work in ten days, the legally prescribed term of leave. Operations are carried out without the use of an anæsthetic and occupy scarcely more than five minutes.

There is general absence of restraints in Russia in the matter of sex relationship. The Soviets allow no commercial exploitation of sex. All houses of prostitution have been closed. There is no display of sex in shop windows or places of amusement.

11

Supremacy of the minority. The old Bolsheviks dominate the Communist Party, and the Communist Party, through the Soviet machinery, dominates Russia.

Russia to-day is spoken of universally as Communist Russia, yet only a percentage of the people are members of the Communist Party. The Communists dominate the machinery of Government much in the manner of the Fascists. Nominally it is the Soviets who, through the All-Russia Congress, are the rulers. But the ultimate supremacy rests with the Party, as Stalin's dictatorship attests, for his official position in the hierarchy of Communism is that of Secretary to the Party, and not, as Lenin was, Chairman of the People's Commissars.

In the Communist Party it is a minority that holds sway—the old Bolsheviks, active revolutionaries of the Czarist days, the intelligentsia of Communism. The machinery of Party and of Soviets is designed to secure power to them. This is attained by the delegation (nominally) of authority from local cells to Party congress, from Party congress to central committee, and within the committee to the dominating coterie organised in two bureaux and a secretariat which are responsible for current administration. The bureaux are the Politbureau, which determines matters of policy, and the Ogbureau, which supervises membership and propaganda.

The old Bolshevik coterie have provided for their dominance within the Party by enforcing a rigid rule of subordination upon all neophytes. Undesirables are removed by the purge which is carried out once a year, and which results in the disappearance of members who are either under-zealous or over-zealous and suspected of careerism.

The hierarchy of the Party are the hierarchy of the State, the personnel of the Party's Central Committee and the Central Executive Committee of the Union of Soviets being largely identical. The first step towards ensuring this dual dominance was made by declaring all political organisations but the Communist Party to be illegal and imposing a rigorous anti-Communist censorship. Local Soviets are not exclusively composed of Communists, but a process of elimination is applied in appointments to the superior bodies to which the Soviets send delegates, so that only Communists reach the Presidium and Council of Commissars.

Russia, or the Union of Socialist Soviet Republics,[1] is a

[1] The Union was formed in 1922 of the Soviet republics of Russia, Ukraine, White Russia and Transcaucasia. Small Asiatic republics joined the Federation—in 1925 Uzbek, to the north of Afghanistan, Turkomar, to the north of Turkey, and in 1929 Tadzhik, to the north of India.

federal State comprising Russia itself and six other republics, and is under the supreme authority of the All-Russia Congress of Soviets. This elected body of two thousand members meets only once in two years and the work is delegated to the Union Central Executive Committee. The Committee in turn delegates its powers to a Presidium which supervises the administrative body, the Council of Commissars, otherwise styled Sovnarkom. The Union machinery is reproduced on small scale in each of the Constituent Republics. The urban workers, the faithful proletariat, whose Communism can be relied upon, are given an initial dominating influence in the appointment of the delegates to the Congress of Republic or Union. In the All-Russia Congress, a deputy is appointed by every 25,000 urban votes, but the rural population have to be content with one deputy to every 125,000 persons. The town voter elects straight to the All-Russia Congress ; the country elector only to the village Soviet, the village Soviet to the district congress (to which the town also appoints direct), the district congress to the regional congress (again furnished with direct town representation) and the regional congress appoints delegates to serve with the directly elected deputies on the All-Russia Congress. There is universal suffrage with a number of disqualifications which nullify the electoral rights of some five per cent of the population. The disfranchised include all who employ hired labour for profit, who have an income not derived from their own labour, and private business men and traders.

In the fact that the members of the Communist Party total only about two millions amongst a population of one hundred and eighty millions[1] may be seen an explanation of the repressive methods which distinguish Communist rule. The Communism of the proletariat is to be relied upon, but the proletariat forms less than a tenth of the population. Russia is the land of peasants, but though they are numerically strong, they are politically weak, because their small communities are scattered. The proletariat may be hopelessly outnumbered, but they are politically stronger, because of their concentration. In the name of the

[1] There are as many Communists outside the official ranks. The youth organisations, Octobrists (children 8–10) Pioneers (10–16) and Komsomol (16 to maturity) have enrolled about 10,000,000.

proletariat, and relying upon their support, the Communists are forcing the vast agricultural community to embrace the Communist faith and become absorbed in the classless order of society. The strict censorship, and the suppression of anti-Communist organisations carried out by the Ogpu reflect not the strength, but the sense of weakness of the Communist rulers. Opposition rouses foes to frenzy, and there is a recrudescence of the Terror such as followed the Kirov assassination.

.   .   .   .

Twenty years will soon have run their course since the November Revolution ushered in Russia's new dynasty. Twenty years of controversy between Marxists and anti-Marxists have run their course, and through the dust of conflicts facts have emerged which give rise to democratic doubt. The reign of the proletariat does not appear to have conferred upon the Russians the liberties enjoyed by democracies not favoured by Soviet inspiration and control. Democrats are left wondering whether the proletariat is after all a good political master. Free speech is seen to be a privilege as jealously guarded in the land of Lenin as in that of Mussolini and of Hitler. There is, indeed, a strange similarity between the political machinery of the totalitarian and the proletarian States, the same strange absence of anxiety concerning the representation of views other than those of the party in power. Whose is the responsibility—the proletariat's? Or is it that despite the vaunted dictatorship, the proletariat is not master in its own house? Must the democrat then look elsewhere for the millennium?

The democrat, now, has not the faith of Russia in 1917 that the millennium is to be reached by way of the gospel of Marx according to Lenin. He has witnessed the application of a rigid materialism more arid than that of the doctrinaires of the Manchester School. He has noted that in the sacred name of equality there has been a levelling down to the lowest denominator ; that the sovereignty of the masses has been exercised with a fine contempt for the " little rickety ego " of the individual. Russia, to adopt a phrase from capitalist sources, seems in a fair way to become a land fit for robots to live in, and only robots will wish to live there. Mechanism has been glorified. Man in the sight of Leninism is less than the machine.

VI

WHAT THEN OF ENGLAND?

Wʜᴀᴛ then is England's fate in this brave new world? Must she too pass under the sway of a dictator? Must the Mother of Parliaments perish? Will democracy fail in the land that gave it birth?

Thirty years ago, when the century was young, such questions would have been received with derision. Then the world's future appeared to be assured. Parliamentary government in British eyes stood unchallenged as the ideal for the world. We had led the van, and progress was for the other peoples who had not advanced so far towards political perfection. The problems of the world would be solved by the spread of democracy. When the backward nations had gained the inestimable benefits of a constitution on the English model, the march of progress would be complete, and the world set in the organisation in which it could endure until the end of time.

Then came the War, then the precarious peace, and now all has changed. The old confidence in democracy has gone. Where there was faith there are now democratic doubts or sheer disbelief. No longer is there blind worship at democracy's shrine. Men have found other idols. The altars of democracy are neglected. The old prophets are despised. Men do not even remember the prophet who foretold democracy's failure, and a century too soon proclaimed the worship of the hero—" Not towards the impossibility, the self-government of a multitude by a multitude, but towards some possibility—government by the wisest does bewildered Europe struggle."

To the late Victorian it would have appeared that civilised society had advanced beyond the stage when constitutional disagreements could lead to a repetition of the civil wars of the Stuarts, Oliver Cromwell and the glorious Revolution of 1688. The contemporaries of Hitler and Mussolini know otherwise, and each time political convulsions are reported from abroad we in England put to ourselves the questions : Could such things happen here ? Could an English Mussolini march on London ? Could an English Hitler manœuvre himself into absolute power ? Shall we, too, witness conflicts in the streets between armed advocates of rival creeds, followers of Marx or Hitler ? We answer in the negative, but it is a dubious negative. We should like to answer with more confidence that English democracy will not fail, but there is a growing body of pessimism.

As State after State has passed under a dictatorship, we have been invited to mark, with scarcely a passing tribute, the setting of the democratic star and to hail the rising of the glory of the dictator. That in so many States an authoritarian régime should have been established has been claimed as evidence that a world movement was in progress —the transition from discredited democracy to the new Fascism. In addition to the dictators whose careers have been considered in this book, the advocates of the authoritarian principle can point to other States whose despotisms of varying degrees of autocracy have been established— Bulgaria, Latvia, Albania and Portugal in Europe. In the East, Japan has continued the policy of westernisation by becoming up-to-date in her political system ; in the West, the Republics of Latin America anticipated the States of the Old World in the establishment of dictatorial régimes, though of a different order of stability.

Because of the many defections from democracy, we are bidden to join with Mussolini in burying economic Liberalism and to follow Hitler in eliminating the last remnants of democracy. And many in England have been prepared to assent to join in this game of following the political leader. Hitler triumphed in Germany and Mussolini in Italy, but must Sir Oswald Mosley inevitably succeed in running up the Black Shirt in place of the Union Jack ? Before joining in the swan song of British democracy it seems profitable to inquire whether events abroad do in fact testify to the failure of democracy as a system. Shall we not find that it is not democracy that has failed, but that these other countries lacked the political sagacity necessary if democracy is to function.

Mussolini and Hitler do not owe their success to the

triumph of a principle. Italy and Germany did not adopt Nazi–Fascism out of admiration for abstract doctrines. The authoritarian State was thrust upon the people and it is not the soundest testimony to the merits of the dictatorial system that the dictated must be kept in subjection lest they rebel. It could at least be submitted in favour of the older Liberal democracy that, whatever the results of its operations, it did, as a system, represent the will of the people.

It was by the will of the people that Liberal democracy was established in Germany and Italy. Why then did it fail ? In large measure because the peoples had not the political experience and traditions of the English. A generation ago John Morley, in his essay designed to scourge our national habit of compromise and deference to the plenary inspiration of majorities, observed :

" Of all societies since the Roman Republic, and not even excepting the Roman Republic, England has been the most emphatically and essentially political. . . . One great tap-root of our national increase has been the growth of self-government, or government by deliberate bodies, representing opposed principles and conflicting interests. With the system of self-government has grown the habit— not of tolerance precisely, for Englishmen when in earnest are as little in love with tolerance as Frenchmen or any other people, but—of giving way to the will of the majority, so long as they remain a majority. This has come to pass for the simple reason that, on any other terms, the participation of large numbers of people in the control and arrangement of public affairs immediately becomes unworkable. The gradual concentration of power in the hands of a supreme deliberative body, the active share of so many thousands of persons in choosing and controlling its members, the close attention with which the proceedings of parliament are followed and watched, the kind of dignity that has been lent to parliamentary methods by the great importance of the transactions, have all tended in the same direction. They have all helped both to fix our strongest and most constant interests upon politics, and to ingrain the mental habits proper to politics, far more deeply than any other, into our general Constitution and inmost character."

With this picture of a nation experienced in self-government contrast the inexperience of the Italians and Germans. The English worked out the methods of parliamentary self-government through the ages. Magna Charta, the Bill of Rights, the Reform Bill and the Representation of the People Acts were steps in political progress spread over seven hundred years. In Germany and Italy, Parliamentary Government on an alien model was bestowed on peoples who had not graduated in self-government. The parliamentary system was introduced in Italy when national unity was achieved in 1871, but though the machinery was created the men to work it were lacking. In Germany after the War there was an abrupt change over from an autocratic government to an advanced democracy, and political indigestion was the result. Neither politicians nor the people had behind them the experience necessary for the proper functioning of the new system. To this initial disadvantage the authors of the Weimar Constitution added other difficulties by the improvements they made on democracy's oldest model—a system of election by Party lists and extreme solicitude for the representation of minorities.

One of the criticisms made against the English Parliament is the lack of quality of the members of the elected Chamber. Financial ability to relieve the local associations of the burden of contesting an election (not to speak of contributions to Party funds and local charities), it is argued, is a recommendation which outweighs the deficiencies of a candidate in the eyes of selection committees, with the result that too many rich mediocrities find their way to Westminster. The authors of Germany's constitution introduced safeguards against this. They provided that candidates should not be directly elected by constituencies, but that from the Party lists members should be returned to the Reichstag in numbers proportionate to the votes polled for the Party. By this means of meeting one defect another was created. The result was to deprive the elector of any feeling of personal interest in the elected, and it is questionable whether the desired end of improving the quality of repretatives was achieved, for the way of the Party hack to the Reichstag was made easy.

Multiplication of parties to a fantastic extent resulted from the provision that, for every 60,000 votes polled, a member could be sent to the Reichstag. The founding of a new society was directly invited by this electoral innovation (it was the original inspiration for Hitler), and there was such a proliferation of splinter parties that in the end no fewer than twenty-six fully fledged political organisations were competing for the suffrages of the electors.

Where there are many parties in the elected chamber, no single one gains a commanding majority. The Government therefore must be formed out of an amalgamation of some of the groups. The chamber gains a determining influence on the course of affairs, but the ministry is dangerously weakened in power. Personal ambitions and group rivalries are the factors which determine the rise and fall of governments. Politicians come to be discredited and the ministries, lacking in authority, suffer a damaging loss of prestige in national eyes. Thus is democracy brought into contempt.

Democracy is not an end in itself, but a contrivance—believed by democrats to be the best contrivance—for getting the task of government performed. Good government, and not a perfect political system, is the people's need. In the new Poland an ultra-democratic constitution was introduced with proportional representation to provide for the adequate representation of varying shades of opinion, but the constitution, though based in theory upon the soundest of democratic principles, did not in practice yield the benefits of good and stable government. Parties multiplied, ministries rose and fell. The Legislative Assembly had been made strong at the expense of the weakness of the executive. Pilsudski stepped in as dictator to redress the balance.

In England we have been invited to avail ourselves of the benefits of the arithmetical perfection of proportional representation, but the advocacy of P.R. has scarcely been enhanced by the spectacle of the working out of the system in other countries. We were in the past made uneasily conscious of the absurdities and anomalies of our present electoral arrangements. We were forced to admit that on the face of it it is not equitable that one set of voters numbering five millions should return 70 per cent or even 80 per cent to the House of Commons, and another set of voters numbering four millions should return 20 per cent or 30 per cent, while a third set of voters numbering three millions should secure only 10 per cent of the representation. The logic of arithmetic is incontestible, but the lessons from abroad suggest that not by mere arithmetical perfection is a nation to find political salvation.

We have had our examples of minority government. We have had a Socialist ministry kept precariously in office by Liberal support. We have seen the spectacle of Liberal leaders performing wonderful evolutions in the political circus—justifying the support of measures to-day which they had condemned at the election yesterday, testifying to the possession of marvellously adaptable political consciences, and to the possession of inimitable talents in casuistry. Politics were diverting in those days, but not edifying.   .

The democratic system on the British parliamentary model will only function effectively when one of the parties is assured of a decisive majority in the House of Commons. Our electoral system promotes that end by reason of the very anomalies which advocates of proportional representation deplore. Our system accentuates the swing of the pendulum, gives to the winning party at the elections representation in the House of Commons in excess of what is proportionately due on the results of the poll. This principle in the past worked from election to election in favour of Conservatives and Liberals. It will ultimately operate in favour of the Socialists. It is an arithmetical imperfection, but it is conducive to the strength of the executive, and a strong government is always better than a weak government, for weakness and indecision bring a government into contempt.

Here is to be found one of the major reasons for the collapse of the parliamentary system in Germany, in Italy, in Austria, in Poland, and in Yugoslavia.

In France the working of the parliamentary machine has been endangered by the group system and its manœuvrings. Cabinet crises are too frequent in France for democracy's well-being, and twice since the War her system has been in peril. There are many parties in France reflecting the niceties of political shadings in the series from Right to Left— Republicans, Republican Democrats, Republican Centre, Republicans of the Left, Radicals, Radical Socialists.· There are groups within groups, so that one party merges almost imperceptibly into the next until the pink of Socialism is lost in Communism's red. The Premier has to form his administration out of this unstable material and to maintain himself, as long as he can, despite the shifting play of personal ambitions and group rivalries, and he is the more at the mercy of the groups because he lacks the power to threaten them with the loss of their parliamentary existence. A British Prime Minister can always appeal over the head of Parliament to the nation. Not so the French Premier, for the constitution denies him the power to dissolve the Chamber and order an election.

Nothing in politics is more ephemeral than the life of a French ministry. In the sixty years of the Third Republic the average life of a ministry has been eight months. In the crisis period between 1923–24, seven ministries rose and fell in eighteen months. Seven more ninepins toppled in the period 1928–30. The budget crisis of 1933–34 accentuated ministerial instability to such a degree that it appeared that the parliamentary system would scarcely survive. Then came the shock of the Stavisky scandal, and the Royalist Riots. The octogenarian ex-President Doumergue was called from his retirement to save the Republic and the Government of National Concentration gave the country a breathing space—but no more, for there is a lack of discipline in the Gallic political make-up.

As the perils receded the rivalries of the political groups reasserted themselves. Deputies would not make sacrifices in the cause of constitutional reforms when M. Doumergue proposed to strengthen the executive and diminish the aggressiveness of the legislature. In particular they resisted the proposed grant to the Premier of the prerogative of dissolution. M. Doumergue went back to his retirement (November, 1934), and French democrats may yet have cause to regret the frustration of his intentions.

British democracy has survived the political discontents of the post-war years of crisis, but what of the social discontents that spring from the hardship of economic distress ? It was social discontent, combined with political inexperience and ineptitude, which brought down democracy in Italy and Germany.

National discontent is the background against which you must view the success of the arch-enemies of democracy. Discontent and disillusion are the conditions most favourable to the growth of hope—most powerful of all forces that guide man as an individual or in the mass. Hope that makes slaves of us all is the most effective weapon in the armoury of the politician. By playing on their hopes he can make slaves of a people. Italy and Germany have been enslaved by rulers who bound them with the fetters of hope. The people delivered themselves to men who cried : " Rally to me all ye who are in distress and I will find a panacea for your ills." They have been encouraged to lift their eyes to far distant hills, so distant that the children of this generation will still have an objective before them. Long term hopes are the safest form of investment for a dictator to recommend. When the objective is distant, the people will be the longer occupied in striving, the longer deferred will be the verdict on the dictator's policy.

England's political history has been the happiest, perhaps, of any of the Powers since the War—or at least since 1926, year of the General Strike, a turning-point in our affairs. The demonstration on the part of the workers in support of the miners provided an occasion for the letting off of political steam.

Relations between employers and employed had not previously been good. The revolution in Russia had infected British agitators with a Soviet virus. Extremists found a certain number of converts for Marxism, not on the scale of Germany or Italy, or even France, but agents from Moscow had a certain influence, and the Communists even achieved representation in the House of Commons. The Communist bogey has been well laid since then, but looking back we can remember how prominently it was displayed before the electors. There was the unhappy election in which the Zinoviev or Red Letter played a prominent part. Communism was all to the fore in those days, and the Trade Unions toyed with the idea of direct action. The mining dispute of 1926 provided the occasion for putting the possibilities of direct action to the test.

The experiment was vastly to the credit of our people, showing to the world an admirable example of how national tempers can be kept even in times of national conflict. There was a valuable demonstration, too, that the General Strike in itself as a means of exercising pressure on the Government is a political mistake. Only as the prelude to more extreme action could anything but failure ha·

resulted, and more extreme action could only have meant an attempt to overthrow the Government by armed revolt. The strike failed in circumstances which left the Labour leaders resolved never again to be inveigled into such an adventure.

In other countries the Socialists and Trade Unionists in their hour of failure might have been humiliated by the action of opponents seeking to exploit the occasion to harass the political enemy. There were advocates of such a policy amongst the Conservative diehards, but the only parliamentary action taken was of a mild nature, of which the principal effect was to remove a grievance of non-Socialist members of Trades Unions. Thereafter non-Socialists found it easier to avoid contributing to the Political Levy.

There were no reprisals. The wounds healed quickly. The political health of the nation was restored. Relations between employers and employed entered upon a new phase of cordiality. Bitterness was removed from the national temper. After the great industrial storm there was a period of tranquillity. In the two years immediately following the General Strike the number of working days lost as the result of industrial disputes totalled no more than 2,600,000. In the two years preceding 1926 the total was 16,300,000. Taking the five year period the same tranquillity is shown. For the years 1921–25 an aggregate of 132,500,000 days of work was lost as the result of strikes ; in the years 1927–31 the days lost were no more than 22,300,000. It may be mentioned that the upheavals of 1926 cost a loss reckoned in working days of 162,233,000.

.   .   .   .

The great steadying and tranquillising influence has been that of Mr. Baldwin. Here is a striking contrast between the democratic leader and the dictator. Mussolini and Hitler exacerbated national feeling and fostered national strife. Mr. Baldwin's role has been that of the great mollifier. Tranquillity was the watchword of one of his elections. His opponents tried to ridicule him for it, but the tranquillity he inspired, the sanity and the good will, enabled British democracy to face and survive the economic blizzard.

Within the Conservative Party they have cavilled sometimes at his leadership for its lack of inspiration. Mr. Baldwin has not been turned from his conception of his duty to democracy.

Ostentatiously—the only form of ostentation to be alleged against him—his public speeches indicate his resolve never to pitch hopes too high, to encourage the belief that things are better than they seem, to promise more than he considers can be fulfilled. The result is that his hearers are rarely roused to enthusiasm by glowing periods or perorations. But he has told democracy the truth, and as Deputy Leader of the National Government—and now once again Prime Minister—has proved the greatest steadying influence in our political life for a century, perhaps since Walpole. Mr. Baldwin is democracy's reply to the dictators.

Another circumstance which has contributed to our escape from unrest and disorder is the existence of the system of unemployment insurance. Mr. Lloyd George was bitterly assailed at the time of the passing of his Unemployment Insurance Act, and was ridiculed as the author of a stamp-licking system. The stamps at which they laughed then are the envy of the world to-day. He advocated this great measure of social reform on humanitarian grounds. Had his eye penetrated through the Welsh mists into the future, he would have been able to foretell that the stamps would, in time of trouble, prove a help whose importance it would be difficult to exaggerate. The existence in Italy and Germany of large numbers of unemployed men was one of the decisive factors in the rise of Nazi-Fascism. Discontented unemployed form a fine recruiting ground for Marxists and anti-Marxists.

In Germany the Communist poll increased in proportion with the roll of unemployed. Hitler enrolled thousands of workless men and put them into brown shirts. Imagine what might have been in England without the Lloyd George fund to ensure the means of existence for those denied the opportunity of work. Since 1921 there have never been less than a million on the unemployment registers and at the height of the economic blizzard there were over two millions and a half. Without the insurance scheme the existence of so vast a body of workless men and women would have been a menace to society. Mr. Lloyd George's scheme proved to be one of the best insurances for national security at home.

Why then should we suppose that Britain should go Fascist and a dictatorship replace our democracy ? Two of the principal factors which contributed to democracy's over-throw abroad are absent here. There is no great volume of political discontent, and although we have our unemployed, conditions of economic distress have been provided against. There is no evidence to suggest the emergence in England of a Fascist Movement comparable with those of Italy and Germany ; no evidence of the existence of a Fascist leader, for the present aspirant to the role is a simulacrum of Mussolini or of Hitler, an elegant shadow of the European despots. The weather-vane has its uses, but it is not customarily regarded as a symbol of determination, far less of ruthlessness. Sir Oswald Mosley is a political weather-vane. He has veered through all the points but one of the political compass. The true blue Conservative who represented Harrow passed by way of Independence to the Socialist fold, and he ascended the front bench as Chancellor of the Duchy in 1929. But he was too independent to ride in the Socialist coach, and he ventured into the political wilderness as leader of the New Party. When this organisa-tion was smashed at the polls in 1931,[1] he founded the Union of Fascists. After trying all the other colours in the political faction ship, he came down to black, symbol of what ? Mourning for his lost consistency, or of despair ? We have the career of Mr. Churchill to remind us that inconsistency is not an unforgivable sin in politics if you are tough enough to brazen it out, but these peripatetics of politics are scarcely of the calibre from which despots are made.

Oswald Mosley has all the trappings of Fascism, the patter of Fascist oratory and an elegance that Mussolini and Hitler lack, but somehow the appearance of conviction contrives to elude him. He may be credited with the possession of more subtle brains than Adolf Hitler, but he has yet to gain

[1] It was a massacre of the innocents. Twenty-two New Party candidates forfeited their election deposits. They polled between them 36,000 votes, about the equal of a popular supporter of the National Government. Even the Communists secured the support of 74,000.

a reputation for such unquestionable sincerity and belief in his own gospel, that absolutely fanatical faith in himself and his movement that distinguishes the Führer of Germany. The leader of the British Fascists is so obviously not a man from the ranks come forward to lead the people. He stands but ill disguised a patrician in Black Shirt clothing, and that so faultlessly tailored.

It is not from Fascist or Communist that British democracy stands in danger, but from the people's own party. *Quis custodiet ipsos custodes?* The Socialists should be democrats of democrats, yet they threaten to adopt methods of dictatorship. Who will be democratic watch-dog over our faltering democrats? We have need here of a croaking Marat, an English *ami du peuple*, to nose out the traitors in the ranks. The Socialists are dissatisfied with our Constitution—not merely with our undemocratic House of Lords, but with the House of Commons, which should be the ark and covenant of democracy. In the event of Socialist success at the polls Parliament would be invited in the terms of the programme of some of the more doctrinaire Left Wingers to transfer emergency powers to the Socialist Government and to stand aside while the Socialist State was brought into being. " There will be no time for superfluous debating while we are busy building the Socialist commonwealth," proclaims Mr. G. D. H. Cole. The Socialist Emergency Powers Act would be a statute without limitations. Orders issued by Ministers under its terms would be " incapable of challenge in the courts," according to Sir Stafford Cripps. The late Mr. E. F. Wise, former Chairman of the National Council of the Socialist League, warned us of the censorship that would be. " Free speech," he said, " a so-called free Press, are no more parts of the eternal verities than is free trade."

There is an ominous similarity between these proposals and the programmes which Mussolini and Hitler have carried into operation—and Socialists denounced Hitler and Mussolini in terms which should only be applied to political barbarians. The democrat cries " A plague on both your houses ! " A dictatorship by Sir Stafford Cripps in the name of the proletariat would be as unpalatable as a dictatorship by Sir Oswald Mosley in the name of British Fascism, and would be even more of an ironic jest of the fates. We may or we may not want Socialism in our time, but we do not want Socialism at the price of the loss of our liberties and the abrogation of the rule of law. There was a time when it appeared that the roads labelled Socialist and democratic travelled in the same direction. Now they are seen to lie apart, unless the promised land flies the red flag, worships at the shrine of Lenin and is subject to the dictatorship, so-called, of the proletariat.

There are milder expressions of Socialist intentions than those of Sir Stafford Cripps. Indeed, the official Party, the Socialism in our time men, have been embarrassed by the declarations of the Left Wingers who want Socialism accomplished to-morrow afternoon. The official Party has declared its disavowal of methods of dictatorship, alarmed by the spectacle of events in Austria and Germany. Nevertheless the less advanced members of the Party have indicated a certain impatience with our parliamentary machinery. Twice a Socialist Government has been in office without achieving an advance towards the Socialist commonwealth. There have been doubts in the Party as to whether Socialism in any time is ever to be arrived at unless a headlong plunge is taken. There is the trouble ; there the danger to the democratic system. Headlong plunges must inevitably lead to the damage of the fabric of our Constitution.

Compromise and the inevitability of gradualness are irksome to earnest social reformers, but it is this very earnestness of conviction which led Hitler to overthrow democracy in Germany. For our democracy to survive and function, compromise is essential. The Conservative safeguarders of things as they are must reconcile themselves to progress and the advocates of advance must temper their impatience. The extension of the franchise indicates the tempo of political progress under our democracy. It took but five years less than a century to complete by the grant of adult suffrage irrespective of sex under the Representation of the People Act, 1928, the movement which was begun by the first Reform Bill of 1832. It took a century to enfranchise the nation. The socialisation of society is a much more complicated affair. Will Socialists accept a rate of gradual progress, or will they sacrifice democracy in their zeal for Socialism ?

·　　·　　·　　·　　·　　·　　·　　·

Except, then, from the zealots of Socialism we have no reason to stand in awe of the menacing shadow of the dictator. Neither from the extreme Left or Right is there evidence of a movement or a leader to cause democrat disquiet. It may be hoped that office, when it comes, will exercise a steadying influence on the Socialists and encourage them to reach a respect for the Constitution which, in opposition, they attack and deride.

We may learn from the dictators how to avoid the political errors which contributed to democracy's overthrow elsewhere. One conclusion is unchallengeable—that the surest safeguard against a dictatorship is efficient democratic government.

Democracy may stoop to learn yet further from the dictators. Fascist Italy has adopted many expedients from Bolshevik Russia and Nazi Germany from Italy. Guided by experience under the new régimes abroad, we may consider the introduction of innovations within the framework of our democratic State.

The task of the man who would govern a nation becomes more difficult year by year. At first it was a matter of politics ; then as the State became less self-contained, problems of international diplomacy as well. Now, to problems of politics and diplomacy are added the complexities of economics. No nation can be contented unless its statesmen are politically adept. No nation can feel secure if its rulers are not diplomatically skilled. No nation can be prosperous unless its rulers are guided by sound economic principles. National prosperity, the riches or poverty of the people, the number of unemployed in the streets, all those elemental features which determine whether the national barometer stands at contentment or despair—these things are determined by the hard facts of economics.

It is the verdict of Mussolini that a dictator is necessary for the proper planning of industrial affairs on national lines, and he has looked towards Russia for an example. Production in Italy, but not distribution, has avowedly been organised on the Bolshevik model, though within the framework of a capitalist State. President Roosevelt made his plans for planning. Even in this country we have made hesitant, tentative moves in planning. We have paid the Bolsheviks the compliment of adopting a Five-Year Plan for the roads. There are national schemes for an incipient control over some of our agricultural products, and there are provisions for a certain measure of rationalisation in coal production. Electricity has been organised on a national scale.

But these measures fall immeasurably short of the programmes of Communism and Fascism, and even these have met with the criticism that we are losing our old individualism. But these are times when the well-being of the individual requires restraint on individualism. The modern nation must plan for prosperity, and planning implies control and restraints.

There is planning for national contentment as well as for national prosperity, which is a matter not of economics, but of politics and psychology. It is the duty of a government not merely to govern well, but to gain the reputation of governing well. Achievement and reputation are not necessarily related. It cannot be gainsaid that our Party system results in an immense wastage of national contentment. Discontent is deliberately fostered by the Party out of office, and we do pay, perhaps, too high a price in dissatisfaction. In the totalitarian States they do not merely discourage discontent ; they incite to contentment.

The duty of a parliamentary opposition is to oppose, a maxim which elevates political fault-finding to the dignity of a principle, and perpetual fault-finding is inevitably damaging to the reputation of our politicians. A people should be encouraged to respect its rulers, to believe in their integrity, their ability, and if possible in their greatness. The effect of Party politics is precisely the reverse.

The attacks of the opposition parties undermined the authority of Ministers in Italy and Germany. There were few politicians left with any shred of reputation for statesmanship. Under the dictatorships, the ban of silence has been imposed upon factious fault-finding. A considerable part of the opinion which has been suppressed is no more than parrot opinion. On democratic principles the suppression of any opinion is to be regretted, but a case can be made for the silencing of the parrots. They are now being trained to use another set of cries—calls of honour for the Führer and the Duce. Parrot cries are worth nothing, but the peoples of Italy and Germany may be the more contented for being trained to have faith in their leaders. If people must be led in their political opinions because they are too indifferent or unskilled to form their own, it is better that they should be led towards contentment than discontentment, better that they should be induced to believe in the greatness and ability of their rulers than to be taught contempt for them. Complete freedom of speech is a privilege only deserved by a people that has learned not to abuse it.

In these new totalitarian States the dictators have not merely suppressed their critics out of existence, they have inaugurated a system of State applause, a matter which appears to have a considerable bearing upon the period of existence of the dictatorships. Democrats with a certain optimistic complacency assure themselves that the dictators will not long survive. They point to history and claim that in the end the people have always overthrown the despot. But despots of the past did not have the skill of our modern dictators in the usage of publicity and propaganda. They did not know how to recommend their rule, to make their very despotism appear a merit in the eyes of their peoples.

Autocrats in the past were satisfied to stamp out criticism. Our modern dictator goes further and appoints a Dr. Goebbels as Minister to train the people in admiration of the Leader, to organise the powerful influences of Press and radio in the cause of the dictatorship. The very children in the schools are reared in reverence of the head of the State. In Russia a generation has almost grown up on Bolshevism. How can the people withstand the influences of this political Coué-ism? How can discontent spread abroad in these hot-houses of political contentment? How can wearers of black shirt, brown shirt and red shirt come to wish for the shirt of liberty when their political fashion plates show nothing but black and brown and red?

Hitler and Mussolini have given their people a new political system, a new economic theory, a new manifestation of the arts of publicity and propaganda. But over and beyond these things they have given their peoples a new psychology. A new spirit is abroad in Italy, in Germany and in Russia to-day. The people have been roused to believe in the supreme importance of themselves and the destinies of their race. Mussolini has called upon the past spirit of

Rome, Hitler upon the spirit of the old Teutons.   They have given their people hope and faith.

Where is the faith in England to-day ?   There is faith in Italy and Germany, in Poland and in Turkey ; the Communists have faith in their creed ; the American was given faith in Mr. Roosevelt and the New Deal.   Where is the faith of England ?   The old faiths have gone.   They are now called shams and shibboleths, but no new faith has taken their place.   There is rather a universal distrust in faith, a universal scepticism and agnosticism.   A people cannot continue in a state of scepticism and agnosticism.   Faith is one of the laws of our being.   Pagan Rome lost faith and became Christian.   The Reformation and revival of faith followed the loss of faith in medieval Christianity.   Wesleyan evangelism was aroused by agnosticism of the eighteenth century.   We have lost faith to-day.   Where shall we find faith to-morrow ?   Italy and Germany lost faith and found a new faith in their dictators.   Who will give faith to England ?

It has emerged from our examination that democracy failed in Italy and Germany because it was an alien tradition introduced on a foreign model.   Let the future leader of England remember that dictatorship is alien to the English race and traditions.

BOOK LIST

For the writing of history almost contemporaneously with the events recorded, the chronicler must inevitably rely upon the newspapers for the basis of his information. This book could not have been written without the invaluable aid of the foreign news services of *The Daily Telegraph* and *The Times*. The literature concerning the dictators and systems of dictatorships is already vast, and is weekly being added to at an alarming rate. It would be a lifetime's work to assimilate the extensive literature concerning the Russian Revolution and the founders of Communism alone.

The book list which follows does not pretend to be more than an outline of some of the more valuable books. Amongst the general surveys, two stand out—*A Guide to Modern Politics*, by G. D. H. and M. I. Cole, and *The World Since* 1914, by Walter Consuelo Langsam. An entire library of books has appeared during recent months devoted to the discussions of the place in world politics of the rival doctrines of Communism and Nazi-Fascism and the future of Liberal Democracy. The majority of them appear to be of little merit, but while this book was in the press there appeared three works of particular value, *Bolshevism, Fascism and the Liberal Democratic State*, by Maurice Parmelee, *Essentials of Parliamentary Democracy*, by R. Bassett, and, for the German struggle, *The Fall of the German Republic*, by R. T. Clark.

HITLER

My Struggle. Adolf Hitler.
History of National Socialism. Konrad Heiden.
My Part in Germany's Fight. Dr. Joseph Goebbels.
Mythos of the Twentieth Century. Alfred Rosenberg.
Germany Enters the Third Reich. C. B. Hoover.
The Brown Book of the Hitler Terror and *The Reichstag Fire Trial.*
Hitler : Whence and Whither and *The Meaning of Hitlerism.*
Wickham Steed.

297

Mussolini

My Autobiography. Benito Mussolini.
Social and Political Doctrine of Fascism. Benito Mussolini.
Economic Foundations of Fascism. Paul Einzig.
Making of the Fascist State. H. W. Schneider.
Fascist Dictatorship. Gaetano Salvemini.
Fascism at Work. William Elwin.

Kemal Ataturk

Mustapha Kemal of Turkey. H. E. Wortham.
Turkey Faces West. Halidé Edib.
Rebirth of Turkey. C. Price.
The Fall of Abd-ul-Hamid. F. McCullagh.
Grey Wolf—Mustapha Kemal. H. C. Armstrong.

Marshal Pilsudski

Memories of a Polish Revolutionary and Soldier. Joseph Pilsudski.
Poland. E. J. Patterson.
The New Poland. N. O. Winter.

President Roosevelt

Looking Forward. Franklin D. Roosevelt.
On Our Way. Franklin D. Roosevelt.
The Roosevelt Revolution. E. K. Lindley.
The New America. Sir A. Steel-Maitland.

Lenin and Stalin

Lenin. V. Marcu.
Lenin. D. S. Mirsky.
Lenin. James Maxton.
My Life : The Rise and Fall of a Dictator. Leon Trotsky.
History of the Russian Revolution. Leon Trotsky.
Mind and Face of Bolshevism. R. Fülop-Miller.
Second Five-Year Plan. W. P. Coates and Zelda K. Coates.
Ten Days that Shook the World. John Reed.
The Russian Revolution. James Mavor.
Murder of the Romanovs. Captain Paul Bulygin.
Stalin. I. D. Levine.

APPENDIX

HITLER ON GERMAN RE-ARMAMENT

[Speech[1] delivered in the Reichstag on May 21, 1935, by Adolf Hitler, Führer and Chancellor.]

Members of the German Reichstag :

At the wish of the Government, General Göring, my party colleague and Chairman of the Reichstag, has called you together for the purpose of hearing from me, as representative of the German nation, some explanatory statements which I consider necessary for the understanding of the attitude taken up by the Government of the Reich and the decisions it has made in regard to certain great issues which affect us all at the present time.

For this purpose I am speaking to you and through you to the German nation. But I wish that my words may also have a wider echo and reach all those in the outside world who, from duty or interest, have endeavoured to obtain an insight into our thoughts on those same problems which also concern themselves.

I consider this to be the fitting place to make such a statement, because experience has shown that it is necessary to guard against the danger of diverse interpretations arising out of conversations which take place between two or only amid a small circle of hearers, the natural result of which is that the public can receive only a fragmentary account of what was said.

I regard this manner of making such a declaration as specially useful because it gives me not only the right, but indeed the sacred duty, to be absolutely open and to speak with all frankness about the various problems. The German nation has the right to demand this from me, and I am determined to comply with the demand. From Anglo-Saxon countries I often hear expressions of regret that Germany should have departed from just those principles of democratic government which such countries consider as specially sacred. This opinion is based upon a serious error. Germany, too, has a " democratic " constitution. The present German Government of the National-Socialist State has also been elected by the people, and feels itself in the same way responsible to the people. It does not matter how many votes a deputy must have in the individual countries. There are countries which consider 20,000 votes necessary for a deputy, others consider 10,000 or 5,000 sufficient, while in others again the number is 60,000 or more.

The German people has elected a single deputy as its representative with 38,000,000 votes. This is perhaps one of the most important differences between ours and the conditions existing in other countries. It means that I feel myself just as responsible to the German people as would any parliament. I act on the trust they have placed in me and I carry out their mandate. The German people therefore have the right to expect that an explanation such as I am about to give to-day should be the unvarnished

[1] Authorised Translation.

truth, and that it should openly discuss those questions which affect not only the rest of the world but also, and at least to the same degree, the German nation itself. And I am glad of this for the following reasons : As Führer and Chancellor of the nation, and as head of the Government of the Reich, unfortunately I have often to make decisions which are of themselves hard enough to decide upon and which are all the more difficult because it is not possible for me to share the responsibility and even less to shift it to someone else's shoulders. And it is for this reason that I desire at least to be able to give to the nation itself an insight into the ideas on which I act and thus make it easier for them to understand the decisions and measures which arise from these ideas. But the more difficult the decisions, so much the more I as a German should like to make sure that my actions are completely uninfluenced by instincts of weakness or fear, and to bring them into harmony with my conscience towards my God and the nation which He permits me to serve.

When the late President entrusted me, on the 30th of January, two years ago, with the formation of a new Government, and the conduct of the affairs of the Reich, many people were sceptical—and among the sceptics were many patriots—about the success of the task laid before me. Envy and anxiety were current among the then distracted German people. For only the inner enemy could draw hope from our position as it then was, whereas friends were unspeakably downhearted. In many spheres national life was in sore jeopardy. Even though for numbers of people—quite naturally—the economic catastrophe was the most serious of all, for those who could think more deeply it was only a consequence. The inner causes which necessarily gave rise to the economic effects were many. Some of them were of a social character. Others were a matter of political organisation, and others again had their origin in the moral order. In view of the overwhelming number of the tasks, the apparent hopelessness of the situation, and the paucity of all means at our disposal, it demanded an enormous amount of courage not to falter—but immediately to set to work to help the nation out of the slough of misery and disruption into which it had fallen.

The economic situation was as follows : After a war which had lasted for four years and had already done untold damage to the national resources the victor Powers imposed upon the German nation a peace dictate devoid of all political and economic reason, and which aimed at making the relation of forces that existed at the end of the War the legal basis for the life of the nations for all time. Without considering the conditions and laws that govern economic life, and even in direct contradiction to them, the victor Powers deprived Germany of every possibility of an economic revival while demanding on the other hand payments and services which lay within the realm of the fantastic. The edifice of German economics was razed to the ground under the watchword " Reparations." This incomprehensible disregard for the most elementary economic laws resulted in the following situation :

1. The nation had a surplus of workers.
2. It was in urgent need of something to replace the values pertaining to the high standard of life to which it had been accustomed and which had been destroyed by the War, the inflation, and the reparations.
3. It suffered from a lack of natural resources of foodstuffs and raw materials.
4. The international market which it needed in order to overcome all these evils was too small, and was further increasingly limited in practice by various measures and by a certain inevitable trend in developments.

It is a very poor testimony to the economic sense of those who were then our political opponents that until their action had not only completely destroyed German economy but had begun to show its ill effects in the economic life of other countries, they did not begin to see that it was impossible for us to fulfil unlimited and sometimes incomprehensible demands.

The result of this madness was that German industry was paralysed, agriculture was destroyed, the middle classes were ruined, trade had shrunk to almost nothing, the whole economic life was overladen with debt, the public finances were rotten to the core, and there were six and a half million unemployed on the register—in reality more than seven and a half millions.

To overcome the economic catastrophe alone very difficult measures were necessary. Formerly the German nation could find room for its ever-increasing population in a limited space, thanks to the adequate conditions of life which resulted from its participation in international trade. As long as this latter condition was fulfilled the 67,000,000 inhabitants of Germany could, in spite of the comparative smallness of the country, feel not only that their livelihood was assured at home, but that they were a useful factor in world economy. The course of the War, and especially the result of post-War politics, will one day serve as a classic, though terrible, disproof of the naïve idea—which unfortunately was held by some statesmen before the War—that the economic advantage of one European state can best be promoted by the economic destruction of another.

For the German nation the economic consequences of the peace on the one hand and the disadvantages from which Germany suffered in her home and foreign trade and commerce, on the other, must inevitably have compelled any government, whether it willed or not, to take the actual situation into account. We are all convinced that the complete carrying out of the idea of economic self-sufficiency for all states, which is threatening us to-day, is, when seen from a higher standpoint, foolish, and can only result in harm for all nations. Economically regarded, it is not very reasonable to endeavour artificially to turn natural agricultural and raw material districts into industrial districts, or, on the other hand, to endeavour to compel the over-populated industrial countries to produce raw materials, or even substitutes, to an adequate degree.

For Europe this development will one day have very unpleasant and evil consequences. But to alter it is unfortunately not within Germany's power. Looked at from the broad economic angle, it is against the dictates of reason. What happens is that in so far as we are deprived of foreign markets for our exports we are forced to restrict our imports. To that extent, so that German productive labour may not stagnate, we must either employ a complicated process for the production of the raw materials that we lack internally, or else we must use substitutes. This task can be undertaken only by means of a planned economic system. And that is a perilous adventure ; for planned economics lead to bureaucratic control, and thus to the suppression of individual creative effort. In the interests of our own nation it was not desirable to risk the eventuality of having the productive efficiency of our people reduced, and the standards of living lowered rather than raised by an economic system not far removed from the communist ideal and by the accompanying paralysis of initiative effort. This danger was accentuated by the following fact : Every planned system of production only too easily invalidates the hard laws of the economic survival of the fittest and elimination of the weak ; or at least it hampers the activity of these laws inasmuch as it guarantees the preservation of the least valuable average, to the detriment of higher efficiency and greater productive power and quality, all of which work out finally to the detriment of the community.

If, despite such knowledge, we have nevertheless taken this path, it was only under the hard pressure of necessity. What we have achieved in two and a half years in the way of a planned provision of labour, a planned regulation of the market, a planned control of prices and wages, was considered a few years ago to be absolutely impossible. We only succeeded because behind these apparently dead economic measures we had the living energies of the whole nation. We had, however, first to create a number of technical and psychological conditions before we could carry out this purpose. In order to guarantee the functioning of the national economy it was necessary first of all to put a stop to the everlasting oscillations of wages and prices. It was further necessary to remove the conditions giving rise to interference which did not spring from higher national economic necessities, i.e. to destroy the class organisations of both camps which lived on the politics of wages and prices. The destruction of the trade unions, both of employers and employees, which were based on the class struggle, demanded an analogous removal of the political parties which were maintained by these groups of interests, which interests in return supported them. Here arose the necessity for a new constructive and vital constitution and a new organisation of the Reich and State. If this was to be more than a purely superficial reorganisation however, then the nation itself had to be educated to a new social way of thinking and living. All these were tasks of which each would require a century for its fulfilment, and in the carrying out of which many a people and state foundered in former times. To bring such a programme to realisation, which either succeeds in its entirety or is bound from the very beginning to fail at every point, success depends upon two conditions :

(a) The extent of peace and quiet at home.

(b) The amount of time at one's disposal.

We Germans can only regret that the rest of the world still takes so little trouble to study objectively what has been going on in Germany within the last two and a half years, and that it does not study the ideals which are solely responsible for these achievements.

For the aims adopted and also the carrying out of the tasks which impart their special stamp to present-day Germany have their origin exclusively in National-Socialist ideas, and are to be ascribed to the National-Socialist Party, its organisation, and to that characteristic energy which emanates from it. In the course of the last two years a revolution has taken place in Germany that is greater than the average man has yet realised. The extent and profundity of this revolution have not suffered owing to the leniency with which its former opponents were treated. For this leniency was by no means due to a feeling of weakness, but on the contrary to a conviction of vast superiority and to a sure confidence in victory. Hence this new Germany cannot be compared with the Germany of the past. Its ideas are just as new as its actions. The spirit of bourgeois jingoism as a decisive political factor has been just as much overcome as the tendencies of Marxist internationalism. If the present Germany advocates peace, it does so neither owing to weakness nor to cowardice. It advocates peace from another standpoint regarding people and state, namely, the standpoint of National Socialism. For National Socialism regards the forcible amalgamation of one people with another alien people not only as a worthless political aim, but in the long run as a danger to the internal unity and hence the strength of a nation. National Socialism therefore dogmatically rejects the idea of national assimilation. That also disposes of the bourgeois belief in a possible " Germanisation."

It is therefore neither our wish nor our intention to deprive alien sections of our population of their nationalism, language or culture, in order to replace these by something German and foreign to them. We issue no directions for the Germanisation of non-German names ; on the contrary, we do not wish that. Our racial theory therefore regards every war for the subjection and domination of an alien people as a proceeding which sooner or later changes and weakens the victor internally, and eventually brings about his defeat. *But we do not believe for a moment that in Europe the nations whose nationalism has been completely consolidated could in the era of the principle of nationalities be deprived of their national birthright at all.* The last 150 years provide more than enough instructive warnings of this. In no future war will the European national states be able to achieve— apart from the temporary weakening of their opponents—more than petty adjustments of national frontiers, of no consequence in comparison with the sacrifices made.

But the permanent state of war that will be established between the various peoples by such intentions may perhaps appear advantageous to various political and economic interests. For the nations, however, it merely means burdens and misfortune. The blood shed on the European continent in the course of the last 300 years bears no proportion to the national result of the events. In the end France has remained France, Germany Germany, Poland Poland, and Italy Italy. What dynastic egoism, political passion and patriotic blindness have attained in the way of apparently far-reaching political changes by shedding rivers of blood has, as regards national feeling, done no more than touched the skin of the nations. It has not substantially altered their fundamental characters. If these states had applied merely a fraction of their sacrifices to wiser purposes the success would certainly have been greater and more permanent.

When I, as a National Socialist, advocate this view perfectly frankly, I am also influenced by the following realisation. The principal effect of every war is to destroy the flower of the nation. But as there is no longer any unoccupied space in Europe, every victory—without making any difference to the fundamental distress in Europe—can at best result in a quantitative increase in the number of the inhabitants of a country. But if the nations attach so much value to that, they can achieve it without tears in a simpler and more natural way. A sound social policy, by increasing the readiness of a nation to have children, can give its own people more children in a few years than the number of aliens that could be conquered and made subject to that nation by war.

No! National Socialist Germany wants peace because of its fundamental convictions. And it wants peace also owing to the realisation of the simple primitive fact that no war would be likely essentially to alter the distress in Europe. It would probably increase it. Present-day Germany is engaged in the tremendous work of making good the damage done to it internally. None of our projects of a practical nature will be completed before a period of from ten to twenty years. None of our tasks of an ideal kind can be completed before fifty or, perhaps, a hundred years have passed. I started the National Socialist Revolution by bringing the movement into being, and since then I have directed the Revolution into the path of action. I know that none of us will live to see more than the very beginning of this great revolutionary development. What, then, could I wish more than peace and tranquillity? But if it is said that this is merely the desire of the leaders, I can reply that if only the leaders and rulers desire peace, the nations themselves will never wish for war.

Germany needs peace and desires peace. And when I now hear from the lips of a British statesman that such assurances are nothing, and that the only proof of sincerity is the signature appended to collective pacts, I must ask Mr. Eden to be good enough to remember that it is a question of an " assurance " in any case. It is sometimes much easier to sign treaties with the mental reservation that one will reconsider one's attitude at the decisive hour than to declare, before an entire nation, and with full publicity, one's adherence to a policy which serves the cause of peace because it rejects anything that may lead to war.

I might have signed ten treaties, but such action would not have been of the same importance as the statement I made to France on the occasion of the Saar plebiscite. When I, as the Führer and representative of the German nation, gave to the world and to my own people the assurance that with the settlement of the Saar question no further territorial demands would be made on France, that was a contribution to peace much greater than many a signature under many a pact. I believe that this solemn declaration really ought to have put an end to a quarrel of long duration between these two nations. We made it in the belief that this conflict and the sacrifices involved were for both nations out of all proportion to the object which has constantly been and would be the cause of so much general suffering and misfortune.

But if such a declaration only receives the answer that it has been "taken cognisance of" then there naturally remains for us nothing else to do but to "take cognisance of" this reply too. But I must protest here against every attempt to interpret statements differently according to requirements. If the German Government gives an assurance in the name of the German people that they wish nothing but peace, then this declaration is either of exactly the same value as their signature under any specially worded pact, or otherwise this signature could not be of more value than the solemn declaration.

It is peculiar that in the history of nations inflated formulæ frequently occur which would hardly withstand exact examination in the light of reason.

For some time the world has been suffering, for instance, from a regular mania for collective co-operation, collective security, collective obligations and so on, all of which seem to have a concrete meaning at the first glance, but which, when regarded more closely, at least allow of manifold interpretations.

What is meant by collective co-operation?

Who shall determine what is collective co-operation and what is not?

Has the term "collective co-operation" not been interpreted in the most different ways for the last seventeen years?

I believe I am right when I say that besides many other rights the victor states of the Versailles Treaty have also arbitrarily assumed the right to decide, without allowing anyone to contradict them, what "collective co-operation" is and what it is not.

In allowing myself to criticise this procedure here, I do so because it is the simplest way in which the essential necessity of the latest decisions of the Government of the Reich can be explained and understanding for our real intentions awakened.

The present idea of collective co-operation among the nations is in essence and fundamentally the intellectual property of President Wilson. The policy of the pre-War period was determined rather by the idea of separate alliances of the nations brought together by common interests. Rightly or wrongly, this policy was formerly held responsible for the outbreak of the World War. Its termination—at least, as far as Germany is concerned—was hastened by the doctrine of Wilson's fourteen points and the three points that supplemented them later. The essential ideas laid down in them to prevent a similar catastrophe happening again to mankind were as follows:

The Peace should not be a Peace of unilateral rights but of general equality and henceforth of universal justice. It should be a peace of reconciliation, of general disarmament, and thereby of general security. From this resulted as crowning achievement the idea of international collective collaboration of all states and nations within a League of Nations.

I should like at this juncture to reaffirm that no nation greeted these ideas more eagerly at the end of the War than Germany. Her sufferings and sacrifices were far more severe than those of any other nation which had taken part in the War. It was in reliance upon these promises that the German soldiers laid down their arms.

When in 1919 the Peace of Versailles was dictated to the German people death sentence was thereby pronounced upon collective collaboration of the nations. For where there should have been equality there was division into victors and vanquished. Instead of equal rights there was discrimination between those with rights and those without. Instead of general reconciliation there was punishment of the defeated. Instead of international disarmament, the disarmament of the vanquished. Instead of general security there was security for the victors.

Yet even in the dictated Peace of Versailles it was expressly provided that the disarmament of Germany should only be carried out first to enable the others to disarm also. Here we are afforded an instance of the extent to which the idea of collective collaboration has been violated by those who are to-day its loudest protagonists.

Germany has fulfilled almost fanatically the requirements imposed upon her by the Peace Treaty, financially to the utter derangement of her finances, economically to the total destruction of her economic life, and in national defence to the point of absolute defencelessness. I reiterate here in broad outline the indisputable facts of Germany's fulfilment of the Treaties.

The following armament was destroyed :

PERTAINING TO THE ARMY :

1.   59,000 guns and gun tubes.
2.   130,000 machine-guns.
3.   31,000 trench mortars and tubes.
4.   6,007,000 rifles and carbines.
5.   243,000 machine-gun tubes.
6.   28,000 gun chassis.
7.   4,390 trench mortar stands.
8. 38,750,000 projectiles.
9. 16,550,000 hand and machine bombs.
10. 60,400,000 priming caps.
11. 491,000,000 rifle projectiles.
12.   335,000 (tons) cartridge cases.
13.   23,515 (tons) cartridge and shell cases.
14.   37,600 tons of powder.
15.   79,000 munition gauges.
16.   212,000 telephones.
17.   1,072 flame-throwers, etc. etc.

In addition to this were destroyed : sledges, portable workshops, anti-aircraft guns, armoured cars, amunition chests, helmets, gas-masks, machines belonging to the old war industries, gun tubes, etc. :

PERTAINING TO THE AIR FORCE :

15,714 chasers and bombing planes.
27,757 aeroplane motors.

PERTAINING TO THE FLEET

26 battleships.
4 armed ships for coastal defence.
4 light cruisers.

19 small cruisers.
21 training and special ships.
83 torpedo boats.
315 submarines.

The following general material was also destroyed :

Waggons of all descriptions.
Material for and against gas attacks.
Material used in the making up of projectiles and explosives.
Searchlights.
Direction finders.
Instruments for measuring distance and for measuring shells. Optical
    instruments of all kinds.
Harness, etc., and all aerodromes for aeroplanes and airships, etc. etc

Germany, on her part, has in almost complete submission paved the way for collective collaboration as it was conceived by the President of the United States.

Now, at any rate, after the completion of German disarmament, the rest of the world ought to have taken similar steps to establish equality. The truth of this view is attested by the fact that voices which warned and admonished were not lacking among the other states and nations, urging the fulfilment of their duty in this respect. I will quote from one or two people who certainly cannot be regarded as friends of the new Germany, so as to refute from their statements the attempts of others to disregard the fact that the contractual obligation in the Peace Treaty to disarm is binding not only on Germany but also on the other states.

Lord Robert Cecil, Member of the British Delegation at the Paris Peace Conference and leader of the British Delegation in the Disarmament Conference, made the following statement, which I quote from the text published in the *Revue de Paris* (No. 5, 1924) :

" The armament stipulations laid down in the Versailles Treaty and other Peace Treaties begin with a preamble which runs as follows : ' To make possible the beginning of a general reduction of armament on the part of all nations, Germany agrees to observe exactly the following stipulations in regard to her land forces, sea power and air power.' This preamble entails a common agreement. It is a solemn promise on the part of the Governments to the Democracies of all the states which signed the Peace Treaty. If it will not be maintained, then the system erected by the Peace Treaty cannot abide, and even partial disarmament will in a short while cease to be observed."

On April 8th, 1927, in the third meeting of the Disarmament Commission, called together by the League of Nations, M. Paul Boncour said :

" It is true that the preamble to Section 5 of the Versailles Treaty refers to the reduction of armaments which Germany was to carry out as an introduction and example for a general reduction of armaments. This differentiates very clearly between the reduction of armaments in Germany and other such reductions which in the course of history were carried out at the close of wars, and which generally proved themselves ineffective. On this occasion such a provision refers for the first time to the whole world, and binds not merely one signatory to the Treaty but establishes a moral and juridical obligation for the other signatories to undertake a general reduction of armaments."

On January 20th, 1931, Mr. Arthur Henderson declared :

" We must convince our parliaments and our peoples that all members of the League of Nations ought to be forced into this policy of a general disarmament which is a sacred obligation laid upon us by international law and national honour. Have I to remind the Council that Article 8 of the Covenant and the preamble to Section 5 of the Versailles Treaty, the final Act of the Locarno Conference and the Resolutions adopted every year since 1920 by the Assembly (of the League) lay down that all the Members of the League are under an equal obligation in this matter ? We have all taken the obligations unto ourselves, and if we do not fulfil them our peaceful intentions may be called in question. The influence and prestige of the League of Nations will suffer thereby."

On January 20th, 1931, M. Briand declared :

" In the name of my country I conclude with the words which were used by our President in opening the session . . . I believe with you, and I have often had the chance of saying so, that the obligations which the nations contractually agreed upon when they signed Article 8 of the Covenant of the League of Nations must not remain a dead letter. They represent a sacred pledge, and any country which should wish to shirk it would do so with dishonour to itself."

On February 27th, 1927, M. Vandervelde, Belgian Foreign Minister and Member of the Belgian Delegation at the Peace Conference, declared :

" From now on we are confronted with the following dilemma : The other Powers must either reduce their armies to a level with the German Reichswehr or the Peace Treaty will collapse and Germany will claim for itself the right to possess striking forces powerful enough to guarantee its territorial integrity. From this fact there are two conclusions to be drawn : that disarmament must be general or not at all."

The same Foreign Minister declared, on December 29th, 1930, as reported in the *Populaire :*

" The Versailles Treaty will become a ' scrap of paper ' if the moral and legal obligations embodied in the Treaty are not fulfilled—those obligations which bound the defeated German nation to disarm as a preliminary to the disarmament of the others."

In his radio address of December 31st, 1930, Lord Robert Cecil said :

" International disarmament is one of the greatest, if not the greatest, of our national interests. Over and over again we have pledged ourselves to the reduction and limitation of the armaments of the victorious nations in return for the disarmament we imposed upon our enemies. If we disregard these pledges we shall make enough scraps of paper to destroy all faith in international obligations. It is almost of minor importance, to my mind, that if we do not disarm we shall have no answer to a claim to rearm by Germany and the other ex-enemy countries."

Once again M. Paul Boncour declared, on April 26th, 1930, as reported in *Le Journal :*

" It is not necessary to prophesy. It suffices to keep one's eyes open in order to perceive that—in case disarmament negotiations are shattered—or even in case they are adjourned to a future date—Germany is rendered free from several obligations. She will get ready to rid herself of this obligation and will no longer submit to the disarmament which the Versailles Treaty laid down as a condition and also as a promise of ' all-round ' disarmament. Then we shall have nothing left to say."

But what happened ?

While Germany faithfully fulfilled the obligations which had been dictated to her in the Treaty, the victor states failed to fulfil their subsequent obligations.

If an attempt is made to-day to excuse this failure on various pretexts, it is really not difficult to dispose of such excuses. We are amazed to hear from foreign statesmen that there was every intention of fulfilment, but that there had not been time to carry out this intention.

What does that mean ?

All the necessary conditions for the disarmament of the other states had then been completely fulfilled.

1. Germany had disarmed. They really could not assert that any danger threatened them from a state which had become completely helpless from a military point of view.

If, on the other hand, the other nations had disarmed, this would have given such a tremendous moral strength to the League of Nations that no state could have dared to have had recourse to violence against a partner in this collective system of general disarmament afterwards.

Then would have been the best opportunity to convert theoretical doctrines into an actual " deed." And this all the more so because :

2. From the political point of view also the necessary conditions had been fulfilled. For Germany was then a democracy such as has never before existed. Everything had been exactly copied and dutifully imitated from the existing great models. It was not National Socialism which ruled in Germany. Even bourgeois nationalism had almost completely disappeared. The world of party politics stretched from Social Democracy by way of the Centre Party to the Democratic Party, and not only resembled outwardly in its " Weltanschauung " the world around it, but felt itself programmatically bound up with it. What, then, were they waiting for ?

Could there have been a better opportunity to set up a collective system of co-operation than at the time when in Germany that spirit ruled exclusively which also inspired the world around her ? No ! The time was ripe, it was there, only the will was not.

In demonstrating the breaches of the Treaty of Versailles by the other side I will not refer at all to the fact that they had not disarmed. Even if one believes that at that time there may have been valid objections to excuse the breach of the obligation to disarm, it will be hard to give the reasons which led to an ever-increasing rearmament.

That is the decisive point.

The other states have not only failed to disarm, but they have on the contrary supplemented their armaments, improved them and increased them.

The reply has been made that there have been to some extent limitations of personnel—but this reply is no valid excuse. These limitations of personnel were more than made up for by the technical and planned improvement of the most modern weapons of warfare. Incidentally they could easily be made good.

And one must pay especial attention to the following :

During the course of the disarmament negotiations the attempt was made to divide armament into weapons which were more suitable for defence and those which were more suitable for attack.

I must here point out that Germany did not possess any of the weapons at all which were designated as suitable for attack. They were all destroyed without exception. And it must further be pointed out that it was these very weapons which were suitable and designed for attack that the partners of the Peace Treaty developed, improved and increased to the very utmost extent.

Germany had destroyed all her aircraft. She not only had no active aerial weapons, but she did not even have any weapons for warding off attack from the air.

At the same time, however, the other partners to the Treaty not only failed to destroy their existing aircraft, but on the contrary they developed it to a vast extent.

The speed of the interceptor fighters, for instance, increased from some 220 km. at the end of the War to nearly 400 km., thanks to improvements of the most modern type. The armament of these planes increased from 2 machine-guns to 3, 4, and 5, and finally to small automatic guns. The maximum altitude at the end of the War was 6,000 m., it has now been extended to 9,000, 10,000 and 11,000 m.

Aeroplane armament increased from 2, 3, and 4 machine guns to 4, 5 and even 8 machine guns, and finally to automatic guns. The sights were improved in such an ingenious way that it was openly admitted that the object aimed at could be destroyed with deadly certainty. The nose-dive bomber was developed in a completely new way. The explosive power of the bombs has been increased continually since the War. The desire for a better system of gassing has been satisfied by new inventions ; and residential quarters are now to be destroyed with inflammatory bombs which, as the technical periodicals of the various air forces assert, cannot possibly be extinguished. The direction-finding apparatuses and aiming gears of these bombing machines have been steadily improved and the latest triumph of disarmament is that, by means of long-distance control without pilots, bombers can now be sent off against defenceless victims.

Not only has there been no reduction in the number of aerodromes and aerial bases ; but these have actually been increased everywhere. Individual battleships have been supplied with fighting and bombing planes as auxiliary weapons and enormous aircraft-carriers have been built. All this has gone on under the catchcry of " disarmament " in regard to all offensive weapons. And it is all in fulfilment of the rule laid down in the Treaty of Versailles that Germany's example should be followed in the destruction of aeroplanes.

Germany has fulfilled the obligation laid upon her to destroy her tanks which remained from the World War. She has thus once more, in loyal fulfilment of the Treaty, destroyed and done away with another " offensive weapon."

It would have been the duty of the other states on their side to begin with the destruction of their tanks. Not only did they fail to do this, but they continued to improve them both as regards speed and as regards resistance and power of attack. The tanks during the War had a speed of from 4 to 12 km. per hour ; this has been increased to 30, 40, 50 and, finally, to 160 km. per hour.

When Germany no longer possessed a single rivet from her former tanks, France first built medium tanks of from 10 to 15 tons, then heavy types of from 25 to 30 tons, and finally the very heaviest types of about 90 tons.

During the War any tank could be pierced by a 13 mm. projectile, but the new war monsters are fitted with armour plate of from 50 to 60 mm., and are thus absolutely protected against the shells of even the field artillery. Hand in hand with this terrible passive improvement in these types of arms as regards speed, weight, wading capacity, field of vision, imperviousness to gas and thickness of armour, there has been an enormous development in the weapons of attack carried by these war engines. The machine guns or guns of 4–5 cm. calibre were superseded by new combinations. Tanks with guns of 7·5 cm., 10 cm. and 15 cm. calibre, and even more, are no longer things of fancy but terrible realities.

At the same time as Germany had destroyed her tanks and waited for the other countries to destroy theirs in fulfilment of their promise, those other countries had built more than 13,000 new tanks and improved and enlarged them into weapons still more frightful.

Under the provisions of the Treaty of Versailles Germany was obliged to destroy her entire heavy artillery. This, too, was done. But while the German howitzers and mortars were being cut up by the acetylene burners and thrown into the blast-furnaces as scrap iron, the other partners to the Treaty failed not only to carry out a similar destruction of their heavy artillery, but on the contrary continued here again with the same constructional development and improvement.

Long after there were no more 42 cm. mortars it was reported that the French factories had succeeded in constructing a 54 cm. howitzer. Long-range guns, firing at a distance of from 60 to 120 km., have been newly constructed. The newest and heaviest artillery has been divided through a most convenient device into portions for road and rail transport in order to increase its mobility to the very utmost with the help of wheel tractors and caterpillar tractors.

This was done in the case of weapons which are really of a very powerful offensive type, and against which we in Germany have not only no counter-weapon, but not even the possibility of any kind of defence.

Gas : Under the Treaty of Versailles Germany had to destroy all her gas weapons, again as a condition preliminary to disarmament on the part of the other signatories. This she has done. In the other states the chemical laboratories were busily working, naturally not to destroy this weapon, but to improve it to the very utmost. From time to time and with absolute full publicity the world was given amazing information as to the successful invention of a new and still deadlier gas, as well of new shells and bombs.

Submarines : Here also Germany has fulfilled her obligations under the provisions of the Treaty of Versailles in order to render possible international disarmament. Anything that even looked like a submarine was completely destroyed by the acetylene burners, dismantled and scrapped.

The rest of the world has, however, not only failed to follow this example, but it has not even retained its war stock at the same figure—on the contrary, it has continually supplemented, improved and increased it. The increase in displacement finally reached the 3000-ton U-boat, and the increase in armament up to 20 cm. guns. The number of torpedo tubes per U-boat was increased, as well as their calibre, and the torpedoes themselves given an increased range and explosive effect. The radius of action of these submarines increased enormously in comparison to that reached during the War. They can now dive deeper, and their periscopes have been improved in an ingenious manner.

This was the contribution to the problem of disarmament on the part of the states which under the Treaty of Versailles had undertaken to follow the example of Germany and destroy their submarine weapon. These are only single facts. They can be supplemented and completed at will in every direction. Taken together, they are a proof, which can be supported by documentary evidence at any time, that contrary to the obligations imposed by the Treaty of Versailles, not only was the disarmament policy ignored by the signatories, but a constant increase and improvement of high-class weapons of war was undertaken.

So they did what was absolutely contrary not only to President Wilson's intentions, but also—in the opinion of the most prominent representatives of the other side—contrary to the obligations to which they had subscribed in the Treaty of Versailles.

If that is not a glaring example of breach of the Treaty and indeed one-sided breach of the Treaty, after the other partner had completely fulfilled his obligations, it will be difficult to see what is the use of signing treaties in future at all.

No. . . . There is no excuse and no glossing over that fact. For Germany, in her completely defenceless and unarmed state, was really anything but a danger for the other states.

In spite of years of waiting in vain for the fulfilment of the Treaty by the other side, Germany was still prepared not to refuse to take part in a plan for genuine collective co-operation. The British Lord Privy Seal, Mr. Eden, says that readiness to arrive at parity in the quantative determination of defensive strengths was to be met with everywhere. If that is so it is all the more to be regretted that no practical steps were taken as a consequence. It was not Germany that wrecked the plan for an army of 200,000 men for all European states, but the other states which did not wish to disarm. And finally it was also not Germany that rejected the British proposal for mediation in the spring of 1934, but the French Government, which broke off the negotiations on the subject on the 17th of March, 1934.

The hope is now frequently expressed that Germany might herself come forward with a constructive plan. I have made such proposals not once but several times. If my constructive plan for an army of 300,000 men had been adopted, then perhaps many a care would have been less and many a burden lighter to-day. But it is almost useless to present constructive plans when their rejection can be regarded as certain from the start. Nevertheless, I propose once more to give a short survey of our views. This is done solely from the feeling that it is our duty to leave no stone unturned in order to restore the necessary internal security to Europe and the feeling of solidarity to the European nations.

After the other states had not only failed to fulfil their obligation to disarm, but in addition all proposals for a limitation of armaments had also been declined, I felt myself obliged, as the Führer of the German nation, responsible to God and my own conscience, in fact of the growth of new military alliances, and after receiving the information that France was introducing a two-year period of service, to restore once more, by virtue of the right to life of the nation itself, the legal equality of Germany, which has been refused her internationally. It was not Germany who thus broke a contractual obligation which had been laid upon her, but those states which had compelled us to adopt this independent action. The introduction of the universal military service and the promulgation of the law for the establishment of the new German army were nothing else than the restoration to Germany of a status of equal rights which threatens nobody but guarantees Germany security.

In this connection I cannot avoid expressing my astonishment here at a statement which was publicly made by the British Prime Minister, Mr. MacDonald, who said—with regard to the restoration of a German defence force—that the other states had been right after all in being cautious about disarmament. If this view is generally adopted, any sort of conduct may be expected in the future. For, according to this view, every breach of a treaty will be subsequently condoned because the other partner is supposed to deduce the same consequences ; that is to say, A and B conclude a treaty. B fulfils his obligation and A fails to observe his obligation : After years of warning B also finally states that the treaty is no longer valid for him, whereupon A is entitled to declare that thereby his previous breach of the treaty has now received subsequent moral justification, in that B has now also abandoned the treaty.

I should like here to deal just briefly with the reproaches and imputations which have been levelled against the restoration of the German military service.

It is stated in the first place that Germany is not menaced by anyone and hence, secondly, that it is not comprehensible why Germany should rearm at all.

This would give rise to the counter-question of why the other side, who in any case could feel less menaced by a disarmed Germany than vice versa, did not stop rearming and finally reduce armaments. But when it is asserted that Germany menaces the other states by rearming, then the increase of the armaments of the other states was at least a much greater menace for a disarmed and defenceless Germany.

I believe that in this case there is only a choice of one thing or the other. If warlike armaments are a menace to peace, then they are a menace for all states. But if they are not a war menace, then they are not a menace for any state. It will not do for one group to represent their armaments as an olive branch of peace and those of the others as the devil's wand. A tank is a tank, and a bomb is a bomb. The opinion that it is possible to divide up the world for all time into states with different rights will always be recognised only by the one side. The German nation, in any case, is not prepared to be regarded and treated for all time as a second-class nation or one with inferior rights. Our love of peace is perhaps greater than that of the other nations, for we suffered most from this unhappy war. Not one of us means to threaten anybody. It is only that we are all determined to secure and maintain equality for the German people. But this equality is also the primary prerequisite for every form of practical and collective co-operation.

So long as there are any mental reservations in this respect, really successful European co-operation will be impossible from the start. Once in possession of absolute equality of rights, Germany will never refuse to participate in those efforts which are intended to serve the cause of human peace, progress and economic welfare. I believe, however, that I must not refrain here from criticising certain methods which have their origin in the dictated Peace Treaty of Versailles, and which are responsible for the failure of so many endeavours that were certainly well meant.

The world is living to-day in the age of conferences. If many of these meetings were completely unsuccessful, then the reason for this disappointment is not infrequently to be found in the way in which the programme was drawn up and in the kind of goal which it was desired to achieve. Some cabinet or other feels—like all the others—that it is necessary to do something for the peace of Europe, which is considered to be menaced. But instead of communicating the general idea to all those whom it is proposed should co-operate, with the wish to learn the views of the various states and of their governments regarding the possible ways and means of dealing with and solving this question, a complete programme is drawn up between two or three chancelleries. In such cases it is frequently difficult to resist the impression that, in fixing the contents of the resolutions to be adopted, the wish is the father of the thought in mingling the possible with the impossible, and thus bringing about certain failure at the cost of those invited to participate later. For, while two or three states agree upon a programme laid down in such detail, the party subsequently invited is merely informed of the contents of such a programme, with the remark that this programme is an inseparable whole, and must either be accepted or rejected in its entirety. As very good ideas may naturally be found in such a programme, the state which does not agree to the whole draft is thereby held responsible for the failure of the useful parts as well. The procedure is very reminiscent of the practice of certain film distributors who adopt the principle of always distributing good and bad films together. But this is comprehensible only as a final atavistic phenomenon which has its origin in the example of the so-called peace negotiations at Versailles. Draw up a programme, hand it as a dictated document to a third party, and then declare that the whole is a solemnly signed treaty. With the aid of this recipe an attempt was made at that time to bring the greatest struggle in the history of the world to the beneficent conclusion so much desired by the nations which had participated in it. The results of this procedure were indeed more than tragic—not only for the conquered but also for the conquerors.

So far as Germany is concerned I can only say the following in regard to such attempts :

We shall take part in no further conference if we have not had our share in the drawing up of the programme from the outset. Because two or three states dish up a draft treaty, we have no wish to be the first to sample it ; which is not, however, to say that we do not reserve the right to give our assent and signature subsequently to a treaty because we were not present when it was drafted or at the conferences themselves. Not at all . . . It is quite possible that in its final shape and form a treaty may satisfy us as being useful, although we were present neither when it was drafted nor at the conference in which it was accepted by a number of states. We would not on that account hesitate to assent to and sign such a treaty afterwards under certain conditions, in so far as it seemed desirable and possible. The German Government must reserve the right to decide for itself when this is the case.

I must, however, again emphasise the fact that to draft programmes for conferences with the heading " All or Nothing " seems to me to be the wrong method.

Such a principle I consider to be altogether unpractical in political life. I believe that much more would have been achieved towards the pacification of Europe if people had been content to accept what was attainable in each instance as it arose. In recent years hardly a draft treaty has come up for discussion where one point or another was not generally accepted. Because, however, it was assumed that these points necessarily hung together with others which for some states were difficult to accept and for other states absolutely unacceptable, the good that could have been accomplished was left unattained and the whole attempt miscarried. It seems to me an equally doubtful procedure to misuse the thesis of the indivisibility of peace as an excuse for interpretations which—intentionally or unintentionally—serve the cause of war preparations rather than that of general security. In this respect the World War should serve as a terrible warning. I do not believe that Europe can survive such a catastrophe for a second time without the most frightful upheaval. But such a catastrophe can arise all the more easily when the possibility of localising smaller conflicts has been rendered less and less by an international network of intersecting obligations, and the danger of numerous states and nations being dragged into the struggle becomes all the greater. So far as Germany is concerned I wish to leave no shadow of doubt in what I am about to say:

Germany has solemnly recognised and guaranteed France her frontiers as determined after the Saar plebiscite. Without taking the past into account Germany has concluded a non-aggression pact with Poland. This is more than a valuable contribution to European peace, and we shall adhere to it unconditionally. We dearly wish that it may continue without interruption, and that it may tend to still more profound and friendly sincerity in the mutual relationships between our two countries. We did all this although we thereby finally renounced, for instance, all claims to Alsace-Lorraine, a land for which we have also fought two great wars. But we did it in particular to spare our own German nation a new and terrible sacrifice of lifes. We are convinced that in so doing we are benefiting not only our own people, but also this frontier territory. We are prepared to do everything on our part to arrive at a true peace and a real friendship with the French nation. With the understanding and heartfelt friendship of genuine nationalists, we recognise Poland as the home of a great and nationally conscious people. While wishing to spare the German nation further bloodshed, even where the renunciation of war implies a certain sacrifice, we certainly have no intention of pledging our blood, without right of choice, for the sake of foreign interests. We do not intend to enable anybody to sell by treaty the people of Germany, her manhood and her sons, in some conflict for which we cannot lay down conditions and which we cannot influence. The German soldier is too valuable and we love our people too well to commit ourselves to mutual assistance pacts where our undertakings are not defined.

We believe that we can thus serve the cause of peace much better. For it can but enhance the necessary feeling of responsibility on the part of every individual state to know from the beginning that it possesses no mighty and powerful military allies in an eventual conflict.

Here, too, of course, there are things which are possible and things which are not.

As an example I should like to deal briefly with the Eastern pact as proposed to us.

In this pact we find a mutual assistance clause which in our view may lead to completely unforeseeable consequences. The German Reich—and in particular the present German Government—have no other wish than to live on friendly and peaceful terms with all neighbouring states. We entertain these feelings not only towards the larger states, but also towards the neighbouring smaller states. Indeed, in so far as they have a really independent existence we welcome them as peaceable neutral factors on our frontiers, which are otherwise from the military standpoint quite open and unprotected. Much as we ourselves love peace, it does not lie in our power to prevent inter-state conflicts breaking out, and especially in the East. In itself it is infinitely difficult in such a case to determine the guilty party. A divinely inspired court, which would be able to discover and pronounce the eternal truth in such a case, does not exist on this earth. As soon as the dogs of war are loosed on the Nations the end begins to justify every means. And then people soon begin to lose all clear sense of Right and Wrong. More than twenty years have passed since the beginning of the World War, and every nation lives in the sacred conviction that right stood on its side and wrong on the side of the opponents. I am afraid that if such a conflict were to break out again treaty obligations would contribute less to the identification of the aggressor than to the support of that state which served his particular interests. It would perhaps be more serviceable to the cause of peace if the other nations were to withdraw at once from both sides at the outbreak of such a conflict rather than to allow themselves to be involved in this conflict from the outset by treaty obligations.

But apart from these considerations of principle we have here a special case. Germany to-day is a National Socialist state. The ideas by which we are governed are diametrically opposed to those of Soviet Russia. National Socialism is a doctrine which applies exclusively to the German people. Bolshevism lays emphasis on its international mission.

We National Socialists believe that in the long run man can be happy only in his own nation. We live in the belief that the happiness and the achievements of Europe are indissolubly connected with the existence of a system of free, independent national states. Bolshevism preaches the constitution of a world empire and only recognises sections of a central International.

We National Socialists recognise that every people has the right to its own inner life according to its own needs and character. Bolshevism on the other hand sets up doctrinaire theories, to be accepted by all nations, without regard for their particular character, disposition and traditions.

National Socialism strives to solve social problems, together with questions and conflicts in its own nation, by methods which are compatible with our general human, spiritual, cultural and economic ideas, traditions and circumstances.

Bolshevism preaches an international class conflict and the carrying out of a world revolution by means of terror and force.

National Socialism aims at bridging over and equalising unfavourable contrasts in social life, and in uniting the whole population in collaborative work.

Bolshevism teaches the overthrow of the rule of one class by means of a forcible dictatorship on the part of another class.

National Socialism places no value upon a purely theoretical rule of the working class, but lays all the more value on the practical improvement of their conditions of life and way of living.

Bolshevism fights for a theory, and to this theory it sacrifices millions of human beings and incalculable cultural and traditional values. In comparison with ourselves it achieves only a very low general standard of living.

As National Socialists we are filled with admiration and respect for the great achievements of the past, not only in our own nation but far beyond it. We are happy to belong to the European community of culture which has inspired the modern world to so large an extent.

Bolshevism rejects this cultural achievement of humanity, and asserts that real culture and human history began with the year in which Marxism was born.

We National Socialists may perhaps not have the same views as our church communities in respect to this or that question of organisation, but we never want to see a lack of religion and faith, and do not want our churches turned into clubrooms and cinemas.

Bolshevism teaches godlessness and acts accordingly.

We National Socialists see in private property a higher grade of human economic development which regulates the administration of rewards in proportion to the differences in achievement, but which in general makes possible and guarantees to all the advantages of a higher standard of living.

Bolshevism destroys not only private property but also private initiative and zest for personal responsibility. In this way it has failed to save millions of men from starvation in Russia, the greatest agrarian state in the world.

The results of such a catastrophe in Germany would be inconceivable. In Russia there are 90 people living on the land to only 10 living in the cities, whereas in Germany there are only 25 peasants to every 75 city dwellers.

One might go on with all this interminably. Both we National Socialists and the Bolshevists are convinced that there is a gulf between us which can never be bridged. But, moreover, there are more than 400 murdered National Socialists between us. Thousands of National Socialists have fallen in other organisations to forestall a Bolshevist revolt. Thousands of soldiers and policemen have been shot and massacred in the fight for the protection of the Reich and the states from the everlasting Communist uprisings, and more than 43,000 members of the National Socialist Party have been wounded. Thousands of them have been either blinded, or crippled for life.

In so far as Bolshevism can be considered a purely Russian affair we have no interest in it whatever. Every nation must seek its salvation in its own way. So far as Bolshevism draws Germany within its range, however, we are its deadliest and most fanatical enemies.

The fact is that Bolshevism feels itself to be a world-revolutionary idea and movement, and freely proclaims this. I have here a mere selection of the revolutionary happenings in the last fifteen years with which the Bolshevist Press, Bolshevist literature, and prominent Bolshevist statesmen and orators openly admit their connection, and even boast of it. Here is the selection :

November, 1918 : Revolution in Austria and Germany.
March, 1919 : Proletarian Revolution in Hungary. Revolt in Korea.
April, 1919 : Soviet Revolution in Bavaria.
September, 1920 : Occupation of business premises by the workers in Italy.

March, 1921 :	Uprising of the Proletarian Leaders in Germany.
Autumn, 1923 :	Revolutionary crisis in Germany.
December, 1924 :	Insurrection in Estonia.
April, 1925 :	Revolt in Morocco.
April, 1925 :	Explosion in the Cathedral of Sophia.
April, 1925 :	Beginning of the Revolutionary movement in China.
December, 1926 :	Communist rising suppressed at the opportune moment in the Dutch East Indies (Java).
July, 1927 :	Revolt in Vienna.
	Extension of the Revolution in China.
	Communist movement among the Negroes in the U.S.A.
	Agitation by Communist agents in the Baltic States.
1928 :	Manifestations by Communist organisations in Spain, Portugal, Hungary, Bolivia, Lithuania, Finland, Estonia, Italy, Japan, Latvia.
	Communist revolt in China.
	Communist agitation in Macedonia.
	Communist bombs in the Argentine.
May, 1928 :	Barricades in Berlin.
August, 1929 :	Communist " World Day against Imperialism."
August, 1929 :	Rising in Colombia.
September, 1929 :	Bomb explosions in Germany.
October, 1929 :	Invasion of Manchuria by Bolsheviks from Russia.
February, 1930 :	Communist manifestation in Germany. " Communist Workers' World Day."
May, 1930 :	Armed Communist rising in China.
June/July, 1930 :	War against the Communist movement in Finland.
July, 1930 :	Communist Civil War in China.
January, 1931 :	War against Communist bands in China.
January, 1931 :	Official revelations about Communism in the United States of America.
May, 1931 :	Revolution breaks out in Spain.
June/July, 1931 :	Renewal of war against Communist bands in China.
August, 1931 :	Campaign against the Communist business agencies in South America—numerous arrests.

It is an endless series !

From the last speech of the British Lord Privy Seal, Mr. Eden, I gathered —if I am not mistaken—that in his opinion such tendencies, and especially aggressive military tendencies, are completely foreign to the policy of the Soviet Union. Nobody would be happier than we if this opinion should prove to be justified in the future. The past, however, does not confirm it. If I may take the liberty of opposing my opinion against this, I can only refer to the fact that the success of my own struggle in life is not entirely due to chance and any especial lack of ability on my part. I believe that there are a few things that I understand in this connection. I began my activities in Germany at about the same time as Bolshevism celebrated its first success in Germany, i.e. the first civil war in Germany. After 15 years Bolshevism counted six million adherents in our country. By that time the number of my adherents had risen to thirteen million. Bolshevism was defeated in the decisive battle. National Socialism has saved Germany, and perhaps the rest of Europe, from the most frightful catastrophe of all times. If the West European critics of this idea had the same practical experience as I have, then I believe that they would perhaps come to quite other conclusions than those which they hold at the present time. If, however, my struggle in Germany had been a failure and the Bolshevist revolt had first overwhelmed Germany, then I know that the greatness of our historic achievement would be understood. As things now stand my part seems to be that of the warner who is perhaps laughed at by the rest of the world. But so far as Germany is concerned, I must, in accordance with my conscience and my position of responsibility, make the following statement :

The Communist uprisings and revolts in Germany could never have taken place without the aid of moral and material preparations on the part of World Bolshevism. The foremost leaders in all these troubles were not only trained and financed in Russia for their revolutionary activities in Germany ; but they received public honours and decorations, and were even appointed to official positions in command of Russian troops. Such are the facts.

Germany has nothing to gain by a European war of any kind. What we want is freedom and independence. For this reason we were ready to conclude pacts of non-aggression with all our neighbours, Lithuania excepted. The sole reason for this exception, however, is not that we wish for a war against that country, but because we cannot make political treaties with a state which ignores the most primitive laws of human society.

It is sad enough that, owing to the way in which the European peoples are split up territorially, very difficult circumstances would be encountered by any practical plan for the delimitation of frontiers which would coincide with the various national groups. It is sad, too, that in the making of certain treaties national affiliations have been consciously disregarded. But this makes it all the more necessary that people who have had the misfortune to be torn away from their national kindred should not be oppressed and maltreated.

A few weeks ago I saw the statement made in a great international newspaper that Germany could easily renounce her claim to the Memel Territory because she is big enough already. But the noble humanitarian author of that statement forgot one thing—namely, that 140,000 people have the right to live in their own way, and that it is not a question whether Germany wants them or not, but whether they themselves want to be Germans or not.

They are Germans. By a surprise attack in the midst of peaceful conditions they were torn away from Germany, and the attack was subsequently sanctioned. As a punishment for still adhering to their German feelings, they were persecuted, tortured and maltreated in a most barbarous way. What would be said in England or France if members of one of these nations were subjected to a similar tragedy ? When people who have been torn away from their own nation, in defiance of every natural right and sentiment, still preserve a feeling of allegiance to their motherland, and that feeling is considered as a punishable crime, then this means that such human beings are denied even the right that is allowed to every beast of the field. By this I mean the right of remaining devoted to the old master and the community in which it was born. In Lithuania 140,000 Germans have been reduced to so low a status that they are even denied this primitive right. Therefore as long as the responsible guarantors of the Memel Statute fail to induce Lithuania to respect the most primitive of human rights, it will be impossible for us to conclude any treaty with that country.

With this exception, however—an exception which can be removed at any time by the Great Powers who are responsible—we are ready, through pacts and non-aggression undertakings, to give any nation whose frontiers border on ours that assurance which will also be beneficial to ourselves. But we cannot supplement such treaties by giving undertakings to assist other countries in case of war. Such undertakings would be inacceptable to us because of the political doctrines in which we believe, and also for technical reasons. National Socialism cannot call upon the German people, who are its adherents, to fight for the maintenance of a system which is looked upon in our own country as deadly inimical. An undertaking to keep the peace ? Yes. We ourselves do not wish for military assistance from the Bolsheviks, and we should not be in a position to render them military assistance.

Moreover, in the concluding of certain assistance pacts which are known to us we see a development that in no way differs from the old type of military alliances. We regret this in a special way because, as a result of the military alliance between France and Russia, an element of legal insecurity has been brought into the Locarno Pact, which is the most definite and most really valuable treaty of mutual assurance in Europe. The points that have recently been raised in various quarters as to the legal obligations arising out of these new alliances are presumably the result of similar misgivings and prove, both in the way the questions are put and the manner in which they are answered, how great is the number of possible eventualities which might give rise to corresponding differences of opinion. The German Government would be specially grateful for an authentic interpretation of the retrospective and future effects of the Franco-Russian military alliance on the contractual obligations of the single parties who signed the Locarno Pact. The German Government also does not wish to allow any doubts to arise as to its own belief that these military alliances are contrary to the spirit and letter of the Covenant of the League of Nations.

The signing of individual non-aggression pacts, as long as it is not clearly defined what this non-aggression means, is just as impossible for us as to undertake the aforementioned unlimited obligations. On our part we, Germans, would have more reasons to rejoice than anyone if finally a way or method could be found to prevent the exercise of influence by outside forces on the inner political life of the nations. Since the end of the War Germany has been the victim of such interferences continually. Our Communist Party was a section of a political movement which had its headquarters abroad, and was directed from abroad. All the revolts in Germany were fomented by teaching from abroad, and were materially supported from abroad. The rest of the world knows this quite well, but has never taken much pains about it.

An army of emigrants is working against Germany from abroad. In Prague and Paris revolutionary newspapers are still being printed in the German language, and are constantly being smuggled into Germany. Public incitements to acts of violence are published not merely in these papers but also in several of the great papers which have a large circulation. What are called " blackleg " radio stations broadcast appeals which call for murderous activities in Germany. Other stations make propaganda in the German language for terror-organisations which are forbidden in Germany. Courts of justice are publicly set up abroad which endeavour to interfere in the German administration of justice. We are interested in seeing all these ways and methods abolished ; but besides our own interest we recognise that if such operations are not defined with great exactitude, a Government which—in its own interior—does not govern by any other right but that of force might attribute any internal revolt to the influence of outside interference, and then, in order to maintain its position, demand such military assistance as had been guaranteed contractually.

The fact that in Europe political frontiers do not correspond to the cultural frontiers is a fact that can be and is very much regretted. Since the rise of Christianity certain ideas have spread in an unbroken tradition throughout Europe. They have formed groups which have had a decided influence on the destiny of Europe. They have bridged across frontiers of states and nations and have created elements of union.

If, for instance, some foreign cabinet minister should express his regret that certain ideas which are held valid in Western Europe are not recognised to-day in Germany, then it will be easier to understand how the doctrines of the German Reich cannot be entirely without their influence in one or other of the German countries.

Germany neither intends nor wishes to interfere in the internal affairs of Austria, to annex Austria, or to conclude an " Anschluß." The German people and the German Government have, however, the very comprehensible desire, arising out of a simple feeling of solidarity due to a common national descent—namely, that the right to self-determination should be guaranteed not only for foreign nations but to the German people everywhere. I myself believe that no régime which does not rest on public consent and is not supported by the people can continue permanently. If there are no such difficulties between Germany and Switzerland, which is to a large extent German, that is due to the fact that the independence and self-reliance of Switzerland is a reality, and because nobody doubts that the Swiss Government represents the real and legal expression of the will of the people.

We Germans have every reason to be glad that there is on our frontier a State, a large percentage of whose population is German, which is firmly established and possesses a real and actual independence. The German Government regret the tension which has arisen from the conflict with Austria all the more because it has resulted in disturbing our former good relations towards Italy, a State with whom we otherwise have no conflict of interests.

Passing from these general considerations to a more precise summing-up of the present issues, I hereby declare that the position of the German Government is as follows :

1. The German Government reject the Geneva resolution of April 17th. It was not Germany which unilaterally broke the Versailles Treaty. The Versailles Dictate was unilaterally broken, and thereby rendered invalid as regards the points at issue, by those Powers who could not decide to carry out in their turn the disarmament which was imposed on Germany and which should have followed in their case by virtue of the Treaty.

The new discrimination introduced at Geneva makes it impossible for the German Government to return to that Institution until the preconditions for a real legal equality of all members have been established. For this purpose the German Government consider it necessary to make a clear separation between the Treaty of Versailles, which was based on a classification of the nations into victors and vanquished, and the League of Nations, which must be constituted on the basis of equal valuation and equality of rights for all the members.

This equality of rights must be extended to all functions and all property rights in international life.

2. The German Government, consequent on the failure of the other states to fulfil their disarmament obligations, have on their part renounced those articles of the Versailles Treaty which, because of the one-sided burden this laid on Germany contrary to the provisions of the Treaty, have constituted a discrimination against Germany for an unlimited period of time. They hereby most solemnly declare that these measures of theirs relate exclusively to the points which involve moral and material discrimination against the German people and of which notice has been given. The German Government will therefore unconditionally respect the articles concerning the mutual relations of the nations in other respects, including the Territorial provisions, and those revisions which shall be rendered necessary in the course of time will be put into effect only by the method of peaceful understandings.

3. The German Government intend not to sign any treaty which seems to them incapable of fulfilment ; but they will scrupulously maintain every treaty voluntarily signed, even though it was concluded before

their accession to power and office. In particular they will uphold and fulfil all obligations arising out of the Locarno Treaty, so long as the other partners are on their side ready to stand by that pact. In respecting the demilitarised zone the German Government consider their action as a contribution to the appeasement of Europe, which contribution is of an unheard-of hardness for a Sovereign State. But they feel bound to point out that the continual increase of troops on the other side can in no way be regarded as a complement to these endeavours.

4. The German Government are ready at any time to participate in a system of collective co-operation for safeguarding European peace, but regard it necessary to recognise the law of perpetual evolution by keeping open the way to treaty revision. In making possible a regulated evolution in the treaty system they recognise a factor for the safeguarding of peace and in the suppression of every necessary change a preparation for future explosions.

5. The German Government are of the opinion that the reconstruction of European collaboration cannot be achieved by the method of imposing conditions unilaterally. In view of the fact that the various interests involved are not always concordant, they believe it right to be content with a minimum instead of allowing this collaboration to break down on account of an unalterable maximum of demands. They have the further conviction that this understanding—with a great aim in view—can be brought about only step by step.

6. The German Government are ready in principle to conclude pacts of non-aggression with their neighbour states and to supplement these pacts with all provisions that aim at isolating the war-maker and localising the area of the war. In particular they are ready to assume all consequent obligations regarding the supply of material and arms in peace or war where such obligations are also assumed and respected by all the partners.

7. The German Government are ready to supplement the Locarno Treaty with an air agreement and to enter upon discussions regarding this matter.

8. The German Government have announced the extent of the expansion of the new German Defence Force. In no circumstances will they depart from this. They do not regard the fulfilment of their programme in the air, on land or at sea, as constituting a menace to any nation. They are ready at any time to limit their armaments to any degree that is also adopted by the other Powers.

The German Government have already spontaneously made known the definite limitations of their intentions, thereby giving the best evidence of their goodwill to avoid an unlimited armaments race. Their limitation of the German air armaments to parity with the individual Great Powers of the West makes it possible at any time to fix a maximum which Germany will be under a binding obligation to observe with the other nations. The limitation of the German Navy is placed at 35 per cent of the British Navy, and therewith still at 15 per cent below the total tonnage of the French Navy. As the opinion has been expressed in various Press commentaries that this demand is only a beginning and would increase, particularly with the possession of colonies, the German Government hereby make the binding declaration : *For Germany this demand is final and abiding.*

Germany has not the intention or the necessity or the means to participate in any new naval rivalry. The German Government recognise of themselves the overpowering vital importance, and therewith the justification, of a dominating protection for the British Empire on the sea, precisely as we are resolved conversely to do all that is necessary for the protection of our continental existence and freedom. The German Government have the straightforward intention to find and maintain a relationship with the British people and State which will prevent for all time a repetition of the only struggle there has been between the two nations hitherto.

9. The German Government are ready to take an active part in all efforts which may lead to a practical limitation of boundless armaments. They regard a return to the former idea of the Geneva Red Cross Convention as the only possible way to achieve this. They believe that first there will be only the possibility of a gradual abolition and outlawry of weapons and methods of warfare which are essentially contrary to the Geneva Red Cross Convention, which is still valid. Just as the use of dum-dum bullets was once forbidden and, on the whole, thereby prevented in practice, so the use of other definite arms should be forbidden and prevented. Here the German Government have in mind all those arms which bring death and destruction not so much to the fighting soldiers as in the first instance to non-combatant women and children.

The German Government consider as erroneous and ineffective the idea of doing away with aeroplanes while leaving bombardment free. But they believe it possible to proscribe the use of certain arms as contrary to international law and to excommunicate those nations still using them from the community of mankind—its rights and its laws.

Here also they believe that gradual progress is the best way to success. For example, there might be prohibition of the dropping of gas, incendiary and explosive bombs outside the real battle zone. This limitation could then be extended to complete international outlawry of all bombing. But so long as bombing as such is permitted, any limitation of the number of bombing planes is questionable in view of the possibility of rapid substitution.

Should bombing as such be branded as an illegal barbarity, the construction of bombing aeroplanes will soon be abandoned as superfluous and of no purpose. If, through the Geneva Red Cross Convention, it turned out possible as a matter of fact to prevent the killing of a defenceless wounded man or prisoner, then it ought to be equally possible to forbid, by an analogous convention, and finally to stop, the bombing of equally defenceless civil populations.

In such a fundamental way of dealing with the problem Germany sees a greater reassurance and security for the nations than in all pacts of assistance and military conventions.

10. The German Government are ready to agree to any limitation which leads to abolition of the heaviest arms, especially suited for aggression. Such are, first, the heaviest artillery, and, secondly, the heaviest tanks. In view of the enormous fortifications on the French frontier such international abolition of the heaviest weapons of attack would *ipso facto* give France 100 per cent security.

11. Germany declares herself ready to agree to any limitation whatsoever of the calibre-strength of artillery, battleships, cruisers and torpedo-boats. In like manner the German Government are ready to accept any international limitation of the size of warships. And finally they are ready to agree to limitation of tonnage for submarines, or to their complete abolition in case of international agreement. And they give the further assurance that they will agree to any international limitation or abolition of arms whatsoever for a uniform space of time.

12. The German Government are of the opinion that all attempts to bring about an alleviation of certain strained relations between individual states by means of international or multilateral agreements must be in vain until suitable measures are taken to prevent the poisoning of public opinion among the nations by irresponsible elements orally or in writing, through the theatre or the cinema.

13. The German Government are ready at any time to reach an international agreement which shall effectively prevent all attempts at outside interference in the affairs of other states. They must demand, however, that such a settlement be internationally effective, and work out for the

benefit of all states. As there is a danger that in countries where the Government does not rest on the general confidence of the people, internal upheavals may all too easily be ascribed to external interference, it seems necessary that the conception of " interference " should be subjected to a precise international definition.

Members of the German Reichstag :

I have been at pains to give you a picture of the problems which confront us to-day. However great the difficulties and worries may be in individual questions, I consider that I owe it to my position as Führer and Chancellor of the Reich not to admit a single doubt as to the possibility of maintaining peace. The peoples wish for peace. It must be possible for the governments to maintain it. I believe that the restoration of the German defence force will contribute to this peace. Not because we intend to increase it beyond all bounds, but because the simple fact of its existence has got rid of a dangerous vacuum in Europe. Germany does not intend to increase her armaments beyond all bounds. We have not got ten thousand bombing planes, and we shall not build them. On the contrary, we have set for ourselves such limits as we are convinced are necessary for the protection of the nation, without coming into conflict with the idea of a collective and regulated security. Nobody would be happier than we if such a regulation should make it possible for us to apply the industry of our people to the production of more useful things than instruments for the destruction of human life and property.

We believe that if the peoples of the world can agree to destroy all their gas, inflammatory and explosive bombs this would be a more useful undertaking than using them to destroy one another.

In saying this I am not speaking any more as the representative of a defenceless state which would have no responsibilities but only advantages as a result of such a procedure. I do not intend to take part here in discussions such as have recently been started in various places as to the value of other armies or one's own army and the cowardice of foreign soldiers and the supreme bravery of one's own.

We all know how many millions of fearless opponents, contemptuous of death, faced us, alas, in the World War. But history has certainly often shown of us Germans that we understand less the art of living reasonably than that of dying nobly. I know that if ever this nation should be attacked the German soldier will do more than his duty, remembering from the experiences of one and a half decades what is the fate of a conquered people. This conviction is for us all a serious responsibility, and at the same time a noble duty. I cannot better conclude my speech of to-day to you, my fellow fighters and trustees of the nation, than by repeating our confession of faith in peace. The nature of our new constitution makes it possible for us in Germany to put a stop to the machinations of the war agitators. May the other nations too be able to give bold expression to their real inner longing for peace. Whoever lights the torch of war in Europe can wish for nothing but chaos. We, however, live in the firm conviction that in our time will be fulfilled, not the decline, but the renaissance of the West. That Germany may make an imperishable contribution to this great work is our proud hope and our unshakable belief.

INDEX

A

Afghanistan, Amanulla King of, 144
Agricultural Adjustment Administration, 213
Alexander, King of Yugoslavia, 117, 142–152
Ali Fouad Pasha, 171, 173
All-Russia Central Committee, 240, 247
All-Russian Congress of Soviets, 239, 243, 244, 247, 273, 276
All Russian Peasant Congress, 250
Almanach de Gotha Cabinet, 46
Amanulla, King of Afghanistan, 144
America, United States of, 199–223
American Bar Association, 210
Anschluss, 121, 122
Anti-Semitism, 25, 30, 67
Arditi, 87
Arif, 173, 180
Aryan, 65
Ataturk, Kemal, 119, 153, 155–183, 186, 187
Atrocities, Nazi, 58
Austria, 118–141
Austrian-Germans, 27
Authoritarian State, 124, 282
" Autobiography " (Mussolini), 89, 101, 110
Avanguardia, 109
Aventine Hill, 100
Azelrod, Paul, 229

B

Balbo, Italo, 95, 105
Baldwin, Stanley, 288, 289
Banking Holiday in U.S., 208, 209
Barthou, M., 67, 142, 149
Baruch, Bernard, M., 211
Bauer, Dr., 127
Bavarian Soviet, 28
Beard, Prof., 212
Beck, Dr., 70
Bergner, Elisabeth, 60
Bianchi, Michele, 95

Bill of Rights, 282
Blue Eagle, 212
Bolshevik, 84, 85, 225, 226, 227, 230, 234, 236, 237, 239, 241, 243, 246, 247, 253, 255, 261, 270, 272, 275, 292
Bonomi, Prime Minister, 93
Boris, King of Bulgaria, 148
Botkin, Dr., 257, 258
Bourgeois Liberals, 225
Boycott, Jewish, 59
Brains Trust, 211, 220
Braun, 47
Braunau-on-the-Inn, 23
Brest Litovsk, 249
British Socialists, 234
Brüning, Dr., 41, 43, 44, 47
Brussilov, 237
Buchanan, Sir George, 255
Bulgaria, Boris King of, 148, 151
Bulygin, Captain Paul, 254, 256, 258, 259

C

Capello, General, 111
Catholic Centre Party, 63
Chamberlain, Houston Stewart, 65
Cheka, 260, 267
Chernozemsky, V. (Georgieff), 151
Christian Socialists, 120
Churchill, Winston, 289
Civilian Conservation Corps, 214
Cole, G. D. H., 290
Commissars, 244, 246, 250, 275, 277
Commodity Credit Corporation, 213
Commons, House of, 283, 284, 290
Communism, 45, 48, 51, 57, 58, 61, 109, 138, 226, 228, 232, 248, 250, 260, 261, 262, 264, 265, 269, 270, 271, 276, 277, 278, 286, 288
Concentration Camps, 61
Concordat, 66
Conservatives, 284, 287, 291
Constantinople, 157, 158, 159, 161, 165, 166, 167, 168, 169, 170, 171, 172, 174, 175